AGE DISCRIMINATION:
THE NEW LAW

AGE DISCRIMINATION: THE NEW LAW

Simon Cheetham
Barrister, Ely Place Chambers

With a Pensions Chapter by
Esther White
Partner, Eversheds LLP

JORDANS

Published by
Jordan Publishing Limited
21 St Thomas Street
Bristol BS1 6JS

British Library Cataloguing-in-Publication Data

A catalogue record for this book is available from the British Library.

ISBN 1 84661 026 5

Typeset by Etica Press Ltd, Malvern, Worcestershire
Printed and bound in Great Britain by Antony Rowe Limited, Chippenham, Wiltshire

PREFACE

The introduction of legislation to outlaw age discrimination has been a long time coming. It is new legislation set in the well-established context of discrimination law and it concerns a basis for discrimination that is very different to discrimination on the grounds of race, sex, disability, sexual orientation, religion or belief. Different treatment on the grounds of age permeates much of what occurs in the workplace, in education and across society. Much of that treatment is necessary and positive. Few would argue that a person of 70 who does not wish to work any more should be provided with a financial safety net; a person of 30 who does not wish to work anymore would have fewer supporters. It is not contentious that the focus of education should primarily be upon those at the start of their lives.

The difficulty with age discrimination lies in establishing at what stage the difference in treatment becomes unnecessary and detrimental. An overt refusal of a job to a person who is aged 55 simply because they are considered too old for the job is discriminatory, in the same as way as refusing someone a job because they are black or gay is discriminatory. However, other questions immediately arise with respect to age: is it likely that older people would not be able to manage the physical demands of that job? How far off is retirement? Is there an impact on the business through additional training costs or inadequate return?

If that is the case with apparently overt discrimination, how much more difficult is the task as the discrimination becomes more subtle, for example, with job advertisements that specify the number of years' experience or contractual benefits related to length of service.

This book can do little more than anticipate how the Employment Equality (Age) Regulations 2006 will work in practice. There is a body of existing case law which provides a framework for construction of the Regulations. There has already been commentary in consultation papers and in notes accompanying the Regulations. There are some things which clearly will be unlawful; there are steps to take to prevent other things becoming unlawful; but there is much that will need to take shape as the new law becomes familiar and tested.

Simon Cheetham
Ely Place Chambers
June 2006

ACKNOWLEDGEMENTS

I am very grateful to Esther White, who is a partner at Eversheds LLP, for kindly agreeing to contribute a chapter on the effect of the Regulations upon pensions. A fortuitous meeting on the train with Esther, who is a friend and former colleague, ensured that this specialist area was left to safer hands than mine.

I am also indebted to my colleague Ali R Sinai, whose encyclopaedic knowledge of European law has been a great resource, which I have exploited, along with his generosity and patience.

A number of people have helped at various stages of the book, including my former pupils Thandi Lubimbi and Amy Stroud and also Jane Liddington (Hextalls), Andrea Nicholls (Howard Kennedy) and Lisa Bryson (Eversheds LLP) who each kindly read various chapters and provided helpful suggestions for improvement, as have my colleagues in the employment group at Ely Place Chambers.

Finally, my wife Maria has endured this latest invasion of our time with her customary grace and understanding.

CONTENTS

Chapter 4
Retirement and dismissal

Chapter 5
Pay and non-pay benefits

TABLE OF CASES

TABLE OF STATUTES

TABLE OF STATUTORY INSTRUMENTS

Those paragraph numbers in **bold** type indicate where a Statutory Instrument is set out in part or in full.

TABLE OF EUROPEAN LEGISLATION

Chapter 1

THE EUROPEAN AND DOMESTIC BACKGROUND TO THE REGULATIONS

1.1 The Employment Equality (Age) Regulations 2006[1] prohibit age discrimination in employment and vocational training. They implement the UK's obligations in relation to Council Directive 2000/78/EC ('the Equality Directive'), which required Member States to extend anti-discrimination legislation to include discrimination on the grounds of sexual orientation, religion or belief and age. The Age Regulations have had a lengthy inception, both within Europe and domestically. This chapter considers the European background in some detail, as it provides the context for understanding how the Age Regulations will work, as well as the domestic background to the implementation of the new law.

1.2 Age discrimination legislation is driven by economics and demographics, as well as by human rights. With an ageing population, there is an economic need to keep people in work longer and to reduce the burden on the state of providing for the retired. It is variously estimated that the cost to the economy of the relatively low levels of employment amongst older workers (ie over 50) is between £19 billion and £31 billion in lost output and taxes and additional spending on benefits.

1.3 Nevertheless, the United Kingdom compares favourably with other European Union states. In 2005, the employment rate in the United Kingdom for those aged between 55 and 64 was 56.9%, which was the highest in the EU and well above the EU target rate of 50% by 2010.[2] However, of the 2.7 million people in the UK aged between 50 and 65 who are not working, it is estimated that between 700,000 and 1 million would like to work.[3] The extent to which the Age Regulations will help to facilitate such a shift remains to be seen.

THE EUROPEAN BACKGROUND

1.4 It took 40 years for the European Union to take a serious interest in age discrimination at an inter-governmental level.

---

[1] SI 2006/1031.
[2] Eurostat, Labour Force Survey; the EU (25 state) average is 42.5%; the comparable rate in France is 37.9%, in Germany 45.4% and in Italy 31.4%.
[3] Report by National Audit Office HC 1026 15 September 2004.

1.5 Primary legislation giving jurisdiction to the Community to legislate in the field was first introduced into the EC Treaty in 1997 by the Treaty of Amsterdam. Article 2(7) of that Treaty inserted a new Art 6a into the EC Treaty (later renumbered Art 13(1) in the consolidated version), as follows:

> 'Without prejudice to the other provisions of this Treaty and within the limits of the powers conferred by it upon the Community, the Council, acting unanimously on a proposal from the Commission and after consulting the European Parliament, may take appropriate action to combat discrimination based on sex, racial or ethnic origin, religion or belief, disability, age or sexual orientation.'

1.6 This is a specific implementation of one of the European Union's founding principles, contained in Art 6 of the Treaty on European Union. This states that the Union is founded on the principles of liberty, democracy, respect for human rights and fundamental freedoms, and the rule of law, as guaranteed by the European Convention for the Protection of Human Rights and resulting from the constitutional traditions of the Member States, such that these are general principles of Community law.

1.7 Article 13(1) was a sign of the Community's jurisdictional growth beyond activity aimed strictly at the smooth functioning of the internal market. It gives the Community the power to adopt anti-discrimination measures regardless of whether such measures are justified by the requirements of the internal market or necessary to promote the free movement of workers. However the wording of Art 13(1) being permissive, no direct rights are conferred on citizens. Furthermore, although action at Community level was allowed, the adoption of secondary legislation was not required. Nonetheless, the Community was quick to exercise its new competence.

1.8 In December 1999, the European Council agreed the European Guidelines for 2000, which stressed the need to foster a labour market favourable to social integration, and emphasised the need to pay particular attention to supporting older workers in order to increase their participation in the labour force. On 6 January 2000, the Commission submitted a proposal to the Council for a Directive establishing a general framework for equal treatment in employment and occupation.[4] The proposal dealt, inter alia, with the principle of equal treatment as regards access to employment and occupation of persons irrespective of age.[5]

1.9 This proposal ultimately led to the adoption by the Council of the Equality Directive[6] on 27 November 2000.[7] The enthusiasm for legislating in

---

[4]   'Proposal for a Council for a Directive establishing a general framework for equal treatment in employment and occupation', COM (1999) 565 final, OJ C 177E (27 June 2000), p 42.

[5]   Art 1.

[6]   Council Directive 2000/78/EC of 27 November 2000 establishing a general framework for equal treatment in employment and occupation, OJ L 303 (2 December 2000), p 16.

[7]   Prior to the enactment of the Directive, age was not included as a specified ground of discrimination in the equality legislation of any EU state, save for Finland and the Republic of Ireland. Only the constitution of Finland specifically identified age as a prohibited ground of discrimination.

this area was evidenced by the fact that the Commission's proposal was adopted some 10 months after being submitted, without many significant substantive amendments. This was notwithstanding the fact that, pursuant to Art 13(1), the Council needed to act unanimously to legislate.

1.10 The scope of the Directive is wide. The instrument deals with discrimination on the grounds of religion or belief, disability, age or sexual orientation.[8] Only a general framework is created, establishing Community goals, and the implementation of detailed rules is left to the Member States. Indeed no meaningful rules are provided by the Directive itself, which perhaps explains why the Community was able to act quickly, or even at all. However, the Council was more realistic than the Commission. Whereas the latter's proposal required implementation by the Member States at the latest by 31 December 2002,[9] the Directive required implementation by 2 December 2003, although with a proviso.[10] In order to take account of 'particular conditions', Member States had the option of taking an additional period of three years to implement the provisions of the Directive. In the event, Member States choosing to use the additional time were required to inform the Commission 'forthwith', and to report annually to the Commission both as regards the steps they were taking to tackle age (and disability) discrimination and on the progress they were making towards implementation.

1.11 Perhaps not surprisingly, given the abstract approach of the Directive, certain Member States, including the United Kingdom, Germany, Sweden, Belgium and the Netherlands, notified the Commission of their intention to use the extra time. However the Community's approach to this additional time was restrictive, as evidenced by the stance of the Commission and the European Court of Justice (ECJ).

1.12 The meaning of 'particular conditions' was not defined in the Directive, but the Commission's view was that this required the Member States to provide reasons as to the particular circumstances necessitating delay and that 'forthwith' in any event meant that notification had to be given by the Member States before the primary deadline for implementation had passed. Therefore, when Austria informed the Commission in January 2004 that four of its Länder wanted to use the additional period for both age and disability discrimination, the Commission refused on the basis that the notification had:

> 'given no information on the particular circumstances that necessitated the extra time, and was received well after the transposition date of the Directive'.[11]

---

[8] Art 1.

[9] Art 15 of the proposal.

[10] Art 18.

[11] See the Report from the Commission to the Council entitled 'Implementation of the age and disability discrimination provisions of Directive 2000/78/EC of 27 November 2000 establishing a general framework for equal treatment in employment and occupation'.

1.13 The ECJ in turn has ruled that interim measures taken by Germany after the Directive came into force but before the extended deadline for implementation had passed, which lowered from 58 to 52 the age whereby the conclusion of fixed-term employment contracts were permitted under national law without objective justification, were unlawful since they were contrary to the aim of the Directive.[12] According to the ECJ, the requirement that a Member State wishing to use the additional period must report annually to the Commission, implied that such a Member State was 'progressively to take concrete measures for the purpose of there and then approximating its legislation to the result prescribed by that directive' and:

> 'that obligation would be rendered redundant if the Member State were to be permitted, during the period allowed for implementation of the directive, to adopt measures incompatible with the objectives pursued by that act'.[13]

The purpose of the Directive: the 'principle of equal treatment'

1.14 The purpose of the Directive is to lay down a general framework for combating discrimination on the grounds of religion or belief, disability, age or sexual orientation as regards employment and occupation, with a view to putting into effect in the Member States the 'principle of equal treatment'.[14] Recital 11 confirms the social policy purpose of the Directive and states that such discrimination may undermine the achievement of the objectives of the EC Treaty, in particular the attainment of a high level of employment and social protection, raising the standard of living and the quality of life, economic and social cohesion and solidarity, and the free movement of persons. To this end, the removal of discrimination is viewed as a factorwhich will remove obstacles to the free movement of persons.

1.15 The purpose of the Directive was explored by the ECJ in *Mangold v Helm*.[15] As mentioned above, the ECJ ruled that Member States were precluded from adopting unlawful interim measures pending implementation. If the reasoning of the judgment had ended at that stage, then any significance would have been limited to 2 December 2006, after which any Member State adopting unlawful national measures would be in breach. However, the Court went on to rule that the 'principle of equal treatment' is not laid down by the Directive itself, since the sole purpose of the Directive is to lay down a general framework. The source of the actual principle underlying the prohibition is to be found in international instruments and in the constitutional traditions common to the Member States. The principle of non-discrimination on grounds of age must thus be regarded as a general principle of Community law,[16] and to that extent:

> 'it is the responsibility of the national court, hearing a dispute involving the principle of non-discrimination in respect of age, to provide ... the legal

---

[12]   Case C-144/04 *Mangold v Helm* [2006] IRLR 143.
[13]   Para 72 of the judgment.
[14]   Art 1.
[15]   [2006] IRLR 143.
[16]   Paras 74–75 of the judgment.

protection which individuals derive from the rules of Community law and to ensure that those rules are fully effective, setting aside any provision of national law which may conflict with that law'.[17]

1.16 That aspect of the judgment is more far-reaching and extends beyond the obligations imposed by the Directive prior to the final deadline for implementation. It may be that the ECJ took the opportunity to confirm that the Directive's purpose in giving effect to the 'principle of equal treatment' is to ensure the application of a principle that imposes wide obligations as a matter of Community law itself. This is an indication that Art 1 of the Directive must be given a wide and purposive interpretation, ensuring that the non-discrimination goal of the Community is achieved.

The concept of discrimination

1.17 Article 2 of the Directive provides guidance on what is termed the 'concept of discrimination'. It does so by defining what is meant by the 'principle of equal treatment'. The principle means that there must be no direct or indirect discrimination 'whatsoever', including on the ground of age.[18] Discrimination is deemed to include an instruction to discriminate on the ground of age.[19] Direct discrimination is taken to occur where one person is treated less favourably than another is, has been or would be treated in a comparable situation, on the ground of age.[20] Indirect discrimination is taken to occur where an apparently neutral provision, criterion or practice would put persons having a particular age at a particular disadvantage compared with other persons.[21]

1.18 The definition of discrimination is extended by the Directive to harassment. Thus harassment on the ground of age is deemed to be a form of discrimination when unwanted conduct related to age takes place with the purpose or effect of violating the dignity of a person and of creating an intimidating, hostile, degrading, humiliating or offensive environment.[22] The Directive also requires Member States to take measures in relation to victimisation which protect employees against dismissal or other adverse treatment by the employer, either as a reaction to an internal complaint, or to any legal proceedings aimed at enforcing compliance with the principle of equal treatment.[23]

1.19 The Directive only lays down minimum requirements of protection against discrimination and Member States are entitled to introduce or maintain provisions which are more favourable to the protection of the principle of equal treatment than those laid down in the Directive.[24] Member

---

[17] Para 77 of the judgment.
[18] Art 2(1).
[19] Art 2(4).
[20] Art 2(2)(a).
[21] Art 2(2)(b).
[22] Art 2(3).
[23] Art 11.
[24] Art 8(1).

States are under no circumstances entitled to reduce the level of protection already afforded in their legal systems against age discrimination as a result of implementing the Directive.[25]

1.20 Member States are also required to take such measures relating to procedural law as are necessary to ensure that the burden of proof lies with the respondent to demonstrate that there has been no breach of the principle of equal treatment.[26] However, Recital 31 of the Directive makes it clear that the complainant must first establish a *prima facie* case of discrimination.

The scope of the protection

1.21 The Directive's protection extends to all persons whether in the public or private sectors,[27] although the protection does not extend to the armed forces.[28] The scope of the protection is limited to the following matters:

(1) conditions for access to employment, to self-employment or to occupation, including selection criteria and recruitment conditions, whatever the branch of activity and at all levels of the professional hierarchy, including promotion;[29]

(2) access to all types and to all levels of vocational guidance, vocational training, advanced vocational training and retraining, including practical work experience;[30]

(3) employment and working conditions, including dismissals and pay;[31]

(4) membership of, and involvement in, an organisation of workers or employers, or any organisation whose members carry on a particular profession, including the benefits provided for by such organisations.[32]

Permissible differences in treatment

1.22 Article 2(1) of the Directive defines the principle of equal treatment as meaning that there shall be no direct or indirect discrimination '*whatsoever*' on the ground of age. In practice, however, the Directive does allow different treatment. In view of Art 2(1)'s prohibition of any discrimination whatsoever, it becomes important to understand how the Directive's approach to permissible differing treatment can be reconciled with the stated aim of the principle of equal treatment, which is to prohibit all discrimination. In particular, it must be examined where differing treatment does not constitute discrimination, and where it constitutes justified discrimination.

---

[25] Art 8(2).
[26] Art 10(1).
[27] Art 3(1).
[28] Art 3(4).
[29] Art 3(1)(a).
[30] Art 3(1)(b).
[31] Art 3(1)(c).
[32] Art 3(1)(d).

Differences in treatment that do not constitute discrimination

1.23 Indirect discrimination can be justified in relation to any of the grounds of discrimination prohibited by the Directive.[33] Article 2(2)(b) states that indirect discrimination 'shall be taken to occur … unless' it is objectively justified under Art 2(2)(b)(i).[34] Therefore in such circumstances, there is no inconsistency between the wording of Art 2(1) and Art 2(2)(b), to the extent that in justified cases no indirect discrimination (and therefore no discrimination 'whatsoever') has occurred. Where an apparently neutral provision, criterion or practice, which has the effect of putting persons of a particular age at a particular disadvantage when compared with other persons, can be objectively justified by a legitimate aim, the different treatment is simply not discriminatory. The neutrality of the provision is no longer apparent, but real.

1.24 The justification must be assessed under two different tests. First, the provision in question must be objectively justified by a legitimate aim. Secondly, even if a provision is proven to be in pursuit of a legitimate aim, it must be appropriate and necessary. What is clear from the Directive is that the tests are intended to mean different things. The first limb requires an objective assessment of the aim being pursued. The second limb requires an assessment of the effect of the actual provision, in order to determine whether, first, it is 'appropriate' – that is to say, whether the legitimate aim is in fact capable of being attained by that provision – and, secondly, whether it is 'necessary'. This presumably requires the effect of the provision to be limited only to what is necessary for the attainment of the aim.

1.25 Article 2(2)(b) of the Directive allows a provision which indirectly discriminates in relation to any of the grounds of discrimination covered by the Directive to be justified under the above mentioned conditions. However, Art 6(1) provides that any measure that discriminates on the ground of age, whether directly or indirectly, shall not constitute discrimination where it can be objectively and reasonably justified by a legitimate aim, and if the means of achieving that aim are appropriate and necessary. Therefore in relation to age discrimination alone, there is an overlap between the justification allowed for indirectly discriminating provisions under Art 2(2)(b)(i), and the justification allowed generally under Art 6(1).

Occupational requirements

1.26 The Directive allows differences of treatment based on a 'characteristic' related to age, where by reason of the nature of the particular occupational activities concerned, or of the context in which they are carried out, such a characteristic constitutes a genuine and determining occupational requirement, provided that the objective is legitimate and the requirement is proportionate.[35] Therefore the exemption applies to differing treatment

---

[33] Art 2(2)(b)(i) and (ii).
[34] And in relation to disability discrimination, also Art 2(2)(b)(ii).
[35] Art 4(1).

regardless of whether it is directly or indirectly founded on the ground of age.

1.27 The occupational requirement exemption applies to any of the grounds of discrimination prohibited by the Directive. Article 4(1) states that 'notwithstanding Article 2(1) and (2)' differences in treatment founded on genuine occupational requirements 'shall not constitute discrimination'. As with indirect discrimination, there is no inconsistency between Arts 2(1) and 4(1), given that a provision covered by Art 4(1) does not actually constitute discrimination. This is because the differing treatment results not from a perception related to age as such, but rather from the actual characteristics of the employment obligations themselves.

1.28 Recital 23 makes it clear that a difference of treatment founded on a characteristic related to age will only constitute a 'genuine and determining' occupational requirement 'in very limited circumstances'. What must be demonstrated is that the employment obligation in question (and not the employer per se) 'requires' workers to be of a certain age.

Differences in treatment which constitute acceptable discrimination

1.29 Certain forms of discrimination are permitted by the Directive, which includes the power given to Member States to permit 'positive action'. Article 7(1) states that, with a view to ensuring 'full equality in practice', the principle of equal treatment shall not prevent any Member State from maintaining or adopting specific measures to prevent or compensate for 'disadvantages linked to age'.

1.30 Given that the aim of such provisions must be to ensure 'full equality in practice', any act which differentiates in favour of certain persons by reference to age must have as its intended effect the removal of the actual disadvantages which flow from persons of that particular age carrying out that particular employment. As such, the discrimination allowed must actually relate to the individual employment relationship. The particular action compensating for a disadvantage is not intended to discriminate in favour of the person concerned, but rather to place him on an equal footing with his competitors in the workforce. In practice however, the effect of affording such an advantage to a person by reference to his or her age may well amount to positive discrimination in favour of that person, to the extent that the allowance made for that person is necessarily a difference of treatment on the ground of age alone, which discriminates against persons who are not within that age group.

1.31 Whereas positive action is permitted in relation to any of the grounds of discrimination prohibited by the Directive, discrimination on the ground of age alone is permitted in certain further situations. To take account of national legislation which differentiates on the ground of age in order to pursue a legitimate national policy or employment objective, Art 6(1) states that, notwithstanding Art 2(2), Member States may provide that differences of treatment on grounds of age shall not constitute discrimination, if, within the context of national law, they are objectively and reasonably justified by a legitimate aim, including legitimate employment policy, labour market and vocational training objectives, and if the means of achieving that aim are appropriate and necessary.

1.32 The aims which may be pursued by national measures are not limited to employment policy, the labour market or vocational training objectives. In theory any legitimate national policy may be pursued. The Directive provides a non-exhaustive list of examples of the type of national measures that may justify differences in treatment. These include:

(1) the setting of special conditions on access to employment and vocational training, employment and occupation, including dismissal and remuneration conditions, for young people, older workers and persons with caring responsibilities in order to promote their vocational integration or ensure their protection;[36]

(2) the fixing of minimum conditions of age, professional experience or seniority in service for access to employment or to certain advantages linked to employment;[37]

(3) the fixing of a maximum age for recruitment which is based on the training requirements of the post in question or the need for a reasonable period of employment before retirement.[38]

1.33 The provision in question must be shown to differentiate on the criterion of age, but such differentiation may result indirectly from age, for example professional experience or seniority in service, or even the age of third persons, such as the young or elderly who are in need of a worker's care. The measures in question must satisfy a two-part test. Firstly, the aim they pursue must be objectively and reasonably justified. Secondly, the means of achieving that aim must be appropriate and necessary.

The interpretation of justifications

1.34 In *Mangold v Helm*,[39] the ECJ confirmed that a measure must satisfy both limbs of the test in order to be justified under Art 6(1). What seems to flow from the ruling of the Court is that any potential justification must be construed restrictively. In the first place, it must be determined whether the aim being pursued is legitimate. Given the ECJ's acceptance of the particular German aim in that case, it may be that as long as the aim of a provision would reasonably appear to be a legitimate one, in particular one related to an employment or vocational training objective, the labour market, or one which genuinely pursues an objective of the employer concerned, then the first limb of the test is likely to be satisfied.

---

[36] Art 6(1)(a).
[37] Art 6(1)(b).
[38] Art 6(1)(c).
[39] [2006] IRLR 143.

1.35 The situation is more complicated in relation to the application of the second limb of the test. In *Mangold*, the Court was not willing to accept that access conditions, which on the face of it made it easier to recruit all persons over the age of 52, did protect the interests of all those persons. While the German measure required fixed-term contracts to be justified when there was a previous period of indefinite employment with the same employer, the measure applied without distinction to all workers over 52 and thus did not protect those workers who were unemployed before turning 52.[40] In practice, the criterion of age applied differently to different members of the same age group (ie those who were previously unemployed and those who were previously employed), since there were no grounds for the previously long-term unemployed workers to resist successive fixed-term contracts. In consequence, the aim being pursued by the relevant measure in relation to a category of persons defined by age, must – even if legitimate – be guaranteed to all persons falling within that category to a similar extent.

1.36 Secondly, the Court's ruling suggests that a measure will not be appropriate and necessary where an age threshold is chosen without consideration for the structure of the market and the situation of those workers who are affected. In other words, it must be demonstrated that the aim being pursued will in fact be achieved in relation to workers of that age category in the context of the market in which they are working and the personal circumstances that are likely to affect their category. For example, different age thresholds may apply to construction workers when compared with IT workers, or to IT workers in industry when compared with IT workers providing higher education services.

1.37 The question still remains whether there is a difference between the test under Art 6(1) and the test under Art 2(2)(b)(i). The former applies to direct discrimination but the latter does not, but is there any difference in justifying direct age discrimination as compared with indirect age discrimination? Article 6(1) is 'notwithstanding Article 2(2)'. This would suggest that, in relation to age discrimination, Art 6(1) is the appropriate basis for justification. As previously suggested, Art 6(1) is concerned with justifying actual instances of discrimination: when a provision falls foul of Art 2(2)(b)(i), it is discriminatory and should therefore fall within the remit of the potential justification provided by Art 6(1).

1.38 However, Art 2(2)(b)(i) and Art 6(1) are concerned with different situations: the former establishes whether an apparently neutral provision discriminates; the latter justifies provisions which do discriminate. As far as indirect discrimination is concerned, there may be no difference in practice; as long as the provision pursues a legitimate aim and is appropriate and necessary under either Article, then it satisfies the controls established under the Directive as a whole. It does not matter in practice whether the provision in question does not discriminate, or whether it discriminates and is justified. The application of the justification test is likely to be merged.

---

[40] It will be recalled that the legitimate aim of the measure as accepted by the ECJ was the facilitation of employment for unemployed older workers.

1.39   But what about directly discriminatory provisions? The UK Government's view is that the same test of justification that governs indirect discrimination also applies in practice to directly discriminatory provisions. Regulation 3(1) of the Age Regulations allows a respondent to justify both direct and indirect discrimination to the same extent under the same test contained in the same provision.[41] Therefore unlike the Directive, reg 3(1) does not distinguish between cases of non-discrimination and cases of justified discrimination.

1.40   It may be that the tests of justification provided under Art 2(2)(b)(i) and Art 6(1) differ, since the latter only applies when a legitimate labour market objective recognised at national level is pursued. On that basis, discriminatory provisions would only be capable of justification under Art 6(1) in the presence of a genuine employment objective, and the test would be more restrictive.

1.41   It therefore remains to be seen whether the United Kingdom's implementation of the Directive in relation to justification of age discrimination, to the extent that it provides the same test under national law for the justification of directly and indirectly discriminatory provisions, and does not distinguish between cases which do not constitute discrimination as opposed to cases where discrimination is justified, will need amplification. It may be that case law will have to impose additional requirements in the application of reg 3(1) to cases that involve the justification of directly discriminatory provisions.

THE DOMESTIC BACKGROUND

1.42   The United Kingdom's age discrimination legislation derives entirely from Europe. Therefore, unlike the parallel legislation in the United States,[42] it is not restricted to older people.

1.43   In 1999, the Government instigated an 'Age Positive' campaign and launched a *Code of Practice on Age Diversity in Employment*, setting standards for 'non-ageist' approaches to recruitment, training and development, promotion, redundancy and retirement. In December 2001, *Towards Equality and Diversity* – the first in a series of consultation papers – sought views on a range of equality legislation, including age, and was followed by proposals for equality legislation in *The Way Ahead* (October 2002).

---

[41]   This is also the approach taken by the French government in relation to the French implementation, which states simply that differences in treatment founded on age do not constitute age discrimination when they are objectively and reasonably justified and the means used are appropriate and necessary (see Article L122–45–3 of the French Labour Code: 'Les différences de traitement fondées sur l'âge ne constituent pas une discrimination lorsqu'elles sont objectivement et raisonnablement justifiées par un objectif légitime, notamment par des objectifs de politique de l'emploi, et lorsque les moyens de réaliser cet objectif sont appropriés et nécessaires.').

[42]   The Age Discrimination in Employment Act (ADEA) was passed in 1967, in the wake of the groundbreaking Civil Rights Law of 1964. Originally, the ADEA protected workers between the ages of 40 and 65, but that cap was raised to 70 and then finally removed in 1986.

1.44 In July 2003, the Department of Trade and Industry published *Age Matters*, which was specifically concerned with age discrimination. At that stage the intended timetable would have seen draft regulations in late 2004, allowing a two-year 'bedding-in' period before implementation in 2006. As with the legislation bringing into force anti-discrimination provisions in respect of religious belief and sexual orientation, the Government chose to transpose that part of the Equality Directive concerning age discrimination into national law as secondary legislation, using its powers under the European Communities Act 1972, with a consequent restriction in the amount of parliamentary consideration of the new law.

1.45 The range of responses to *Age Matters* and the contentious issues that were being considered delayed the process of implementation, which might be seen as confirmation of the European Commission's general view that:

> 'of all the grounds of discrimination, age and disability are particularly difficult to transpose into national law primarily because of the potential impact on the labour market. Prohibiting discrimination on grounds of age and disability also challenges long-held assumptions about people's abilities and their place in society.'[43]

Coming of Age in July 2005 sought views on the draft Age Regulations, which were finally laid before Parliament in April 2006. The commencement date is 1 October 2006.

1.46 The Age Regulations extend to Great Britain. Separate regulations implement the Directive in Northern Ireland. They do not extend to Gibraltar, the Channel Isles or the Isle of Man.

1.47 The Equality Act 2006 establishes a new single Commission for Equality and Human Rights to replace the Commission for Racial Equality, the Disability Rights Commission and the Equal Opportunities Commission. The Commission, which will include age discrimination within its remit, should be operational by 2007, with the existing commissions being incorporated by 2008/2009.[44]

The effect upon other legislation

1.48 Article 16 of the Equality Directive requires the abolition of legislation contrary to the principle of equal treatment. The amendments to legislation are set out in Sch 8 to the Age Regulations. The most significant consequential changes are to the Employment Rights Act 1996 in respect of unfair dismissal and redundancy and also to the National Minimum Wage legislation. These are dealt with separately,[45] as are certain other amendments, which are considered in context. The remaining significant amendments are as follows.

---

[43]   Report from the Commission to the Council, supra, p 4.
[44]   The Equality Act 2006 has been amended by the Age Regulations to extend its scope to include the Age Regulations.
[45]   Chapters 4 and 5 respectively.

1.49 The Parliamentary Commissioner Act 1967 is amended so that the appointment is changed from one with a retirement age of 65 to a non-renewable fixed term of seven years. A similar change is made to the Health Service Commissioners Act 1993.

1.50 Age is no longer a characteristic that a harbour authority may require of a potential pilot under the Pilotage Act 1987, s 3(2).

1.51 The Social Security Contributions and Benefits Act 1992 is amended so as to remove age limits relating to entitlement to sick, maternity, paternity and adoption pay. So, for example, the upper age limit of 65 for entitlement to statutory sick pay is removed.

1.52 There are also changes to secondary legislation, which are dealt with as they arise in context, where relevant.

Chapter 2

THE CONCEPT OF AGE DISCRIMINATION

2.1 Age discrimination can occur to anyone at any age. There is no intrinsic factor that defines the group, compared with race, sex, disability, sexual orientation or religious belief. A 40-year-old might be considered old within one set of circumstances and young within another. Moreover, discrimination against younger people is of a different nature from discrimination against older people. As Fredman says: [1]

> 'While young people will necessarily grow out of the group, and may therefore shake free of any discrimination attaching to their youth, older people cannot escape their age and the attached stigma and stereotyping, material disadvantage, and social exclusion.'

Benjamin Franklin's observation that all would live long, but none would be old, remains apposite.

2.2 This chapter considers the concepts that have become common to all forms of discrimination and which now apply to age discrimination under the Employment Equality (Age) Regulations 2006 and which are contained within Part 1 of the Regulations. References to discrimination within the Regulations are to any discrimination falling within reg 3 (direct and indirect discrimination on the grounds of age), reg 4 (discrimination by way of victimisation) and reg 5 (instructions to discriminate). References to harassment relate to the definition contained within reg 6.[2] There is an extensive body of case law behind those common concepts, which will be equally relevant to age discrimination.

REGULATION 3: DISCRIMINATION ON THE GROUNDS OF AGE

Direct discrimination

2.3 Under reg 3(1)(a), direct discrimination occurs when, on the grounds of B's age, A treats B less favourably than he treats or would treat other persons. The reference to B's age includes B's apparent age, so that discrimination based upon A's assumptions about B's age is included, even where the assumptions are incorrect.[3] In contrast with, for example, the

---

[1]   Fredman *Discrimination Law* (OUP, 2002).
[2]   Reg 2(2).
[3]   Reg 3(3)(b).

parallel provisions relating to religion or belief and sexual orientation,[4] the less favourable treatment is on the grounds of B's age, not on the grounds of age. Therefore, it is not unlawful for A to treat B less favourably on the grounds of someone else's age, such as an older colleague.

2.4 There are common concepts in direct discrimination which can be distilled down to identifying why someone was treated less favourably and whether age was the reason (conscious or unconscious) which caused the treatment.[5] Direct discrimination in employment arises where age is the reason for subjecting someone to a detriment. In *Law Society v Bahl*,[6] Elias J summarised the 'undisputed principles' of direct discrimination in the following terms:

(1) The onus lies on the claimant to show discrimination in accordance with the normal standard of proof.[7]

(2) The discrimination need not be conscious; sometimes a person may discriminate on these grounds as a result of inbuilt and unrecognised prejudice of which he or she is unaware.

(3) The discriminatory reason for the conduct need not be the sole or even the principal reason for the discrimination; it is enough that it is a contributing cause in the sense of a 'significant influence'.[8]

(4) In determining whether there has been direct discrimination, it is necessary in all save the most obvious cases for the tribunal to discover what was in the mind of the alleged discriminator. Since there will generally be no direct evidence on this point, the tribunal will have to draw appropriate inferences from the primary facts that it finds.

(5) In deciding whether there is discrimination, the tribunal must consider the totality of the facts.[9] Where there is a finding of less favourable treatment, a tribunal may infer that discrimination was on the proscribed grounds if there is no explanation for the treatment or if the explanation proffered is rejected.

(6) The need to identify a 'detriment' is in addition to the need to finding less favourable treatment on the prohibited ground, though in many cases the detriment will be obvious. Indeed, in most cases the fact that there is less favourable treatment will strongly suggest that there is a detriment. However, this does not necessarily follow, and the more a course of conduct is broken down into a series of discrete elements, each of which is alleged to be discriminatory, the more likely it is that a

---

[4] Employment Equality (Religion or Belief) Regulations 2003, SI 2003/1660; Employment Equality (Sexual Orientation) Regulations 2003, SI 2003/1661.
[5] See, for example, *Shamoon v Chief Constable of the Royal Ulster Constabulary* [2003] IRLR 285, HL.
[6] [2003] IRLR 640, EAT; the case was subsequently heard by the Court of Appeal: see [2004] IRLR 799.
[7] Reg 37; see Chapter 8.
[8] See Lord Nicholls in *Nagarajan v London Regional Transport* [1999] IRLR 572, at 576.
[9] See the observations of Mummery J in *Qureshi v Victoria University of Manchester* [2001] ICR 863, which were followed by the Court of Appeal in *Anya v University of Oxford* [2001] IRLR 377.

tribunal will properly be able to conclude that certain elements of the overall conduct, even if discriminatory, are so minor or insignificant as not to give rise to any detriment. The test for establishing detriment is in general easily met and was defined by Lord Hope in *Shamoon*[10] as follows (para 35): 'Is the treatment of such a kind that a reasonable worker would or might take the view that in all the circumstances it was to his detriment?'

(7) Finally, a tribunal should not make findings of unlawful discrimination in respect of any matter that was not in the originating application or the subject of subsequent amendment. It is not for the tribunal to extend the range of complaints of its own motion.

Corporation

2.5 For direct discrimination to occur, A must treat B less favourably than he treats, or would treat, other persons, so there must be a comparator, either real or hypothetical. This may be a more difficult concept in age discrimination. For example, B (aged 20) says that A treats him less favourably than A treats older workers. There may be no specific age that B has in mind when he refers to 'older' workers. Comparing like with like, the relevant circumstances of B and the comparator must be materially the same, apart from age. The comparator must be older, which may mean simply above B's particular age.

Indirect discrimination

2.6 Indirect discrimination is defined in terms that are common to other discrimination legislation. A person ('A') discriminates against another person ('B') if A applies to B a provision, criterion or practice which he applies or would apply to persons not of the same age group as B, but which:

(1) puts or would put persons of the same age group as B at a particular disadvantage when compared with other persons, and

(2) puts B at that disadvantage.

The reference to 'age group' means a group of persons defined by reference to age, whether by reference to a particular age or a range of ages.[11]

2.7 The term 'provision, criterion or practice' is not defined, but discrimination case law gives it a broad definition. The ACAS Guide refers to selection criteria, policies, benefits, employment rules 'or any other practices which, although they are applied to all employees, have the effect of disadvantaging people of a particular age'. Some specific examples are considered in Chapter 3 in the context of recruitment.

2.8 It is for a claimant to show that the provision, criterion or practice puts persons of the claimant's age group at a disadvantage and therefore

[10] [2003] IRLR 285.
[11] Reg 3(3)(a).

statistical and factual evidence may be needed to demonstrate this. Staying with recruitment, if an employer requires all applicants to take a physical aptitude test, which the claimant maintains put persons of the claimant's age group at a disadvantage, statistical evidence would show the ages of those who took the test. It would be impossible to establish statistically the number of applicants capable of doing the particular job who were deterred from applying by the need to take the test, but statistics might be available relating to the national workforce.

2.9 If the claimant in that example is aged 50, then he could say that his age group is those aged 50 and above. Of course, 'age group' is a flexible concept and the claimant will try to define his age group in whatever way is best supported by the statistics or other evidence. If nobody over the age of 35 passed the physical aptitude test, then the claimant's age group might be those aged over 35.

Defence of justification

2.10 In contrast with other forms of discrimination, there is a justification defence applying to both direct and indirect discrimination. It is open to A to show that the treatment or, as the case may be, provision, criterion or practice was a proportionate means of achieving a legitimate aim.[12] This is in contrast to other forms of discrimination, where direct discrimination cannot be justified.

2.11 Article 6 of the Equality Directive[13] states that:

> 'Notwithstanding Article 2(2), Member States may provide that differences of treatment on grounds of age shall not constitute discrimination, if, within the context of national law, they are objectively and reasonably justified by a legitimate aim, including legitimate employment policy, labour market and vocational training objectives, and if the means of achieving that aim are appropriate and necessary.'

2.12 The Government does not consider that the words 'objectively and reasonably justified' add anything to the requirement that the discriminator must show the existence of a legitimate aim, hence their omission from reg 3(1).[14] Similarly, the term 'proportionate' is used in reg 3(1), whereas 'appropriate and necessary' is the term used in Art 6. It is pointed out that the European Court of Justice has used the two terms interchangeably, explaining that proportionality requires that the means used to achieve an aim must not exceed the limits of what is appropriate and necessary to achieve that aim.[15] The Government's Notes to the Regulations conclude that the term 'proportionate' is clearer than 'appropriate and necessary' in implementing the Directive, in that the former term sets the requirement of

---

[12]   Reg 3(1).
[13]   2000/78/EC.
[14]   Notes on Regulations, para. 13.
[15]   *R v MAFF, ex p NFU* [1998] ECR I-1211; *Johnston v RUC* [1986] ECR 1651; *Mangold v Helm* [2006] IRLR 143.

necessity in its proper context, which is one in which the discriminatory effects of a measure are balanced against the importance of the aim being pursued, rather than any stricter concept of necessity. This echoes the words of Balcombe LJ in *Hampson v Department of Education and Science*:[16]

> 'In my judgment "justifiable" requires an objective balance between the discriminatory effect of the condition and the reasonable needs of the party who applies the condition.'

2.13 As discussed in chapter 1, the Directive goes on to provide examples of justifiable differences of treatment and these will be useful in considering the scope of the justification defence:[17]

> 'Such differences of treatment may include, among others –
>
> (a) the setting of special conditions on access to employment and vocational training, employment and occupation, including dismissal and remuneration conditions, for young people, older workers and persons with caring responsibilities in order to promote their vocational integration or ensure their protection;
> (b) the fixing of minimum conditions of age, professional experience or seniority in service for access to employment or to certain advantages linked to employment;
> (c) the fixing of a maximum age for recruitment which is based on the training requirements of the post in question or the need for a reasonable period of employment before retirement.'[18]

Legitimate aims

2.14 The consultation paper *Age Matters* provides the Government's thinking on legitimate aims:[19]

> 'A wide variety of aims may be considered as legitimate. The aim must correspond with a real need on the part of the employer (or other person or organisation wishing to apply a discriminatory practice). Economic factors such as business needs and considerations of efficiency may also be legitimate aims. However, discrimination will not be justified merely because it may be more expensive not to discriminate.'

2.15 The consultation paper goes on to give six examples of legitimate aims:

(1) health, welfare and safety;

(2) facilitation of employment planning;

(3) particular training requirements;

(4) encouraging and rewarding loyalty;

---

[16] [1989] IRLR 69, CA.
[17] The draft Regulations also provided examples, which did not survive into the final version.
[18] The application of these examples is considered in Chapter 3.
[19] At para. 4.1.16.

(5) the need for a reasonable period of employment before retirement;

(6) recruiting or retaining older people.

2.16 It then provides one example of what would not amount to a legitimate aim, where a retailer of trendy fashion items wants to employ young shop assistants because it believes that this will contribute to its aim of targeting young buyers. The conclusion given is that trying to attract a young target group will not be a legitimate aim, because this has an age discriminatory aspect. One might comment that trying to attract a young target group may have an age discriminatory aspect, but not one that is unlawful. The example suggests that an aim is not legitimate if it is associated with any age discriminatory purpose.

2.17 That example also raises a question about what will often be the most pressing aim, namely the business needs of the person wishing to apply a discriminatory practice. Saving costs will not amount to a legitimate aim on its own. The extent to which costs will be a factor is harder to define. In *Cross v British Airways*,[20] Burton P said that:

> 'It seems to us, as a matter of obvious common sense (and in accordance with the principle of the concept of proportionality), ... that, albeit that, in the weighing exercise, costs justifications may often be valued less, particularly if the discrimination is substantial, obvious and even deliberate, economic justification such as the saving, or the non-expenditure, of costs (which must, for example, include the avoidance of loss) must be considered. It would, in our judgment, need clear reasoning and binding authority to prevent that occurring.'

Therefore an employer seeking to justify a discriminatory practice cannot rely solely on considerations of cost as a legitimate aim. Savings in cost can, however, be placed into the balance, but may be valued less if the discrimination is more substantial.

Proportionate means

2.18 Even if the aim is a legitimate one, the means of achieving that aim must be proportionate. *Age Matters*[21] considers a number of aspects of proportionality. First, the discriminatory treatment must actually contribute to the pursuit of the legitimate aim. For example, if an employer wishes to use an age-related provision in order to encourage loyalty, it must be satisfied that it actually does so. Secondly, the importance of the legitimate aim that is being pursued should be weighed against the discriminatory effects. The more important the aim, the greater the permissible discriminatory effect. Where the aim is protecting people's lives and safety, a proportionately greater discriminatory effect would be justified than where the aim is rewarding loyalty. Thirdly, one should not discriminate more than necessary, so that where a legitimate aim can be achieved by differing

---

[20]   [2005] IRLR 863, EAT.
[21]   At para 4.1.20.

measures with differing discriminatory effects, the measure with the least effect will be appropriate.

2.19 In *Mangold v Helm*,[22] the European Court of Justice stated that:

> 'Observance of the principle of proportionality requires every derogation from an individual right to reconcile, so far as is possible, the requirements of the principle of equal treatment with those of the aim pursued.'

In that case, the blanket exclusion of employees aged 52 and over from legislative protection for fixed-term workers was held not to be a proportionate means of achieving what was accepted as a legitimate aim, namely encouraging greater vocational integration of unemployed older workers.[23]

REGULATION 4: VICTIMISATION

2.20 Regulation 4 refers to discrimination by way of victimisation and is parallel to victimisation provisions elsewhere in discrimination law, with the same protected acts.

2.21 A person ('A') discriminates against another person ('B') if he treats B less favourably than he treats, or would treat, other persons in the same circumstances by reason of B making one of four protected acts. First, B has brought proceedings against A or any other person under or by virtue of the Age Regulations. Secondly, B has given evidence or information in connection with proceedings brought by any person against A or any other person. This provides the example of victimisation given in the ACAS Guide, namely where a work colleague gives evidence against her employer at the employment tribunal. When that person applies for promotion, the application is rejected, even though she is able to show she has all the necessary skills and experience. Her manager maintains she is a 'troublemaker' because she gave evidence and therefore should not be promoted. As the ACAS Guide says, this is victimisation.

2.22 The third protected act is where B has otherwise done anything under, or by reference to, the Regulations in relation to A or any other persons. Fourthly, B has alleged that A or any other person has committed an act that (whether or not the allegation so states) would amount to a contravention of the Regulations. A discriminates against B either because B has done one of the protected acts or because A knows or suspects that B intends to or suspects that he has done so.

2.23 The claim for victimisation is subject to the proviso that it does not apply to treatment of B by reason of any allegation made by him, or evidence or information given by him, if the allegation, evidence or information was false and not made or given in good faith.[24] Unlike direct

---

[22]   (C-144/04) [2006] IRLR 143.
[23]   See further discussion in Chapter 4.
[24]   Reg 4(2).

and indirect discrimination – but in common with victimisation in other legislation – there is no defence of objective justification.

REGULATION 5: INSTRUCTIONS TO DISCRIMINATE

2.24   Article 2.4 of the Equality Directive deems an instruction to discriminate as falling within the definition of discrimination and this is provided by reg 5. Therefore, A discriminates against B if he treats B less favourably than he treats, or would treat, other persons in the same circumstances and does so by reason that B has not carried out an instruction to do an act which is unlawful under the Regulations or has complained to A or any other person about that instruction. The comparison is therefore the same as with victimisation, namely 'other persons in the same circumstances'.[25]

REGULATION 6: HARASSMENT

2.25 Under reg 6, a person ('A') subjects another person ('B') to harassment where, on grounds of age, A engages in unwanted conduct which has the purpose or effect of either violating B's dignity or creating an intimidating, hostile, degrading, humiliating or offensive atmosphere.[26] Conduct shall be regarded as having that effect only if, having regard to all the circumstances, including in particular the perception of B, it should reasonably be considered as having that effect.

2.26 Harassment is therefore defined as an unlawful act distinct from direct and indirect discrimination and in terms that are common to discrimination on grounds of sexual orientation, religion or belief, race and disability. Unlike direct age discrimination, harassment relates to treatment 'on grounds of age', not 'on grounds of B's age'. The distinction is shown in an example from the ACAS Guide of potential harassment on grounds of age. An employee has a father working in the same workplace. People in the workplace often tell jokes about 'old fogies' and tease the employee about teaching 'old dogs new tricks'. This may amount to harassment on the grounds of age, even though it is not the employee's own age that is the subject of the teasing.

2.27 Another example from the ACAS Guide is of a young employee who is continually told he is 'wet behind the ears' and 'straight out of the pram', which he finds humiliating and distressing. This is an example that shows the difficulties that may arise. One can easily think of racist remarks, for instance, that are automatically offensive to most people and which would not be accepted in any work place. However, remarks that are related to age

---

[25]   See also *Weathersfield v Sargent* [1999] IRLR 94, CA.
[26]   Art 2.3 of the Equality Directive refers to harassment as occurring when: 'unwanted conduct ... takes place with the purpose or effect of violating the dignity of a person *and* of creating an intimidating (etc.) environment'.

are less likely to be intrinsically offensive and may frequently be viewed as neutral or even acceptable in many circumstances. Further, ageist remarks will often relate to a person's capabilities, which are perceived as either diminishing with age or yet to be acquired as a result of the person's youth and which reflect commonly held assumptions. There is not, as yet, the widespread social intolerance of ageist remarks that exists with regard to sex, race and, disability and – perhaps to a lesser extent – sexual orientation and religion or belief.

2.28 A tribunal must take into account the employee's perception of the conduct and Morison J's words in *Reed v Stedman*[27] (in the context of sexual harassment) remain relevant:

> 'Because it is for each individual to determine what they find unwelcome or offensive, there may be cases where there is a gap between what a tribunal would regard as acceptable and what the individual in question was prepared to tolerate. It does not follow that because the tribunal would not have regarded the acts complained of as unacceptable, the complaint must be dismissed.'[28]

2.29 It may well be that the individual will have to establish the parameters of what is acceptable more obviously than with other grounds of harassment. For example, the use of the word 'wrinkly' may seem harmless or humorous, but the person on the receiving end of the remark or within a working environment in which it is used will need to make it clear that the word is objectionable. Subsequent repetition of the word would be unwanted and more likely to be reasonably considered as having the purpose or effect of creating an offensive atmosphere (for example). The question is not whether the tribunal finds the word offensive.

2.30 A further example from the ACAS Guide is as follows: George is in his 60s and works in an office with a team of younger colleagues in their 20s and 30s. The team, including the manager, often go out socialising. They do not ask George because they feel that he would not like the venues they choose for such events. However, George finds out that many workplace issues and problems are discussed and resolved during these informal meetings. George feels undervalued and disengaged by this unintended action. The Guide suggests that the treatment could amount to harassment as George is being excluded from the team, but it is not obvious that this office practice violates George's dignity or creates an intimidating, hostile, degrading, humiliating or offensive atmosphere. It may, however, amount to a detriment.

2.31 As with direct and indirect discrimination, an employer's liability for harassment is limited by reg 25(3), which provides a defence if the employer can prove that it took such steps as were reasonably practicable to prevent the employee from doing whatever act(s) of which complaint is made. As with victimisation, there is no defence of objective justification.

---

[27]   [1999] IRLR 299, EAT.
[28]   See also *Driskel v Peninsula Business Services Ltd* [2000] IRLR 151, EAT, cited in the Notes to the Regulations.

Chapter 3

DISCRIMINATION IN EMPLOYMENT

APPLICANTS AND EMPLOYEES

3.1 Part 2 of the Age Regulations is entitled 'Discrimination in Employment and Vocational Training'. This chapter considers the application of this Part of the Regulations to employment. The provision of vocational training and also the effect upon institutions of further and higher education are considered in Chapter 7. Three of the general exceptions from Part 2 – statutory authority, national security and positive action – are also discussed in this chapter.

Employment

3.2 Regulation 7 makes it unlawful for employers to discriminate against those they employ at an establishment in Great Britain, starting with the arrangements they make to determine to whom employment should be offered. With one addition, reg 7 mirrors the comparable provisions in the other discrimination laws and regulations.

3.3 The term 'employment' covers those employed under a contract of service or of apprenticeship or a contract personally to do any work.[1] The law in this area has recently been considered by the House of Lords in *Percy v Church of Scotland Board of National Mission*,[2] which reaffirms the breadth of the term 'employment' in discrimination law, and in which it was emphasised (per Lady Hale) that 'the essential distinction is … between the employed and the self-employed'.

Establishment in Great Britain

3.4 'Great Britain' includes such of the territorial waters of the United Kingdom as are adjacent to Great Britain.[3] Employment is regarded as being at an establishment in Great Britain if the employee does his work wholly or

---

[1]   See generally: *Quinnen v Hovells* [1984] IRLR 227, EAT; *Mirror Group of Newspapers v Gunning* [1986] ICR 706, EAT; *Mingeley v Pennock and Ivory t/a Amber Cars* [2004] IRLR 373, CA.
[2]   [2006] IRLR 195.
[3]   Reg 2(2).

partly in Great Britain.[4] If he does his work wholly outside Great Britain, then his employment is still regarded as being at an establishment in Great Britain if: (a) the employer has a place of business at an establishment in Great Britain; (b) the work is for the purposes of the business carried on at that establishment; and (c) the employee is ordinarily resident in Great Britain at the time when he applies for, or is offered, employment, or at any time during the course of the employment.[5] In deciding whether an employee does his work wholly outside Great Britain, the whole period of employment is relevant.[6]

3.5 Employment on board a ship is included if the ship is registered at a port of registry in Great Britain, as is employment on an aircraft or hovercraft if it is registered in the United Kingdom and operated by a person who has his principal place of business, or is ordinarily resident, in Great Britain.[7] There are special provisions for employment concerned with exploration of the sea bed or sub-soil[8] and the Frigg gas field.[9]

Recruitment and selection

3.6 Under reg 7(1)(a), it is unlawful for an employer to discriminate against a person in the arrangements it makes for the purpose of determining to whom it should offer employment. Such arrangements would operate in a discriminatory manner if age limits were applied in recruitment (subject to objective justification). They would also operate in a discriminatory manner if they applied a provision, criterion or practice that was to the detriment of a particular age group, for example, by requiring a minimum number of years' experience. Recruitment and selection has been a major strand of the Government's 'Age Positive' campaign, with its catchphrase, 'Focus on potential, skills and abilities ... not age'.

Job requirements

3.7 The Equality Directive[10] provides examples of differences of treatment on the grounds of age that may be justified. Although the draft Regulations also provided these examples, they have not found their way into the final version. One of the examples in the Directive is:[11]

> 'the fixing of a maximum age for recruitment which is based on the training requirements of the post in question or the need for a reasonable period of employment before retirement.'

---

4   Reg 10(1)(a).
5   Reg 10(2).
6   *Saggar v The Ministry of Defence* [2005] IRLR 618.
7   Reg 10(3).
8   Reg 10(4).
9   Reg 10(5) and Sch 1.
10 2000/78/EC, Art 6.
11 Ibid, Art 6(1)(c).

3.8 A good example is airline pilots. If it takes an airline two years to train a pilot, and a further three years to recoup the training costs through that pilot's subsequent service, then it will probably wish to set a maximum age for recruitment that is five years lower than the normal retirement age. This is a legitimate aim, but must be objectively justified. It may be easier in respect of training requirements than where an employer has to decide what is 'a reasonable period of employment' before retirement. The economic value of an employee is not always readily measurable, so the amount of time is likely to be carefully considered to see whether it is a genuine reflection of the business needs of the employer.

3.9 The example of the airline pilots also illustrates health and safety and performance issues, as the airline may claim that pilots above a particular age pose a health and safety risk and/or that their performance levels decline beyond a particular age. Maintaining health, safety and performance may be legitimate aims but, in the absence of compelling evidence, it may be difficult to justify setting specific age limits to achieve those aims. A better approach would be to assess the needs of the job and require applicants to meet whatever tests measured those needs. This is subject to the potential difficulty for the employer if it sets a test that is physically so demanding that it indirectly discriminates against older workers.

3.10 In the DTI's consultation paper *Age Matters*, another legitimate aim that was canvassed was the facilitation of employment planning: for example, a small company has a disproportionately high number of employees approaching retirement age, therefore wishes to recruit younger applicants. Again, it may be difficult to justify the specific age limit that is chosen to achieve this legitimate aim, particularly as there is no guarantee than younger staff, once recruited, will stay any longer than older staff.

Advertising

3.11 To comply with the requirement that recruitment and selection should be non-discriminatory, employers need to shift emphasis from age-specific requirements to those which emphasise the specifications of the job and the skills required. The wording of advertisements for jobs will need to avoid phrases such as 'applicants should be 25–35', as well as less obvious potentially discriminatory requirements, such as 'mature person'. Although the problem will be more apparent at the stage of advertising, clearly this also goes to the particular job specification.

3.12 In the first Irish case brought under the Employment Equality Act 1998 on grounds of age, the Office of the Director of Equality Investigations found against Ryanair after the airline advertised that it needed 'a young and dynamic professional' and 'the ideal candidate will be young [and] dynamic'. The Equality Officer found that the use of the word 'young', 'clearly indicated, or might reasonably be understood as indicating, an intention to exclude applicants who were "not young"', a finding supported by evidence at the hearing, which showed that, of the 28 of 30 applicants who indicated their age, none was over 40 years old.[12]

3.13 Defined periods of experience could discriminate against a particular age group that could not, or was less likely to, attain that experience. For example, an advertisement by a driving school for driving instructors who must be qualified and have a minimum of 10 years' driving experience would effectively prevent someone under 28 applying, and could therefore be discriminatory. This is an example contained within the ACAS Guide, where it is suggested that the driving school would need to justify this 10-year experience, especially as only four years is required to qualify as a driving instructor.[13]

3.14 As well as considering the wording of advertisements, employers may also need to consider where they place advertisements (for example, magazines predominantly read by a particular age group). Similarly, using an employment agency that targets a particular niche of the market might be problematic. The consultation paper *Coming of Age* gives the example of an employment agency stating that it specialises in finding work for people above 50. While this in itself would be unlikely to constitute difference of treatment on grounds of age, the employment agency would have to objectively justify refusing its services on the grounds of age to a 30-year-old.

3.15 A question arises over recruitment of potential graduates at university 'milk rounds', which is a practice that is likely to expose far more young people to recruitment than older people. There is also the use of the word 'graduate' itself, which the ACAS Guide suggests may be a discriminatory term as it can be interpreted as code for someone in their early twenties.[14] *Coming of Age* suggests that an employer wishing to recruit graduates may not be able to justify setting a requirement of a certain maximum age, but states that it will be easier for employers to justify indirect discrimination at universities, provided employers do not exclude applications from other sources.[15]

Interviews

3.16 Although the consultation paper *Coming of Age* does not consider that requiring a date of birth on job application forms is discriminatory, the ACAS Guide suggests that age/date of birth should be removed from the main application form.[16] Of course, removing that information is pointless if the applicant's age can easily be deduced from (for example) dates of education, so the references to age throughout the form need to be

---

12   *Equality Authority v Ryanair* DEC-E/2000/14; see also *O'Connor v GTS Reprographics DEC –*
      E/2003/24.
13   *ACAS: Age and the Workplace*, p 12.
14   *ACAS: Age and the Workplace*, p 14.
15   *Equality and Diversity: Coming of Age*, para 4.2.7.
16   *ACAS: Age and the Workplace*, p 11.

considered, and the risk assessed, of requiring information that is surplus and arguably unnecessary, but which might give rise to an adverse inference when challenged by an unsuccessful applicant.

3.17 There are two aspects to consider in respect of the interview itself: making the arrangements for the interview, and conducting the interview. Selecting a shortlist for interview based upon age would be discriminatory even if the post were not filled.[17] In the same way, if an applicant did not get a job for non-discriminatory reasons, he could still bring a claim in respect of discriminatory questions asked during the interview. Where an interviewer conducts an interview in a discriminatory way, it is not necessary to show that there was discrimination in the actual making of the arrangements for the interview.[18]

3.18 'Age Positive' advises interviewers to ask job-related questions, rather than questions reflecting stereotypical views, which is sound, if not illuminating, advice. In another Irish case, a 53-year-old complainant applied for a cabin crew position with Aer Lingus and was asked in her interview how she would feel about working and being directed by younger employees. She was not offered the job on the basis that she was over qualified. The Equality Officer held that although her non-selection was not discriminatory, the question was and may have affected her interview performance.[19] (The remedy, which was an order that she be offered a fresh interview with a differently composed interview board or offered a position with the airline within 12 weeks, would not be available to an employment tribunal in the United Kingdom.)

3.19 Employers will also need to ensure that they do not make assumptions about the capability or medical fitness of someone based purely on their age, for example by seeking medical references from an older person and not from a younger person.

Offers of employment

3.20 It is also unlawful to discriminate against a person in the terms in which that person is offered employment[20] or by refusing to offer employment, or deliberately not offering employment.[21]

Exception

3.21 However, in one of the major derogations from the principle of age discrimination, the provision making it unlawful to discriminate in the making of arrangements and the provision making it unlawful to refuse to offer or deliberately not offer employment do not apply in two circumstances:

---

[17]   *Brennan v J H Dewhurst Ltd* [1983] IRLR 357, EAT.
[18]   *Nagarajan v London Regional Transport* [1999] IRLR 572, HL.
[19]   *Hughes v Aer Lingus* DEC-E/2002/49; see also *Margetts v Graham Anthony* DEC-E/2002/50.
[20]   Reg 7(1)(b).
[21]   Reg 7(1)(c).

(1) if the person's age is greater than the employer's normal retirement age or, in default, 65;

(2) if the person would, within a period of six months from the date of his application to the employer, reach the employer's normal retirement age or, in default, 65.[22]

3.22 The term 'normal retirement age' is defined in s 98ZH of the Employment Rights Act 1996 (as amended under Sch 8 to the Regulations) and means 'the age at which employees in the employer's undertaking who hold, or have held, the same kind of position as the employee are normally required to retire'. For the purposes of this Regulation, however, 'normal retirement age' is an age of 65 or more.[23]

3.23 The effect of reg 7(4) is that it is not unlawful for an employer to discriminate against a person in deciding to whom to offer employment and by refusing to offer employment where the person is 65 (or whatever is the normal retirement age if that is over 65) or will reach that age within six months of the application to the employer. Any such discrimination against a person under 65 would require objective justification to be lawful.

3.24 The rationale for this provision is to make it consistent with the exception for retirement under reg 30. There is no point in an employer being required not to discriminate against an applicant for a job when, if it was to employ him, that person could be lawfully retired within six months. Regulation 7(5) applies this exception only to persons to whom reg 30 could apply, which is the exception for retirement.

Employment opportunities and benefits

3.25 An employer may not discriminate against a person he employs in the terms of employment that he affords him,[24] in the opportunities which he affords him for promotion, a transfer, training or receiving any other benefit,[25] or by refusing to afford him, or deliberately not affording him, any such opportunity.[26] The term 'benefits' includes facilities and services.[27]

3.26 This does not apply to benefits of any description if the employer provides such benefits to the public (with or without payment) or a section of the public that includes the particular employee. For example, an employer that is a health insurance provider can provide that benefit to its employees in the same way as it offers the service to the general public. However, the prohibition on acting in a discriminatory way will apply where there is a material difference between the benefits provided to the public and to the employee; the provision of benefits is regulated by the contract of employment; or where the benefits relate to training.

---

[22]   Reg 7(4).
[23]   Reg 7(8).
[24]   Reg 7(2)(a).
[25]   Reg 7(2)(b).
[26]   Reg 7(2)(c).
[27]   Reg 2(2).

Dismissal or detriment

3.27 It is unlawful for an employer to discriminate against a person on the grounds of age by dismissing them or subjecting them to any other detriment.[28] The provision regarding dismissal is qualified by the exception for retirement.[29] It includes expiry without renewal of a fixed-term contract and also constructive dismissal.[30] The test for detriment draws upon Lord Hope's frequently invoked question: 'Is the treatment of such a kind that a reasonable worker would or might take the view that in all the circumstances it was to his detriment?'.[31]

Harassment

3.28 Under reg 7(3), it is unlawful for an employer to subject to harassment an employee or someone who has applied for employment.[32]

Genuine occupational requirement

3.29 Regulation 8 provides an exception for genuine occupational requirement and is similar to the parallel provision in the sexual orientation and religion or belief regulations. It allows an employer, when recruiting for a position, to treat job applicants differently on grounds of their age if possessing a characteristic related to age is a genuine and determining occupational requirement for that post. It must be proportionate to apply that requirement in the particular case and either the person to whom that requirement is applied does not meet that requirement or the employer is not satisfied (and it is reasonable not to be satisfied) that the person meets it. The employer may also rely upon this exception when promoting, transferring or training persons for a post and when dismissing.

3.30 Article 4 of the Equality Directive allows an exception for genuine occupational requirement and the wording of reg 8 follows the article, save for requiring the objective to be legitimate. However, if an occupational requirement is established as genuine, then it is implicit that it must also pursue a legitimate objective.[33] As it is a derogation from the principle of equal treatment, the exception has to be construed strictly.

3.31 The Government believes that this exception is likely to be less significant in age discrimination than in other areas of discrimination, where genuine occupational requirement and positive action are the only instances of justifiable direct discrimination. It anticipates that it will apply in only a

---

[28] Reg 7(2)(d).
[29] See Chapter 5.
[30] Reg 7(7).
[31] *Shamoon v Chief Constable of Royal Ulster Constabulary* [2003] ICR 337, HL.
[32] See Chapter 2.
[33] *R (on the application of Amicus et al) v Secretary of State for Trade and Industry* [2004] IRLR 430, QBD.

very few cases and gives the sole example of acting:[34] King Lear must look older than his daughters and make-up can only go so far. Modelling is perhaps another example, although a youthful appearance would not automatically be a genuine requirement. The ACAS Guide gives a further example, where an organisation advising on, and promoting rights for, older people may be able to show that it essential that its chief executive – as the organisation's public face – is of a certain age.[35]

CONTRACT WORKERS

Definitions

3.32 A 'principal' is a person who makes work available ('contract work') to be done by individuals who are employed by another person, who supplies them under a contract with the principal. The individual supplied to the principal under that contract is the contract worker.[36] Regulation 9 protects the contract worker from discrimination by the principal.

3.33 From case law on this provision in other anti-discrimination legislation, one can anticipate the scope of this regulation. The existence of a contract to provide labour between the principal and the contract worker's employee is essential.[37] The protection would extend to the in-store employees of a concessionaire operating in a department store, where the store discriminates against those employees.[38] An employee of an investment company selling the products of a life assurance company was held to be a contract worker, although the court considered it doubtful whether it is sufficient for a complainant to establish merely that the principal benefited from the work done by them.[39]

Unlawful acts

3.34 It is unlawful for a principal, in relation to contract work, to discriminate on grounds of age against a contract worker in the terms in which he allows him to do that work; by not allowing him to do it or continue to do it (subject to a genuine occupational requirement); in the way he affords him access to any benefits or by refusing or deliberately not affording him access to them; or subjecting him to any other detriment. It is also unlawful to subject a contract worker to harassment. These categories are similar to the categories of discrimination against applicants and employees. They do not include discrimination in recruitment, selection, engagement and dismissal, because that would be the liability of the contract

---

[34]   *Equality and Diversity: Coming of Age*, para 4.2.6.
[35]   *ACAS: Age and the Workplace*, p 35.
[36]   Reg 9(5).
[37]   *Rice v Fon-A-Car* [1980] ICR 133, EAT.
[38]   *Harrods Ltd v Remick* [1997] IRLR 583, CA.
[39]   *Jones v Friends Provident Life Office* [2004] IRLR 783, CA(NI).

worker's employer. Regulation 9 applies to contract work 'at an establishment in Great Britain', which is defined as for employment at an establishment in Great Britain under reg 10.

3.35 As with the parallel provision for applicants and employees,[40] the provisions for contract workers do not apply to benefits of any description if the principal is concerned with the provision (for payment or not) of benefits of that description to the public or a section of the public to which the contract worker belongs, unless the provision differs in a material respect from the provision of the benefits by the principal to his contract workers.[41] 'Benefits' includes facilities and services.[42]

PENSION SCHEMES

3.36 The application of the Regulations to pension schemes is considered in Chapter 7.

OFFICE HOLDERS

Definitions

3.37 Regulation 12 sets out the provisions relating to those holding an office or post. As with the equivalent rules under other discrimination laws, they are complex.

3.38 The terms 'office' and 'post' are not defined, but the regulation applies to any office or post to which persons are appointed to discharge functions personally under the direction of another person and in respect of which they are entitled to remuneration.[43] For this purpose, the holder of an office or post is to be regarded as discharging his functions under the direction of another person if that other person is entitled to direct him as to when and where he discharges those functions. He is not to be regarded as entitled to remuneration merely because he is entitled to payments either in respect of expenses incurred by him in carrying out the function of the office or post or by way of compensation for the loss of income or benefits he would or might have received had he not been carrying out the functions of the office or post.[44] Holding an office and being an employee are not inconsistent; a person may hold an office on the terms of, and pursuant to, a contract of employment.[45]

---

[40] Reg 7(6).
[41] Reg 9(4).
[42] Reg 2(2).
[43] Reg 12(8)(a).
[44] Reg 12(9).
[45] *Percy v Church of Scotland Board of National Mission* [2006] IRLR 195, HL.

3.39 Regulation 12 also applies in part to any office or post to which persons are made by or on the recommendation of or subject to the approval of a Minister of the Crown, a government department, the National Assembly for Wales or any part of the Scottish Administration.

3.40 It does not apply to a 'political office', which is given an extensive list of definitions, as follows:[46]

- any office of the House of Commons or House of Lords held by a member of it;

- a life peerage;

- specified ministerial offices;

- the offices of Leader of the Opposition, Chief Opposition Whip or Assistant Opposition Whip;

- any office of the Scottish Parliament or Welsh Assembly held by a member of it;

- a member of the Scottish Executive or a junior Scottish minister;

- any office of a county council, London borough council, district or parish council in England;

- any office of a county council, county borough council or community council in Wales;

- any office of a council or community council in Scotland;

- any office of the Greater London Authority held by a member of it;

- any office of the Council of the Scilly Isles held by a member of it;

- any office of a political party;

- any office of the Assembly held by a member of it (Northern Ireland);

- any officer of a district council held by a member of it (Northern Ireland).

3.41 Regulation 12 also does not apply where regs 7 (applicants and employees), 9 (contract workers), 15 (barristers), 16 (advocates) or 17 (partnerships) apply or would apply but for the operation of any other provision of these regulations.

Unlawful acts

3.42 Unlawful acts are committed by 'a relevant person', the definition of which becomes apparent with each unlawful act. Appointment to an office or post does not include election to an office or post.

---

[46]   Reg 12(10).

Offer of appointment

3.43 First, it is unlawful for a relevant person, in relation to an appointment to an office or post, to discriminate on the grounds of age in the arrangements he makes for the purpose of determining to whom the appointment should be offered. Secondly, it is unlawful for a relevant person to discriminate against a person on the grounds of age in the terms in which he offers him the appointment. Thirdly, it is unlawful for a relevant person to discriminate against a person on the grounds of age by refusing to offer him the appointment (which includes a deliberate omission). The 'relevant person' here is the person with power to make an appointment or to determine the terms of the appointment.

3.44 None of these would apply to any act in relation to an office or post where, if the office or post constituted employment, that act would be lawful by virtue of the exception for genuine occupational requirement under reg 8.

Recommendation or approval of appointment

3.45 There are two potentially unlawful acts in respect of any office or post to which appointments are made by, on the recommendation of, or subject to, the approval of a Minister of the Crown, a government department, the National Assembly for Wales or any part of the Scottish Administration. First, it is unlawful for a relevant person to discriminate against a person on the grounds of age in the arrangements he makes for the purpose of determining who should be recommended or approved in relation to the appointment. Secondly, it is unlawful for a relevant person to discriminate against a person on the grounds of age in making or refusing to make a recommendation, or giving or refusing to give an approval in relation to the appointment. Refusal includes a deliberate omission and 'recommendation' includes making a negative recommendation. The 'relevant person' here is the person or body on whose recommendation or subject to whose approval appointments are made to the office or post.

3.46 Again, neither of these would apply to any act in relation to an office or post where, if the office or post constituted employment, it would be lawful by virtue of the exception for genuine occupational requirement to refuse to offer the person such employment.

Appointment

3.47 Once appointed, the holder of the office or post is potentially subject to four unlawful acts. First, it is unlawful for a relevant person to discriminate on the grounds of age against a person who has been appointed to an office or post in the terms of the appointment. The relevant person is the person with power to determine the terms. Secondly, it is unlawful for a relevant person to discriminate against a person on the grounds of age in the opportunities which he affords him for promotion, a transfer, training or receiving any other benefit, or by refusing to afford him any such opportunity. The relevant person here is any person with power to determine these 'working conditions'. However, this does not apply to benefits of any description if the relevant person is concerned with the provision (for payment or not) of benefits of that description to the public or a section of the public to which the office- or post-holder belongs, subject to three exceptions. These are: (1) unless the provision differs in a material respect from the provision of the benefits to persons appointed to offices or posts which are the same or not materially different from that which the appointed person holds; (2) the provision of the benefits to the person appointed is regulated by the terms and conditions of his appointment; or (3) the benefits relate to training.

3.48 Thirdly, it is unlawful for a relevant person to discriminate against a person on the grounds of age by terminating the appointment, the relevant person being the person with power to terminate. The reference to termination of an appointment includes expiry of a fixed term and a constructive termination. Fourthly, it is unlawful for a relevant person to discriminate on the grounds of age against a person who has been appointed to an office or post by subjecting him to any other detriment in relation to the appointment. The relevant person is any person or body with the power to make, recommend, approve or terminate the appointment or determine its terms or its working conditions.

3.49 As above, none of these would apply to any act in relation to an office or post where, if the office or post constituted employment, that act would be lawful by virtue of the exception for genuine occupational requirement under reg 8.

Harassment

3.50 Finally, it is unlawful for a relevant person – with the same broad ambit – to subject to harassment, in relation to an office or post, a person who (1) has been appointed, (2) is seeking or being considered for appointment, or (3) is seeking or being considered for recommendation or approval in relation to an office or post. This last applies to any office or post to which appointments are made by, on the recommendation of or subject to the approval of, a Minister of the Crown, a government department, the National Assembly for Wales or any part of the Scottish Administration

POLICE

3.51 For the purposes of Part 2 of the Age Regulations (Discrimination in Employment and Vocational Training), the holding of the office of constable is to be treated as employment by either (1) the chief office of police as respects any act done by him in relation to a constable or that office or (2) the police authority as respects any act done by him in relation to a constable or that office.[47] This gives police officers the same rights under Part 2 as other employees. The chief officer of police is also vicariously liable for the acts of a police officer and anything done by a person holding such an office in the performance, or purported performance, of his functions shall be treated as done in the course of that employment. These provisions apply equally to a police cadet and appointment as a police cadet as they apply to a constable and the office of constable.

3.52 Any compensation, costs or expenses awarded against a chief officer of police in any proceedings brought against him under the Regulations and any costs or expenses incurred by him in such proceedings so far as not recovered are to be paid out of the police fund. Any sum required by a chief officer of police for the settlement of any claim made against him is also to be paid out of the police fund if the settlement is approved by the police. In such cases, and to such extent as appears to it to be appropriate, a police authority may pay out of the police fund any compensation, costs or expenses awarded against a person under the direction and control of the chief officer of police; any costs or expenses incurred and not recovered by such a person in such proceedings; and any sum required in connection with the settlement of a claim that has or might give rise to such proceedings.

SERIOUS ORGANISED CRIME AGENCY

3.53 Under reg 14, any constable or other person seconded to the newly-formed Serious Organised Crime Agency ('SOCA')[48] to serve as a member of its staff shall be treated as employed by SOCA for the purposes of reg 25 (Liability of employers and principals).

BARRISTERS

3.54 Regulation 15 makes it unlawful for barristers or their clerks to discriminate against, or harass, pupils and tenants (including applicants for pupillage and tenancy). As well as covering recruitment, selection, terms, opportunities and benefits, the regulation includes terminating pupillage or subjecting the person to any pressure to leave the chambers or to other detriment. It also makes it unlawful for any person to discriminate in the giving, withholding or acceptance of instructions to a barrister. It is therefore unlawful for a solicitor to refuse to use a barrister because that person is too old or too young.

3.55 A barrister's clerk includes any person carrying out the function of a barrister's clerk. The terms 'pupil', 'pupillage' and 'set of chambers' have the meanings commonly associated with their use in the context of barristers practising in independent practice. So do 'tenant' and 'tenancy', but they

---

[47] Reg 13.

[48] SOCA came into operation on 1 April 2006.

also include reference to a barrister permitted to work in a set of chambers who is not a tenant (eg a 'squatter' or door tenant).

ADVOCATES

3.56 Since the provisions in respect of barristers extend to England and Wales only, reg 16 prohibits discrimination by advocates in Scotland in the same way. The only difference lies in the definition of advocates and pupils, which recognises that in Scotland advocates do not practise in sets of chambers.

PARTNERSHIPS

3.57 Partnerships are brought within the scope of Part 2 under reg 17, the result being to give partners and those applying for partnership similar rights to those of an employee. The provisions apply to a firm and to a limited liability partnership, with references to a partner in a firm being references to members of a limited liability partnership. They also apply to persons proposing to form themselves into a partnership. In the case of a limited partnership, references to a partner are to be construed as references to a general partner.

Unlawful acts

3.58 It is unlawful for a firm, in relation to a position as a partner in the firm, to discriminate against a person on the grounds of age in the arrangements they make for the purpose of determining to whom they should offer that position, in the terms on which they offer him that position, and by refusing to offer, or deliberately not offering him that position. In a case where the person already holds the position of partner, it is unlawful for the firm to discriminate against him in the way they afford him access to any benefits or by refusing to afford him, or deliberately not affording him, access to them.

3.59 It is also unlawful to discriminate against a person holding the position of partner by expelling him from that position or subjecting him to any other detriment. Expulsion includes the termination by expiry of a fixed-term partnership or a constructive termination. Finally, it is unlawful to subject to harassment a person who holds or has applied for the position of partner. The exception of genuine occupational requirement applies to partnerships.

TRADE ORGANISATIONS

Trade organisations

3.60 A 'trade organisation' is given a broad definition: [49]

> 'an organisation of workers, an organisation of employers, or any other organisation whose members carry on a particular profession or trade for the purposes of which the organisation exists'.

Organisation of workers

3.61 An organisation of workers will include a trade union, which is defined as a temporary or permanent organisation which consists wholly or mainly of workers and whose principal purposes include the regulation of relations between workers and employers or employers' associations.[50] A 'worker' is an individual who works – or seeks to work – under a contract of employment or under any other contract for the personal performance of any work or services or in Crown employment.[51]

3.62 In *Sadek v Medical Protection Society*,[52] the Court of Appeal held that the Medical Protection Society, a mutual medical protection organisation whose members are doctors, dentists and other healthcare professionals, was an organisation of workers within the equivalent provision of the Race Relations Act 1976. A member of a profession can be a 'worker'. However, having been defined as an organisation of workers, the organisation could not also be defined as falling into the third category, 'any other organisation whose members carry on a particular profession'.

Organisation of employers

3.63 An 'organisation of employers' is defined as a temporary or permanent organisation which consists wholly or mainly of employers or individual owners of undertakings and whose principal purposes include the regulation of relations between employers and workers or trade unions. The definition also includes an organisation consisting wholly or mainly of constituent or affiliated organisations, or representatives of such organisations, with the same principal purpose.[53]

Other organisation

3.64 Regulation 18 includes 'any other organisation whose members carry on a particular profession or trade for the purposes of which the organisation exists'. 'Profession' includes any vocation or occupation, while 'trade'

---

49   Reg 18(4).
50   TU&LR(C)A 1992, s 1.
51   TU&LR(C)A 1992, s 296(1).
52   [2005] IRLR 57.
53   TU&LR(C)A 1992, s 122(1).

includes any business.[54] This would include chartered professional institutions and bodies such as the Law Society and General Council of the Bar.

Unlawful acts

3.65 It is unlawful for a trade organisation to discriminate against a person on the grounds of age in the terms on which it is prepared to admit him to membership of the organisation or be refusing to accept, or deliberately not accepting, his application for membership. Therefore, a professional institution that requires a minimum number of years' practice in order for a person to qualify as a chartered member of that institution may be applying a discriminatory practice.

3.66 Once a person is a member of a trade organisation, there are three ways in which the trade organisation can potentially act unlawfully: (1) in the way it affords him access to any benefits or by refusing or deliberately omitting to afford him access to them; (2) by depriving him of membership, or varying the terms on which he is a member; or (3) by subjecting him to any other detriment. 'Benefits' includes facilities and services.[55] It is also unlawful for a trade organisation, in relation to a person's membership or application for membership, to subject that person to harassment.

QUALIFICATIONS BODIES

3.67 A qualifications body means any authority or body that can confer a professional or trade qualification, but does not include the governing body of institutions of further and higher education or the proprietor of a school. Examples of such bodies would include the General Medical Council, Royal Pharmaceutical Society, the UK Central Council for Nursing, Midwifery and Health Visiting, the Institute of the Motor Industry and the Driving Standards Agency. 'Professional or trade qualification' means any authorisation, qualification, recognition, registration, enrolment, approval or certification which is needed for or facilitates engagement in a particular trade or profession.[56]

3.68 It is unlawful for such bodies to discriminate on the grounds of age in the terms in which it is prepared to confer a professional or trade qualification (which includes renew or extend), by refusing or deliberately not granting a qualification or by withdrawing or varying the terms of the qualification.[57] Harassment is also unlawful.

---

[54]   Reg 18(4).
[55]   Reg 2(2).
[56]   Reg 19(3).
[57]   Reg 19(1).

EMPLOYMENT AGENCIES AND CAREERS GUIDANCE

3.69 An employment agency cannot discriminate against a person on grounds of age in the terms on which it provides any of its services, by refusing, or deliberately not providing, any of its services or in the way it provides any of its services.[58] Nor can it harass a person to whom it provides its services.[59] The genuine occupational requirement exception applies and would extend to an agency reasonably relying upon a statement from the employer that the exception applied (and it is a criminal offence for the employer to make a false statement).

THE ARMED FORCES

3.70 The Age Regulations do not extend to service in the armed forces.

ASSISTING PERSONS TO OBTAIN EMPLOYMENT

3.71 Regulation 22 makes it unlawful for the Secretary of State to discriminate against any person by subjecting him to a detriment or harassment in the provision of services under s 2 of the Employment and Training Act 1973. This section requires the Secretary of State, 'to make such arrangements as he considers appropriate for the purpose of assisting persons to select, train for, obtain and retain employment suitable for their ages and capacities or of assisting persons to obtain suitable employees'. There is an analogous requirement for the Scottish Enterprise and Highlands and Islands Enterprise. The Regulation does not apply in a case where reg 20 (the provision of vocational training) applies or where the Secretary of State is acting as an employment agency under reg 21 (employment agencies, careers guidance, etc).

RELATIONSHIPS WHICH HAVE COME TO AN END

3.72 Under reg 24, it is unlawful to discriminate after a relevant relationship has come to an end, either by subjecting the ex-employee to a detriment or harassment. A 'relevant relationship' is one during which an act of discrimination is unlawful. For example, an employer who refused on grounds of the employee's age to provide a reference to that employee would be acting unlawfully. This regulation follows the House of Lords' decision in *Rhys-Harper v Relaxion Group plc*[60] that an employment tribunal had jurisdiction under other discrimination statutes to consider a complaint

---

[58]   Reg 21(1).
[59]   Reg 21(2).
[60]   [2003] IRLR 484.

of discrimination which related only to acts which were alleged to have taken place after the complainant's employment had come to an end.

GENERAL EXCEPTIONS FROM PART 2

Exception for national security

3.73 Regulation 27 provides that the Regulations do not render unlawful any act done in order to comply with a requirement of any statutory provision. 'Statutory provision' means legislation emanating from central government at Westminster or Edinburgh. This is an absolute defence, but only applies to acts done in necessary performance of an express obligation (for example, a requirement that persons under 18 should not be employed in bars[61]). If a provision gives permission or the discretion to act, then that discretion must be exercised lawfully.[62]

3.74 Regulation 24 provides that the Age Regulations do not render unlawful an act done for the purpose of safeguarding national security, if it is justified.

Exception for positive action

3.75 Article 7.1 of the Equal Treatment Directive states that the principle of equal treatment shall not prevent a Member State from maintaining or adopting specific measures to compensate for disadvantages linked to age. Regulation 29 sets out this exception, whereby the Regulations do not render unlawful any act done in or in connection with: (1) affording persons of a particular age or age group access to facilities for training, which would help fit them for particular work; or (2) encouraging persons of a particular age or age group to take advantage of opportunities for doing particular work. The proviso is that it must reasonably appear to the person doing the act that it prevents or compensates for disadvantages linked to age suffered by persons of that age or age group doing that work or likely to take up that work.

3.76 There is a similar provision for a trade organisation (as defined in reg 18) in respect of members of a particular age or age group, who can be given access to facilities for training which would help fit them for holding a post of any kind in the organisation or who can be encouraged to take advantage of opportunities for holding such posts in the organisation.[63] This is subject to the same proviso, as is a provision allowing trade organisations to encourage only persons of a particular age or age group to become members of the organisation.[64]

---

[61] Licensing Act 1964, s 170.
[62] *Hampson v Department of Education and Science* [1991] 1 AC 171, [1990] IRLR 302, HL.
[63] Reg 29(2).
[64] Reg 29(3).

3.77 Positive action allows an employer who, for example, advertises only in a magazine for young people, to do so lawfully if it reasonably appears to him that this will compensate for a disadvantage suffered by that age group, namely under-representation in that business. However, he could not exclude applications from other age groups without crossing the line between positive action and positive discrimination.

3.78 The test is that it must reasonably appear to the person taking the positive action that it prevents or compensates for disadvantages. This would appear to be an easier test than objective justification under reg 3. If the employer can show that what it has done falls within reg 29(1)(a) or (b), then it need only show that it considered it was reasonable to take that action.

Chapter 4

RETIREMENT AND DISMISSAL

BACKGROUND

4.1 At a time when life expectancy in the United Kingdom is rising, the average retirement age is falling. In 1950, the average retirement age for men and women in the United Kingdom was 67 and 64 respectively; in 2001 it was 63 and 61 respectively.[1] Yet a man aged 60 is now likely to live for another 20 years and a woman aged 60 for over 23 years.[2] Economically, this is an unsustainable paradox.

4.2 Currently, only about 30% of people are still in employment at the age of 65, although it is unclear to what extent this results from employers imposing earlier retirement ages. According to research carried out for the DTI's *Impact Assessment on Retirement Ages* (July 2005), 'there is no evidence that employers' fixed retirement ages exert a widespread influence on decisions to retire before state pension age'.[3]

4.3 At present, 49.9% of men are in a workplace with a fixed retirement age of 65, 16% in a workplace with lower ages (the largest percentage being 11.3% at the age of 60) and 1.3% where the retirement age is above 65. The remainder are in workplaces with no fixed retirement age. For women, a large percentage (31%) are in a workplace with a fixed retirement age of 60, 1.1% where it is below that, 0.5% at 63, 19.3% at 65 and 0.5% over 65, with the remainder again in workplaces with no fixed retirement age.[4]

4.4 Removing fixed retirement ages below 65 unless they can be objectively justified will allow workers who are currently being retired earlier to stay at work longer, if they want to do so and are capable of doing the work. Similarly, giving employees the opportunity to request continued working beyond their retirement date will encourage some employees to remain at work. However, the likely impact of this increased flexibility can only be guessed, with the statistics showing that more women are likely to be affected than men, but that the numbers affected may, in any event, be relatively low. At present, only 19% of all those with a fixed retirement age retire at that retirement age and, of these, perhaps half do so against their will.

---

[1]   European Commission *Employment in Europe 2003 Recent Trends and Prospects* (2005).
[2]   Government Actuaries Department Life Tables.
[3]   A Humphreys et al *Factors affecting the labour market participation of older workers* (DWP Research Report, 2003).
[4]   Ibid.

4.5 Nevertheless, apart from the political and social need to comply with the Equality Directive and the economic need to encourage people to work longer, there are benefits to both employers and employees in encouraging employees to remain at work as they grow older:

(1) Research suggests that older workers are no less productive than younger workers, save in limited jobs and circumstances. In addition, experience, better inter-personal skills and motivation (for example) could compensate for any loss of speed or strength.[5] This has been the much-publicised experience for B&Q, the DIY and home improvement chain, which has an age-positive recruitment strategy and now has 21% of its workforce aged over 50. However, it will at least be the perception of many employers that a significant number of older workers 'mark time' as they approach retirement and/or have a higher number of days absent through sickness.

(2) A lower turnover of staff reduces recruitment costs and allows for more efficient staff planning.

(3) Older employees will benefit from increased earnings and the opportunity to save.

4.6 Therefore, while the impact on employers and employees is numerically uncertain, the social and economic benefits are easier to predict.

4.7 A major impact of the Employment Equality (Age) Regulations 2006 will be upon retirement. For the first time, there is a default retirement age of 65, which an employer may choose to raise, but which it must objectively justify if it wishes to lower. Dismissals on the ground of retirement will be fair, if retirement is the reason for dismissal and a set procedure is followed. The key feature of the procedure is the employee's right to request to continue working beyond the intended retirement date. This chapter considers these different elements.

THE DEFAULT RETIREMENT AGE

4.8 While the Equality Directive applies to dismissals[6] and so prohibits mandatory retirement on grounds of age, Recital 14 states, 'the Directive shall be without prejudice to national provisions laying down retirement ages'. In order to allow retirement dismissals – which would otherwise be discriminatory – the Age Regulations have provided a national default retirement age of 65, which permits an employer to dismiss an employee on the ground of retirement at or above 65 without the need for objective justification.

---

[5]   P Meadows *Retirement ages in the UK: a review of the literature on key issues* (DTI Research Series No18, 2003).

[6]   Article 3.1(b).

Regulation 30 – exception for retirement

4.9 Regulation 30 sets out the exception for retirement and applies in relation to 'an employee', which has the same meaning as in the Employment Rights Act 1996, s 230, where it is defined as meaning 'an individual who has entered into or works under (or, where the employment has ceased, worked under) a contract of employment'. Therefore, it does not apply – for example – to office-holders, including the police, or to partners. Regulation 30(1) applies to employees working under a fixed-term contract, but excludes employees who are in Crown employment and House of Commons and House of Lords staff.

4.10 Regulation 30(2) then goes on to state the exception, namely that:

> 'Nothing in Part 2 or 3 shall render unlawful the dismissal of a person to whom this regulation applies at or over the age of 65 where the reason for the dismissal is retirement.'

Justifying a default retirement age

4.11 In the responses to the DTI's 2003 consultation paper *Age Matters*, opinion was divided over the need for a national default retirement age, but only 24% of the responses were in favour of a suggested national default retirement age of 70. In part, this reflected the existing practices of businesses and the time that will be needed to accommodate changes to the workforce. The default retirement age of 65 was therefore considered a pragmatic response to economic and social realities, but it will be reviewed in 2011. As the Rt Hon Margaret Hodge, Minister for Employment and Welfare Reform, said in Parliament during an adjournment debate on retirement: [7]

> '… under the legislation, there is a default retirement age of 65, although we have promised that we will review that, as the measure beds in, over five years. I tend to agree with [the initiator of the debate] that if we can get rid of that default age, we will improve the ability of older people to participate in the labour market. However, I hope he accepts that as we try to transform cultural attitudes in our society towards the employment of older people, we should bring all the stakeholders with us. As we set the default retirement age, we were conscious of the concerns of business. There were fears among those in the business community that if there was no retirement age, they would find it difficult to manage their work force and ensure that younger people had the opportunity to develop in the workplace.'

4.12 The national default retirement age is therefore not a compulsory age for retirement. There is nothing to stop an employee from choosing to terminate his employment at a lower age. An employer can set a retirement age that is above 65 and is not forced to retire employees at 65. However, when an employer sets a retirement age of below 65, this will have to be

---

[7] HC Deb, Vol 445, Part 135, col 46WH.

objectively justified under reg 3(1),whereas a retirement age of 65 or above need not be.

4.13 The decision by the Government whether to keep or to abolish the default retirement age will focus upon two main factors: (1) whether it remains appropriate and necessary to keep a default retirement age to facilitate workforce planning and to avoid adverse effects on pensions and other employment benefits; and (2) the influence of any other social policy objectives.

Objective justification

4.14 A major impact of the Age Regulations initially will be upon employers who have contractual retirement ages of below 65, as these will have to be objectively justified. Without such justification, any contract of employment that currently has a term that permits the employer to retire the employee at an age below 65 will be unenforceable against the particular employee.[8]

4.15 It is likely that employers will find it difficult objectively to justify a lower retirement age than 65. Industry practice would not be sufficient, nor would an employer's perception of itself as a 'young' company, as neither would amount to a proportionate means of achieving a legitimate end. The following may be relevant factors in justifying a lower retirement age than 65:

(1) *Health, welfare and safety*. For example, an airline might be able to show that there were deficiencies in performance linked to age which meant that a person over 60 was more likely to fail relevant competence tests.

(2) *Capability*. There is little evidence that older workers are less productive than younger workers, except in a limited range of jobs. An example might be a company that requires heavy labouring skills from employees and which could show that employees over a certain age would be unlikely to perform the work adequately.

(3) *'Job blocking'*. At least in the short term, an extension of the retirement age to 65 where it has previously been set at – for example – 60 could cause economic or personnel problems for an employer, where it 'blocks' other employees from promotion or leads to duplication of roles.

4.16 Whilst it is instructive to look at the arguments the Government deploys to justify the default retirement age, as these may be used by employers to satisfy the objective justification test, one also wonders whether the Government itself might have some difficulties in justifying the default retirement. In the DTI's Notes on the Regulations,[9] it states that:

---

[8]   Sch 5, para 1(1), (2).

[9]   At para 99.

'This exception for retirement ages of 65 and over is considered to be within the exemption contained in Article 6(1) of the Directive as being justified by reference to a legitimate aim of social policy in accordance with the test in *R v Secretary of State for Employment ex parte Seymour-Smith & Perez*.'[10]

The legitimate aim

4.17 The legitimate aim of social policy is to meet the concern of employers in relation to (1) workforce planning and (2) avoiding an adverse impact on the provision of occupational pensions and other work-related benefits.

4.18 However, is that sufficient? Workforce planning is said to include a number of aspects. Firstly, it means that a retirement age is a target age against which employers can plan their work and employees can plan their careers and retirement. In response it might be said that a greater benefit to the employee would be the flexibility of choosing when to retire.

4.19 Secondly, employers gain by being able to rely upon a set retirement age, thus allowing the recruitment, training and development of employees and the planning of wages structures and occupational pensions against a known attrition profile. Reference is made to Art 6(1)(c) of the Directive,[11] which recognises justifiable differences of treatment in respect of the fixing of a maximum age for retirement, although that is a specific example that relates to the training requirements of a particular post, not a general exemption.

4.20 Thirdly, for both employers and employees, being able to rely on a set retirement age avoids the blocking of jobs – often the more senior jobs – from younger workers.

4.21 Fourthly, knowing there is a set retirement age means that employees cannot be certain that they will be in work after that time, thereby encouraging them to make savings now.

4.22 The other concern of employers – avoiding an adverse impact on the provision of occupational pensions and other work-related benefits – is said to be that, if employers only had the option of individually objectively-justified retirement ages, there would be a risk of adverse consequences for occupational pension schemes and other work related benefits. Employers might reduce or remove benefits to offset the cost of providing those benefits to all employees, including those over 65.

Proportionality

4.23 If the exception for retirement ages can be justified as a means of achieving a legitimate aim of social policy (whether by workforce planning or avoiding an adverse impact on pension and benefits), the next question that arises is whether setting a default retirement age of 65 is an appropriate and necessary way of achieving that objective.

---

[10]   [2000] 1 WLR 435.
[11]   DTI's Note on the Regulations, para 100.

4.24   In *Mangold v Helm*,[12] the European Court of Justice considered German legislation which placed curbs on fixed-term contracts of employment, requiring an objective reason justifying the fixed term or, alternatively, imposing limits on the number of renewals and on total duration. These restrictions did not apply to contracts with workers aged 58 and over (and to workers aged 52 and over until the end of 2006). The purpose of the difference in treatment for older workers was to promote the vocational integration of unemployed older workers, in so far as they encounter considerable difficulties in finding work. The Court accepted that 'The legitimacy of such a public interest objective cannot reasonably be thrown in doubt.'[13]

4.25   The Court went on:

> 'An objective of that kind must as a rule, therefore, be regarded as justifying, "objectively and reasonably", as provided for by the first subparagraph of Article 6(1) of Directive 2000/78, a difference of treatment on grounds of age laid down by Member States. It still remains to be established whether, according to the actual wording of that provision, the means used to achieve that legitimate objective are "appropriate and necessary".'[14]

4.26   The Court concluded that the means were not proportionate and, in terms that may have resonance for the United Kingdom's default retirement age of 65, made this statement of principle:

> 'In so far as such legislation takes the age of the worker concerned as the only criterion for the application of a fixed-term contract of employment, when it has not been shown that fixing an age threshold, as such, regardless of any other consideration linked to the structure of the labour market in question or the personal situation of the person concerned, is objectively necessary to the attainment of the objective which is the vocational integration of unemployed older workers, it must be considered to go beyond what is appropriate and necessary in order to attain the objective pursued. Observance of the principle of proportionality requires every derogation from an individual right to reconcile, so far as is possible, the requirements of the principle of equal treatment with those of the aim pursued ... Such national legislation cannot, therefore, be justified.'[15]

4.27   Therefore, the question will be whether a default retirement age of 65 is appropriate and necessary in order to attain what may be the legitimate aim of a social policy that seeks to meet the concerns – primarily – of employers.

---

[12]   Case C-144/04; [2006] IRLR 143.
[13]   Ibid, para 60.
[14]   Ibid, paras 61, 62.
[15]   Ibid, para 65.

THE DUTY TO CONSIDER WORKING BEYOND RETIREMENT (REG 47, SCH 6)

4.28 In every case, before an employer can dismiss an employee on the grounds of retirement, irrespective of the age of the employee or the employer's normal retirement age, it must follow a statutory procedure. This procedure is analogous to the statutory dismissal and disciplinary procedures implemented by the Employment Act 2002 for dismissal on other grounds.

4.29 The statutory dismissal procedures under the Employment Act 2002 do not apply to retirement dismissals.[16] That Act has been amended to add the Age Regulations to Schs 3, 4 and 5 of the 2002 Act:

(1) Schedule 3 is the list of jurisdictions to which s 31 of the 2002 Act applies ('Non-completion of statutory procedure: adjustment of awards'). It requires a tribunal to reduce or increase an award by between 10% and 50% for non-completion of 'one of the statutory procedures'.

(2) Section 32 prevents a tribunal from having jurisdiction to hear a complaint unless the statutory grievance procedure has been followed.

(3) Section 38 is the tribunal's duty to make a minimum award of two weeks' pay where there has been a failure by the employer to give the employee a statement of employment particulars.

(The amendment to include the Age Regulations under ss 32 is dealt with elsewhere.[17])

4.30 The procedure that an employer must follow before dismissing an employee on the grounds of retirement is set out in Sch 6 to the Regulations.

4.31 At para 1, the definitions include two important terms. The 'operative date of termination' means:

(1) where the employer terminates the contract by notice, the date on which the notice expires, or

(2) where the employer terminates without notice, the date on which termination takes effect.

The 'intended date of retirement' will normally mean the date on which the employer intends to retire the employee as notified to the employee, but there are also provisions for when the employer fails to notify.

The duty to inform the employee

4.32 Schedule 6, para 2 creates a duty upon an employer who intends dismissing an employee by reason of retirement. The duty on the employer is to notify the employee in writing of:

---

[16] Employment Act 2002 (Dispute Resolution) Regulations 2004, SI 2004/752, reg 4(1)(h), as amended by Sch 8, para 64.

[17] See Chapter 8.

(1) the employee's right to make 'a request'; and

(2) the date upon which it intends the employee to retire.

'A request' means a request not to retire, as set out in para 5.[18]

4.33   The duty to inform the employee in accordance with the Age Regulations is absolute. It applies regardless of any term in the employee's contract indicating when his retirement is expected to take place; any other notification or information given by the employer at any time; or any other information provided at any time about the employee's right to make a request. In other words, a reference to the right to make a request in a handbook or in written terms and conditions or during any discussion will not be sufficient.

4.34 The notice must be given not more than one year and not less than six months before the intended retirement dismissal, although there is a continuing duty to notify the employee in writing until the 14th day before the operative date of termination.[19]

> **Example**: AB Ltd wishes to dismiss K on her 65th birthday, which falls on 31 December. It must therefore notify K of its intention that she should retire on that date and of her right to make a request not to retire on that date no earlier than 1 January and no later than 30 June of that year. If it fails to do so, AB Ltd is still under a continuing duty to notify K until 17 December, which is the 14th day before the date of dismissal.

4.35 Paragraph 3 applies if the employer has notified the employee of the right to make a request or the employee has made a request before being notified and:

(1) the employer and employee agree without holding a meeting that the employment will continue for an agreed period (or, if the employee has appealed a refusal, there is an agreement as to when the employee will retire without an appeal meeting), or

(2) the employer has given notification to the employee after a meeting or an appeal in the same terms as requested, or

(3) the parties have agreed that the dismissal will take effect earlier than the intended date.

4.36 If any one of these alternatives applies and either the extension of time is for six months or less or the dismissal will take place earlier than the intended date, there is then no need for any further notification from the employer. In these circumstances, the new date supersedes the intended date of retirement.

> **Example**: K makes a request to continue working for a further three months beyond the intended date of retirement. AB Ltd agrees (with or without holding a meeting) and gives notice to K that her employment will continue for three

---

[18]   See the pro forma letter in the Annexes to the ACAS Guide *Age and the Workplace*, in Appendix 2.

[19]   Sch 6, para 4.

months beyond 31 December. As this is less than six months, AB Ltd does not need to give further notification to K to retire her on the new date, which supersedes 31 December.

4.37 It follows from this that there is therefore a requirement to repeat the statutory procedures where the employer agrees to an indefinite extension of the intended date of retirement or an extension exceeding six months. Whether or not this will act as a disincentive to employers to reach such agreement remains to be seen.

Failure to comply with duty to inform

4.38 Failure by the employer to comply with the duty to inform no more than one year and no less than six months before dismissal entitles an employee to seek compensation from the employment tribunal, which may make an award not exceeding eight week's pay (at the statutory limit for a week's pay[20] calculated at the date on which the complaint was presented or, if earlier, the operative date of termination) as the tribunal considers just and equitable in all the circumstances.[21] Therefore, an employer who notifies after six months and carries out a fair retirement dismissal is still liable to pay compensation for this failure. Although the decision to make an award and its amount (up to eight weeks' pay) lie within the tribunal's discretion, one presumes that the length of delay and the employee's knowledge of likely retirement will be factors in the exercise of that discretion.

4.39 A complaint must be brought before the end of the period of three months beginning with the last day permitted to the employer for complying with the duty to notify (ie six months before the intended date of retirement). If the employee did not know the intended date of retirement, then time runs from the first day he knew or should have known that date. The discretion to extend time is that it was not 'reasonably practicable for the complaint to be presented before the end of that period of three months'.[22] Despite this, the Age Regulations do not impose a requirement that an employer informs an employee of the procedural steps and time limits that must be observed (for example, by adding this information to the information required under s 3 of the Employment Rights Act 1996).

The employee's request

4.40 The employee's request (under Sch 6, para 5) must be in writing and 'state that it is made under this paragraph'. It must propose that the employment should continue, following the intended date of retirement, (1) indefinitely, (2) for a stated period, or (3) until a stated date. Where the employer has failed to notify the employee in accordance with para 2 (not more than one year, not less than six months before the intended date of

---

[20]   ERA 1996, s 227(1).
[21]   Sch 6, para 11(3).
[22]   Sch 6, para 11(2).

retirement) and not yet notified under the continuing duty, then the request should identify the date the employee believes to be the intended date of retirement.

4.41 An employee may make one request only in relation to any one intended date of retirement and may not make a request in respect of a date that has superseded the intended date. There is no requirement to provide any reasons for the request. However, one imagines that, in many cases, such further information is more likely to encourage a genuine consideration of the request.

4.42 Where the employer has complied with the duty to notify under para 2, the employee's request should be made more than three months but not more than six months before the intended date of retirement. Where the employer has not notified the employee within that specified period, the employee can make the request at any time in the six months up to the intended date of retirement.

4.43 It is difficult to see what advantage there would be to the employee in leaving his request late where he has been notified by his employer in good time. Where that has happened – for example, nine months pre-intended date of retirement – he is likely to have his request considered more favourably in many cases if he makes his request as soon as possible (which is six months pre-intended date) so that the employer has time to make any necessary arrangements. It might therefore encourage better employment relations if time to make the request ran from the date of the employer's notice.

The duty to consider the request

4.44 The employee's request to continue working beyond the retirement date creates a further duty on the employer, which is to consider the request.[23] No duty arises where the employer has served on the employee, not more than one year and not less than six months pre-retirement, notice of the right to make a request and its intention to retire and the employee has failed to make a request up to three months before the intended retirement date.

4.45 Whereas under the draft Regulations, the duty to consider a request was to be done 'in good faith', this requirement has been dropped from the final version of the Age Regulations. There is now only a set of procedural requirements and no guidance for the employer on what would be relevant to considerations in making the decision. So long as the employer has considered the request, its reasoning is irrelevant.

4.46 A meeting should be held to discuss the request with the employee, within a reasonable period after receiving it and which both parties must take all reasonable steps to attend.[24] There is no parallel provision in these procedures to those in the statutory dismissal and disciplinary procedures

---

[23]   Sch 6, para 6.
[24]   Sch 6, para 7.

requiring an employer to allow an employee two opportunities to attend the meeting.[25] The duty to hold a meeting does not apply if the parties have already reached agreement, nor where it is not practicable to hold a meeting, so long as the employer considers the requests and any representations made by the employee.

4.47 There is a right to be accompanied to the meeting, under para 9. This is in similar terms to the statutory right to be accompanied under the Employment Relations Act 1999, s 10.[26] If the employee reasonably requests to be accompanied at the meeting, then he may choose a companion who is a worker employed by the same employer. His choice would therefore not extend to a trade union representative if that person was not an employee. The companion may address the meeting, but not answer questions on behalf of the employee, and he may confer with the employee during the meeting. If the companion is not able to attend the meeting, the employee may propose a convenient alternative time within seven days after the proposed meeting date. The companion is entitled to time off work to attend the meeting.

4.48 If the employee is denied the right to be accompanied, the employee can bring a complaint to the employment tribunal (under para 12) within three months of the date of failure or threat of failure, or within a further three months in a case where it was not reasonably practicable to do so earlier. The remedy is an amount not exceeding two weeks' pay at the statutorily capped level.

4.49 There is also a right not to be subjected to any detriment by any act of the employer done on the ground that the employee exercised the right to be accompanied.[27] The companion is similarly not to be subjected to any detriment. Enforcement of that right follows the procedures under the Employment Rights Act 1996, s 48 (under Part V of that Act, 'Protection from suffering detriment in employment'). Any dismissal on this ground will be an automatically unfair dismissal and there is a right to interim relief. It is also a dismissal for which there is no qualifying period of continuous employment.[28]

The employer's response

4.50 The employer is under a duty to consider the request and the meeting is 'to discuss the request with the employee'.[29] In contrast to the statutory dismissal and disciplinary procedures, there is no requirement that the employer provide any information in preparation for this meeting (apart from the intended retirement date).

---

[25]   Employment Act 2002 (Dispute Resolution) Regulations 2004, SI 2004/752, reg 13.
[26]   The right to be accompanied to disciplinary and grievance hearings.
[27]   Sch 6, para 13(1).
[28]   ERA 1996, s 108(3)(m).
[29]   Sch 6, para 7(1).

4.51 If the employer agrees, it is agreeing to a request not to retire the employee on the planned retirement date and the outcome will be either that the employment continues for a stated period or indefinitely. The employer does not have to agree to the particular period that the employee has requested, if such a specific request has been made. Therefore, an employer has acted lawfully if it agrees to the request not to retire on the intended date of retirement but decides to allow the employee to continue working for a further one year, where the employee wishes to work for a further two years.

4.52 Notice of the employer's decision must be given in writing, dated and – if it is a refusal – confirm that the employer wishes to retire the employee and the date on which dismissal shall take effect. Crucially, there is no requirement to provide reasons for the refusal. As noted above, all the employer must do is consider the response. The employee has no right to know why it has been refused. The notice shall also inform the employee of the right to appeal. Where the request is agreed, the notice must state either that the employment will continue indefinitely or that it will continue for a stated period. Where that stated period is less than the employee proposed, the employee should also be informed of the right to appeal.

4.53 It is important to note that the contract of employment remains in force for all purposes until the day following the day on which the notice is given.[30] However any such continuation of the contract of employment is disregarded when determining the operative date of dismissal for the purposes of unfair dismissal (see below). Therefore, where an employer has dismissed an employee for retirement, but has not responded to the unsuccessful request to work beyond retirement, the employee remains in employment until the day after the notice refusing the request is given. If the employee is bringing a claim arising from the dismissal, then time still runs from the actual date of dismissal.

The appeal

4.54 The employee should notify the employer that he wishes to appeal as soon as is reasonably practicable after he has received the employer's notice. The notice of appeal should be in writing and set out the grounds of appeal. In the absence of a reasoned refusal, this may be difficult to do.

4.55 An appeal meeting should be held within a reasonable period after notice of appeal is given and both parties should take all reasonable steps to attend. As with the request meeting, there is no need to hold an appeal meeting if the parties have reached agreement. There is also no duty to hold the meeting where it is not practicable to do so, so long as the employer considers the appeal and any representations. If an appeal meeting is held, there is the same right to be accompanied.

---

[30]   Sch 6, para 10.

4.56 Written and dated notification of the outcome of the appeal should be given as soon as reasonably practicable after the meeting. Consideration of the appeal need not take place before the dismissal takes effect.

Transitional provisions

4.57 Schedule 7 sets out the transitional provisions in respect of the duty to consider working beyond retirement. They are surprisingly complex and employers will do well to find their way through the procedural labyrinth. There are four different sets of circumstances.

4.58 The first is where an employer has given notice of dismissal before 1 October 2006 of at least the contractual notice period or, where that exceeds four weeks, of at least four weeks, and the notice of dismissal expires before 1 April 2007. If the employer has made the employee aware (prior to 1 October 2006) that he is being retired on the expiry date, the employer should notify the employee on, or as soon as practicable after, 1 October 2006 of the right to make a request to continue working. This prevents the employer from being in default of the notice provisions.

4.59 The employee should then make a request as per Sch 6, para 5 and do so, where practicable, at least four weeks before the expiry date. Where that is not practicable, the request must be made as soon as reasonably practicable after being notified of the right to make a request, but not more than four weeks after the expiry date. This does not delay the operative date of termination.[31] Where a request is made, the employer must comply with the rules regarding a meeting to consider the request, any appeal and the right to be accompanied to meetings.[32]

4.60 Where the employer fails to notify the employee in writing of the right to make a request, or does not do so as soon as practicable after 1 October 2006, then the employee can still make a request (so long as it satisfies the procedural requirements of Sch 6, para 5).

4.61 The second set of circumstances differs from the first through the failure by the employer (1) to provide minimum notice or (2) to make the employee aware, before 1 October 2006, that the employer considers that the employee is being retired on the expiry date. In this case, there is a continuing duty on the employer to notify and a right for the employee to make a request anyway.

4.62 The third set of circumstances covers notice of dismissal given on or after 1 October 2006 of at least the contractual notice period or, where that exceeds four weeks, of at least four weeks, with the notice of dismissal expiring before 1 April 2007. Here, the employer complies with its duty by notifying the employee before or on the same day as the notice of dismissal. The employee should then make a request as per Sch, 6 para 5 and do so, where practicable, at least four weeks before the expiry date. Again, where

---

[31]   Sch 7, para 6(a).
[32]   Sch 7, para 6(b).

that is not practicable, the request must be made as soon as reasonably practicable after being notified of the right to make a request, but not more than four weeks after the expiry date.

4.63 Finally, where s notice is given after 1 October 2006 which is less than the contractual notice period or, if longer, the statutory notice period[33] and it expires before 1 April 2007, there is a continuing duty to notify and the option for the employee of requesting to work beyond the retirement date.

4.64 The scenario that is not covered by the transitional provisions is where the employee is due to be retired on or soon after 1 April 2007. Given that the duty of the employer to inform the employee of the right to make a request must be made not more than one year and not less than six months before the intended date of retirement, an employee who is due to be retired on – for example – 2 April 2007, needs to be notified by 1 October 2006.

DISMISSAL FOR RETIREMENT

4.65 As discussed earlier in this chapter, reg 30 states that:

> 'Nothing in Part 2 or 3 shall render unlawful the dismissal of a person to whom this regulation applies at or over the age of 65 where the reason for the dismissal is retirement.'

The Regulation applies to employees.[34]

4.66 Prior to the Age Regulations, an employee who had reached the age of 65 did not have the right to claim unfair dismissal.[35] At about the same time as Parliament finally approved the Age Regulations, the House of Lords finally buried the long-running case of *Secretary of State for Trade and Industry and Rutherford et al,*[36] in which the upper age limit on bringing a claim for unfair dismissal and redundancy payments was challenged on the grounds that it indirectly discriminated against the male claimants. While the principles of indirect discrimination remain in issue, the question of age limits for both unfair dismissal and redundancy payments is now academic, with their removal by the Age Regulations. An employer now has a right to dismiss an employee on grounds of retirement at or over the age of 65, but an employee also has a right to claim unfair dismissal at any age.

4.67 Under the Employment Rights Act 1996, s 98(2)(ba) as amended, retirement of the employee is a potentially fair reason for dismissal, along with capability, conduct, redundancy and contravention of an enactment, as well as 'some other substantial reason' under s 98(1)(b). It is for the employer to prove that the reason – or, if more than one, the principal reason – relied upon for dismissal was retirement.

---

33   ERA 1996, s 86.
34   Per ERA 1996, s 230(1), not including those in Crown employment, House of Commons or House of Lords staff.
35   ERA 1996, s 109(1), now omitted.
36   [2006] UKHL 19.

4.68 In any case where the employer has shown that the reason for dismissal is retirement, the question whether the dismissal is fair or unfair is determined by s 98ZG, not by applying the test of reasonableness under s 98(4) of the 1996 Act. Therefore, the tribunal does not have to decide whether the employer acted reasonably in treating retirement as a sufficient reason for dismissing the employee.

4.69 Under s 98ZG, the employee shall be regarded as unfairly dismissed only if there has been a failure on the part of the employer to comply with the following obligations under Sch 6:

(1) notification of the employee under para 4 (in other words, failure to comply with the duty to notify by the 14th day before the operative date of termination where the employer failed to notify within one year and six month's of that date);

(2) the duty to consider the employee's request not to be retired under paras 6 and 7, which would include holding a meeting where appropriate;

(3) the duty to consider an appeal under para 8.

4.70 These are the only grounds upon which a dismissal for retirement will be regarded as an unfair dismissal and, as the employee 'shall be regarded' as unfairly dismissed, will therefore be automatically unfair. It follows that if an employer can show that the reason for dismissal was retirement and it observes the procedures correctly, the dismissal will be fair. As the DTI's Notes state: [37]

> 'If the employer wishes to be able to rely on retirement as a reason for dismissal, the chances of successfully doing so are greatly increased if he follows the procedures set out in para 2 of Sch 6 to the Regulations.'

4.71 On the basis that the Employment Act 2002, s 31 (which allows adjustment of awards) only applies to non-completion of 'statutory procedures' under that Act, it will not apply to a failure to follow statutory procedures under different legislation, such as the Age Regulations. It does not appear, therefore, that a tribunal has the power to increase any award it makes to the employee by 10% and up to 50% where the retirement dismissal is automatically unfair.

4.72 Section 98ZG needs to be read alongside ss 98ZA–ZF. These set out factual scenarios which may apply to the dismissal and will determine whether or not the reason for dismissal is retirement; they are considered more fully below.

---

[37]   At para 283.

Circumstances where retirement will be the only reason for dismissal

4.73 There are three circumstances in which retirement will be deemed to be the only reason for dismissal:

(1) First, s 98ZB(2) applies where the employee has no normal retirement age and the operative date of termination falls on or after the date the employee reaches 65. If the employer has notified the employee in accordance with Sch 6, para 2 and the contract terminates on the intended date of retirement, then retirement shall be taken to be the only reason for the dismissal and 'any other reason shall be disregarded'.

(2) Secondly, s 98ZD applies to the dismissal of an employee where there is a normal retirement age of 65 or above and the operative date of termination falls on or after the date when the employee reaches that age. Under s 98ZD(2), again, if the employer has notified the employee in accordance with Sch 6, para 2 (notice to the employee of the right to make a request served between one year and six months prior to the intended date of retirement) and the contract terminates on the intended date of retirement, then retirement shall be taken to be the only reason for the dismissal.

(3) Finally, where an employee has a retirement age that is below 65, that earlier retirement date must first be objectively justified under reg 3(1). As discussed earlier in this chapter, that may be a difficult test to meet. However, when the test of objective justification is met and the employer has notified the employee in accordance with Sch 6, para 2 and the contract terminates on the intended date of retirement then, under s 98ZE(4), retirement shall be taken to be the only reason for the dismissal

Circumstances where retirement cannot be the reason for dismissal

4.74 There are nine sets of circumstances where retirement cannot be the reason for dismissal. Section 98ZA applies where the employee has no normal retirement age and the operative date of termination falls before the date when the employee reaches the age of 65. In that case, retirement shall not be taken to be the reason (or a reason) for the dismissal. The 'operative date of retirement' is defined as the date on which notice expires or, where the contract is terminated without notice, the date on which termination takes effect.[38]

4.75 Section 98ZB(3) applies where the employee has no normal retirement date and the operative date of termination falls on or after the date the employee is 65. If the employer has notified the employee in accordance with Sch 6, para 2, but the contract terminates before the intended date of retirement, then retirement shall not be taken to be the reason for dismissal.

---

[38]   ERA 1996, s 98ZH.

Under s 98ZB(4), where the employer does not notify the employee and there is an intended date of retirement, but the contract terminates before that date, then retirement shall not be taken as the reason for dismissal.

4.76 Under s 98ZH, 'intended date of retirement' means the date as defined in para 1(2) of Sch 6, which itself has five different definitions. Where there is a failure to notify under para 2, that could be a date notified under para 4 (under the continuing duty to notify), or it could be where the employee has made a request before the employer has notified a date or a date that supersedes the original date.

4.77 Under s 98ZC, if the employee has a normal retirement age and the operative date of termination falls before the date the employee reaches that age, then retirement cannot be the reason.

4.78 Where there is a normal retirement age of 65 or over, the employer has notified the employee in accordance with Sch 6, para 2, but the contract terminates before the intended date of retirement, then – under s 98ZD(3) – retirement shall not be taken to be the reason for dismissal. Similarly, under s 98ZD(4), where the employer does not notify the employee and there is an intended date of retirement, but the contract terminates before that date, then retirement shall not be taken as the reason for dismissal.

4.79 Where the employee has a normal retirement age below 65 and the operative date of termination falls on or after that date, then, if that normal retirement age has not been objectively justified under reg 3(1) and is therefore unlawful, it follows that retirement shall not be taken to be the reason for dismissal (s 98ZE(2)).

4.80 Where there is a normal retirement age below 65 that can be objectively justified and the employer has notified the employee in accordance with Sch 6, para 2, but the contract terminates before the intended date of retirement, then – under s 98ZE(5) – retirement shall not be taken to be the reason for dismissal. Likewise, under s 98ZE(6), where the employer does not notify the employee and there is an intended date of retirement, but the contract terminates before that date, then retirement shall not be taken as the reason for dismissal.

4.81 These 12 sets of circumstances are summarised in the table below:

Does the employee have a normal retirement age?	What is the operative date of retirement?	Further requirements	Is retirement the reason for dismissal?	ERA 1996 section
No	Before the employee reaches 65	–	No	98ZA
No	Operative date of termination falls on or after	Employer has notified and contract	Yes	98ZB(2)

Does the employee have a normal retirement age?	What is the operative date of retirement?	Further requirements	Is retirement the reason for dismissal?	ERA 1996 section
	employee reaches 65	terminates on intended date of retirement		
No	Operative date of termination falls on or after employee reaches 65	Employer has notified *but* contract terminates *before* intended date of retirement	No	98ZB(3)
No	Operative date of termination falls on or after employee reaches 65	Employer has failed to notify and contract terminates before intended date of retirement	No	98ZB(4)
Yes	Before the employee's normal retirement age	–	No	98ZC
65 or higher	Operative date of termination falls on or after employee reaches retirement age	Employer has notified and contract terminates on intended date of retirement	Yes	98ZD(2)
65 or higher	Operative date of termination falls on or after employee reaches retirement age	Employer has notified *but* contract terminates *before* intended date of retirement	No	98ZD(3)
65 or higher	Operative date of termination falls on or after employee reaches retirement age	Employer has failed to notify and contract terminates before intended date of retirement	No	98ZD(4)

Does the employee have a normal retirement age?	What is the operative date of retirement?	Further requirements	Is retirement the reason for dismissal?	ERA 1996 section
Below 65	Operative date of termination falls on or after employee reaches retirement age	Retirement age below 65 cannot be objectively justified	No	98ZE(2)
Below 65	Operative date of termination falls on or after employee reaches retirement age	Objectively justified and employer has notified and contract terminates on intended date of retirement	Yes	98ZE(4)
Below 65	Operative date of termination falls on or after employee reaches retirement age	Objectively justified; employer has notified *but* contract terminates *before* intended date of retirement	No	98ZE(5)
Below 65	Operative date of termination falls on or after employee reaches retirement age	Objectively justified; employer has failed to notify and contract terminates before intended date of retirement	No	98ZE(6)

Circumstances where the tribunal must determine the reason

4.82 There are limited circumstances in which the tribunal must decide whether retirement is the reason for dismissal. Where an employer has not notified an employee in accordance with Sch 6, para 2, 'particular regard shall be had to the matters in s 98ZF when determining the reason (or principal reason) for dismissal'.[39] That section sets out three matters:

(1) whether or not the employer has notified the employee in accordance with Sch 6, para 4, which is the continuing duty to notify up to the 14th day pre-dismissal;

(2) if the employer has done, how long before the notified retirement date it did so;

(3) whether or not the employer has followed the procedures in Sch 6, para 7, which relate to consideration of a request.

4.83 The tribunal will also have to determine whether retirement is the reason for dismissal where there has been notification of the employee under para 2, but the dismissal takes effect after the intended date of retirement. It may take into account the matters listed above.

4.84 Having reached a decision as to the reason for dismissal, the tribunal will have to go on to consider fairness (under s 98ZG) in the usual way.

Other amendments to the unfair dismissal legislation

4.85 As well as removing the upper age limit on bringing unfair dismissal claims, there are other consequential amendments to the legislation.

4.86 The tapering of the basic award for unfair dismissal after the age of 64 is removed.[40] However, the different basis of calculation for those aged 41 and over (1½ weeks' pay) and those aged 21 and under (½ week's pay) remains.[41] In line with an automatically unfair dismissal for failing to follow the statutory dismissal and disciplinary procedures, the basic award can be increased to four weeks' pay for an automatically unfair retirement dismissal.[42]

4.87 Finally, s 211(2) of the 1996 Act is repealed, so that an employee's period of continuous employment is no longer treated as beginning on the employee's 18th birthday.

---

[39] ERA 1996, ss 98ZB(5), ZD(5) ZE(7).
[40] ERA 1996, s 119(4) and (5) are omitted.
[41] ERA 1996, s 119(2).
[42] ERA 1996, s 120(1A).

Chapter 5

PAY AND NON-PAY BENEFITS

5.1 Part 4 of the Employment Equality (Age) Regulations 2006 contains the General Exceptions from Parts 2 (Discrimination in Employment and Vocational Training) and 3 (Other Unlawful Acts). The exceptions for statutory authority, national security and positive action (regs 27, 28 and 29 respectively) have been considered in Chapter 3 and the exception for retirement in Chapter 4. The four remaining exceptions relate to minimum pay, benefits, enhanced redundancy payments and the provision of life assurance and are considered in this chapter.

NATIONAL MINIMUM WAGE

5.2 Article 6.1(a) of the Equality Directive[1] provides, as an example of a legitimate employment aim, the setting of special conditions on access to employment, including 'remuneration conditions for young people'. These conditions are contained within the National Minimum Wage Act 1998 and the National Minimum Wage Regulations 1999,[2] which prescribe a minimum hourly rate for 16- and 17-year-olds, which is less than that for 18 to 21 year olds, which is itself less than the rate for 22 year olds and over.[3] As these contain differentials based upon age, they are discriminatory.

5.3 Regulation 31 provides the exception to allow this differential treatment, thereby meeting concerns that the application of a single rate to all ages would have adverse employment consequences, in that it would discourage employment of younger people.[4] In the consultation paper *Age Matters*, the Government stated its view that maintaining the age bands was objectively justified because many employers would be unwilling to pay younger employees the same (higher) minimum wage that employees over 21 would be getting, so the age bands make it easier for younger workers to find employment. The age bands also encourage young people to stay in education.[5]

5.4 Applying the exception, it remains lawful for a person ('A') to be paid in respect of his work at a rate which is lower than the rate at which another such person ('B') is paid where:

---

[1]   2000/78/EC.
[2]   SI 1999/584.
[3]   From October 2006, the rates are £3.30, £4.45 and £5.35 respectively.
[4]   See Low Pay Commission Report 2005, 'National Minimum Wage'.
[5]   At para. 5.2.1.

(1) the hourly rate of the national minimum wage for a person of A's age is lower than that for a person of B's age, and

(2) the rate at which A is paid is below the prescribed single hourly rate for the national minimum wage (ie the minimum adult rate).

5.5 This means that an employer can pay someone aged 22 and over more than it pays someone aged under 22, so long as the person under 22 is paid less than the minimum adult rate. Similarly, someone aged between 18 and 21 can be paid more than someone who is under 18, so long as the person under 18 is paid less than the minimum adult rate. So, for example (and taking the minimum adult rate of £5.35 from October 2006), an employer would not be permitted to pay a 17-year-old £6 per hour and a 23-year-old £7 per hour for doing the same job (subject to objective justification), but would be allowed to pay the 17-year-old £5 per hour.

5.6 Therefore, this exception does not allow different rates of pay within the same age band for doing the same job (subject to objective justification) or different rates for doing the same job between the age bands (again, subject to objective justification) where the younger person receives a rate of pay equivalent to or exceeding the minimum adult rate. To take an example from *Age Matters*, if an employer pays those aged 16 to 17 £10 per hour, those aged 18 to 21 £12 per hour and those above 21 £14 per hour, the exemption does not apply and the employer could only maintain those pay differences if they could be objectively justified.

5.7 Taking another example, A (aged 20) is paid £5.45 per hour, which is the national minimum wage for that age band from October 2006 (£4.45) plus London weighting (£1), which together exceed the adult minimum wage of £5.35. B (aged 22) is paid £6.35, which is the adult minimum wage, plus the same London weighting. As A's pay exceeds the adult national minimum wage, reg 31 does not apply and the differential must be justified. If it is a legitimate aim to recruit/retain workers in London by paying them a weighting allowance and that allowance can statistically be shown to relate to the additional cost of living in London, then it is suggested that the differential would be objectively justified.[6]

5.8 Regulation 31(2) deals with apprentices and allows an employer to pay an apprentice who is not entitled to the national minimum wage (ie he is under 19 or within the first 12 months of his apprenticeship[7]) less than an apprentice who is entitled to the national minimum wage.

PROVISION OF BENEFITS BASED ON LENGTH OF SERVICE

5.9 Most employers reward length of service by giving employees benefits. As well as incremental pay increases related to years of service, 'non-pay'

---

[6] The author is grateful to Christina Tolvas-Vincent of Bond Pearce LLP for this example.

[7] National Minimum Wage Regulations 1999, SI 1999/584, reg 12(2) as amended by the Employment Equality (Age) Regulations 2006, SI 2006/1031, Sch 8 para 58.

benefits such as entitlement to health insurance, enhanced sickness benefits or additional days of holiday will frequently be 'earned' upon completion of a certain period of service. Since such provisions are likely to disadvantage younger workers who cannot meet the length of service requirements, reg 32 contains the exception for provision of certain benefits based on length of service. It derives from Art 6.1(b) of the Equality Directive[8] which provides for differences of treatment which include: 'the fixing of minimum conditions of … seniority in service for access … to certain advantages linked to employment'. This exception is separate to the test for objective justification in reg 3.

5.10 The legitimate aim justifying the retention of service-related benefits is employment planning, according to the Government's Notes accompanying the Age Regulations,[9] which state that service related benefits maintain workforce stability by rewarding loyalty as distinct from performance and by responding to employees' reasonable expectation that their salary should not remain static.

5.11 Service-related benefits have been considered by the European Court of Justice in the context of sex discrimination.[10] Most recently, the Advocate General has given his opinion in *Cadman v Health and Safety Executive*.[11] Mrs Cadman originally brought a claim before an employment tribunal in 2001, arguing that the HSE's pay system, under which she received less than male counterparts in the same pay bracket due to differences in length of service, was indirectly discriminatory, and as a result her contract should be amended in line with Equal Pay Act 1970, s 1(2)(b). The Court of Appeal referred the question of justification to the European Court of Justice, noting the uncertainty caused by apparently conflicting ECJ judgments.

5.12 The Advocate General's conclusion (which is not binding on the Court) was that where an employer uses length of service as a determinant of pay, and this has a disparate impact on male and female employees, it should be required to demonstrate that the way in which the length of service criterion is used takes into account the business needs of the undertaking and is applied proportionately so as to minimise the disadvantageous impact it has on women. If an employer cannot justify the use of a length of service criterion as a whole, it should provide specific justification for the difference in pay levels between the employee raising the complaint and others performing the same job.

5.13 As will be seen, reg 32 requires an employer to demonstrate that using length of service as a criterion for awarding benefits fulfils a business need of the undertaking, but only where length of service exceeds five years. It remains to be seen whether the European Court of Justice upholds the Advocate General's opinion and, if it does, whether there is a sufficient

---

[8] 2000/78/EC.
[9] Para 113 et seq.
[10] See *Handels- og Kontorfunktionaerernes Forbund Danmark v Dansk Arbejdsgiverforening (acting for Danfoss)* [1989] IRLR 532; *Nimz v Freie und Hansestadt Hamburg*, [1991] IRLR 222.
[11] Case C-17/05.

distinction between service-related benefits in the context of equal pay and age discrimination so that the exception under reg 32 is unaffected.

5.14 It should be noted that reg 32 relates only to the provision of benefits based on length of service. It does not, for example, affect the provision of benefits following a performance review or appraisal or passing a health check. Any basis for providing benefits other than length of service is not exempted and will need to be objectively justified if it is discriminatory. The most obvious example is an entitlement to benefits (such as insurance) which is directly age-related, for example providing free health insurance up to a maximum age of 60.

Providing benefits

5.15 This is a two-stage process. The first stage is the application of the exception, namely that nothing in Part 2 or 3 of the Age Regulations shall render it unlawful for a person ('A'), in relation to the award of any benefit by him, to put a worker ('B') at a disadvantage when compared with another worker ('C'), if and to the extent that the disadvantage suffered by B is because B's length of service is less than that of C.[12]

> **Example**: AB Ltd provides an additional two days' annual leave for all employees upon completion of two years' service and private health insurance entitlement after four years' service. This is lawful as it falls within reg 32(1) and there is therefore no need objectively to justify these service-related benefits.

5.16 For the purposes of this regulation, the term 'benefits' does not include any benefit awarded to a worker by virtue of his ceasing to work for A.[13] Therefore it does not include redundancy payments (which are covered by reg 33) or other payments on termination. There is also the general definition of 'benefit', which includes facilities and services.[14]

5.17 The second stage only arises where B's length of service exceeds five years. Where that is the case, it must reasonably appear to A that the way in which he uses the criterion of length of service, in relation to the award in respect of which B is put at a disadvantage, fulfils a business need of his undertaking. The examples are given of encouraging the loyalty or motivation, or rewarding the experience, of some or all of A's workers.[15]

> **Example**: AB Ltd provides a further three days' annual leave for all employees upon completion of seven years' service. In order to fall within the exception, it must reasonably appear to AB Ltd that it is fulfilling a business need (for example, rewarding loyalty) in using the length of service criterion.

---

[12]   Reg 32(1).
[13]   Reg 32(7).
[14]   Reg 2(2).
[15]   Reg 32(2).

5.18 The ACAS Guide suggests that an employer would need evidence from which it could conclude there was a benefit to the organisation and gives the example of information gathered through monitoring, staff attitude surveys or focus groups. Presumably an employment tribunal will want some evidence that the employer has not simply assumed that there is an advantage to the business in using length of service beyond five years to reward loyalty, but has gone through some reasoning process. Nevertheless, it may not be difficult to persuade a tribunal that a business benefit will result from rewarding a higher level of experience or from encouraging the motivation of workers who have been doing the same job for a number of years.

Definitions

5.19 Regulation 32 sets out the calculations that A – the person awarding the benefit – must make. In calculating a worker's length of service, A shall calculate one of two things, either:

(1) the length of time the worker has been working for him doing work which he reasonably considers to be at or above a particular level (assessed by reference to the demands made on the worker, for example, in terms of effort, skills and decision making); or

(2) the length of time the worker has been working for him in total.

On each occasion on which A decides to use the criterion of length of service in relation to the award of a benefit to workers, it is for him to decide which of these definitions to use to calculate the lengths of service.[16] The second definition is much simpler than the first, which might apply where a worker has been promoted from the shop floor to a managerial position.

5.20 The calculation of the length of time the worker has been working for A is set out at reg 32(4).

(a) A shall calculate the length of time in terms of the number of weeks during the whole or part of which the worker was working for him. This would seem to cover a worker who has worked on separate occasions for an employer, subject to (b) below.

(b) Any period during which the worker was absent from work may be discounted, unless in all the circumstances it would not be reasonable for A to do this. This includes any period of absence which at the time it occurred was thought by A or the worker to be permanent. In deciding whether it would be reasonable to discount, the way in which other workers' absences occurring in similar circumstances are treated by A in calculating their lengths of service will be relevant.

(c) A may also discount any period during which the worker was present at work (called 'the relevant period') where the relevant period preceded a

---

[16] Reg 32(3).

period during which the worker was absent from work and in all the circumstances it is reasonable for A to discount the relevant period. The circumstances include the length of the worker's absence, the reason for his absence, the effect his absence had on his ability to discharge the duties of his work, and the way in which other workers were treated by A in similar circumstances.

5.21 The potential difficulties within these definitions are shown by an example from *Age Matters*. A law firm uses a four-year pay scale for trainees, a five-year pay scale for junior associates and a five-year pay scale for senior associates. The natural progression for lawyers at the firm is to rise automatically through each of these scales in turn. The question then arises whether, for the purposes of the five-year exemption, the scale should be seen as a single pay scale of 14 years (in which case the last nine years would not be covered by the automatic exemption) or three separate scales of five years or less, each covered by the automatic exemption.

5.22 This example was provided before the final drafting of reg 32 and the answer lies in reg 32(3). Arguably, the firm could calculate the length of time the senior associate (for example) has been working, not by calculating the total length of time he has worked for the firm (reg 32(3)(b)), but by calculating length of service from when he became a senior associate and differentiating between the demands made upon a senior associate compared with those made upon an associate (reg 32(3)(a)). This argument should succeed where there is a measurable difference between the demands of different positions.

5.23 To complete the definitions in reg 32, when calculating the length of time the worker has been working for A in total, a worker shall be treated as having worked for A during any period which he worked for another if that falls within the Employment Rights Act 1996, s 218, which sets out the rules for continuity of employment upon change of employer, for example where a trade, business or undertaking is transferred. Finally, were the worker to be made redundant by A, the period he worked for another and the period he worked for A would amount to 'relevant service' under s 155 of the 1996 Act (the two-year qualifying period for a redundancy payment).

Pay

5.24 *Age Matters* gives as an example an employer offering a pay scale where the employee gets an increase in pay at the end of each year up to four years of service. Beyond the fourth year, further pay increases depend on the performance appraisal of the employee. The pay rises related to length of service will come within the five-year exemption and therefore be lawful. The fact that the employer then uses performance as a criterion for pay rises after the fourth year is outside the scope of the Regulations and also lawful. This would seem the most obvious way of avoiding the requirement of showing a business need to justify service-related pay increases after five years.

REDUNDANCY

5.25 Through an amendment to the Employment Rights Act 1996, the upper age limit (65) for receiving a redundancy payment is removed.[17] The tapering provisions for calculating redundancy payments for individuals aged 64 are also removed.[18] As set out below, the minimum qualifying period of two years remains, as do the existing age bands and the maximum of 20 years' service.

5.26 In the Explanatory Memorandum that accompanied the Age Regulations when they were laid before Parliament, the Government stated that:

> 'Evidence demonstrates that younger, prime age and older workers fall into three distinct economic categories, with older workers facing a particularly difficult position in the employment market. We now believe that there is, therefore, a good case for providing different levels of compensation for each of these groups under the scheme.'

Exception for provision of enhanced redundancy payments to employees

5.27 The amount of a statutory redundancy payment is dependent upon an employee's age, length of service and weekly pay, and the scheme is set out in Part XI of the Employment Rights Act 1996 ('the 1996 Act'). It is helpful at the start of this section to set out how the statutory scheme works, since any enhanced scheme operates by reference to the statutory scheme. Under s 162(1)–(3) of the 1996 Act an employee is entitled to an 'appropriate amount' for each year during which the employee has been continuously employed, reckoning backwards from the effective date of termination. The 'appropriate amount' is one and a half weeks' pay for each year of employment in which the employee was not below 41; one week's pay for each year he was not below the age of 22; and half a week's pay for each year he was 21 or under. The amount is limited to the last 20 years of employment. There is also a statutory cap on the amount of a week's pay.[19]

5.28 An employer who makes a redundancy payment in accordance with Part XI of the 1996 Act does not have to justify itself, because the exemption for statutory authority applies and, according to the Government, the scheme can be objectively justified.[20]

5.29 However, employers who wish to pay more than the statutory scheme allows also need to be protected from any challenge if they are using age-based criteria. Regulation 33 is aimed at those employers and contains the exception in respect of enhanced redundancy payments. It applies to 'qualifying employees', who are defined as follows:

---

[17]   S 156 is repealed.
[18]   Ss 162(4), (5) and (8) are repealed.
[19]   Employment Rights Act 1996, s 227(1); since 1 February 2006, the amount has been £290.
[20]   Notes on Regulations, para 127.

(a) an employee who is entitled to a redundancy payment by virtue of the 1996 Act, s 135. That entitlement is for an employee who is dismissed by reason of redundancy or who is eligible for a redundancy payment by reason of being laid off or kept on short-time;

(b) an employee who would have been entitled but for the requirement under s 155 of the 1996 Act for two years' continuous employment;

(c) an employee who agrees to the termination of his employment in circumstances where, had he been dismissed, he would have been entitled under either of sub-paras (a) or (b).[21]

5.30 Regulation 33(1) allows an employer to give a qualifying employee an enhanced redundancy payment which is less in amount than the enhanced redundancy payment which he gives to another such employee if both amounts are calculated in the same way. For example, if an employer calculates redundancy payments by reference to age and length of service, then two employees with the same length of service, but with different ages, may receive different amounts, subject to this regulation. It also allows the employer to give enhanced redundancy payments only to an employee falling within sub-para (a) above or who would have fallen into that category, had he been dismissed, but who agrees to the termination of his employment.

5.31 An 'enhanced redundancy payment' means a payment of an amount calculated in accordance with one of two methods. To fall within the first method, it must be calculated in accordance with s 162(1)–(3) of the 1996 Act, as set out above.[22] Once that calculation has been made, the employer may pay the resultant amount. That may therefore include a payment to an employee who would not qualify under the statutory scheme through insufficient continuing employment.

5.32 If the employer wishes to enhance the amount, it must follow the second method of calculating the amount. The same steps are followed as in the first, up to the application of the statutory limit. However, the employer may then do one of three things:

(a) It may treat a week's pay as not being subject to a maximum amount or as being subject to a maximum amount that is above the statutory cap (for example, calculating it by using the employee's actual weekly rate of pay).[23]

(b) Alternatively, it may multiply the number of weeks' pay allowed for each year of employment by a multiplier of more than one.[24]

(c) As a further alternative, it may multiply the total amount produced by the statutory calculation with or without the variations in sub-para (b) by a multiplier of more than one.[25]

---

[21]   Reg 33(2).
[22]   Reg 33(3).
[23]   Reg 33(4)(b)(i).
[24]   Reg 33(4)(b)(ii).

5.33 A question arising in respect of sub-para (b) is whether the same multiplier must be used for each year of service.

> **Example**: AB Ltd wishes to enhance redundancy payments for a number of employees with differing length of service. It has previously operated a scheme which multiplies the weekly rate of pay by differing multipliers, that increase with length of service. Under reg 33, it first calculates entitlement following the statutory scheme. Must it then use the same multiplier, so that – for example – a multiplier of two would mean that each year of service between the ages of 22 and 40 would count as two week's pay and each year above 41 would count as three week's pay?

5.34 Since many employers will have enhanced redundancy schemes with varying multipliers, this is an important question. One argument would be that, if the same multiplier must be used for each year of service, then sub-para (c) would cover that enhancement, because the application of the same multiplier to each year has the same effect as application of that multiplier to the whole. That would make sub-para (b) otiose and would also run counter to the Government's recognition of the need for flexibility.[26]

5.35 However that purposive approach is not necessarily supported by a strict construction of reg 33(4)(b)(ii) ('he may multiply the appropriate amount allowed for each year of employment by a figure of more than one'). Further, the Department of Trade and Industry has issued an explanatory note stating that, if the employer chooses to enhance the statutory redundancy scheme as described above, it can only rely on the exemption if it makes the same adjustments to each of the three age bands. In other words, any increase in the multipliers must be applied across the board to each of the three age bands. That also suggests use of the same multiplier.

5.36 This leads on to a further issue. Many UK employers operating enhanced redundancy schemes do not follow the age bands in the statutory scheme. Regulation 33 provides for enhanced redundancy schemes that mirror the statutory scheme, because the initial calculation, which is then enhanced, follows the 1996 Act. This means that employers whose enhanced redundancy schemes do not follow the statutory age bands will have to be able to objectively justify their schemes.

> **Example**: CD Ltd's enhanced redundancy scheme has previously paid 200% of the statutory scheme for those aged 50 and over. Having first calculated entitlement following the statutory scheme, can it still apply that multiplier to those in that age bracket?

5.37 CD Ltd would need to be able to justify this enhancement objectively. If the Government believes that the age differentials in the statutory schemes can be justified, it may be difficult to show that going beyond those differentials is a proportionate means of achieving a legitimate aim. Even though the aim would be one of rewarding loyalty and long service and

---

[25]   Reg 33(4)(c).
[26]   Explanatory Memorandum to the Age Regulations.

therefore arguably legitimate, the use of a relatively arbitrary age limit to achieve this may not be proportionate.

5.38   It is therefore difficult, at the stage of implementation of the Age Regulations, to see the scope for flexibility in respect of enhanced redundancy payments that was requested by employers' groups during consultation. There are additional problems for employers as they amend their schemes to fit in with reg 33 and find their employees unhappy with the changes to their contractual entitlements.

PROVISION OF LIFE ASSURANCE COVER TO RETIRED WORKERS

5.39   Where a person ('A') arranges for workers to be provided with life assurance cover after their early retirement on grounds of ill health, reg 34 allows that cover to cease when the worker reaches 65 or the normal retirement age if that is different. This is a pragmatic provision that recognises the increased cost for such cover in respect of older people and the likelihood that those providing that cover for workers would otherwise simply stop offering life assurance.

Chapter 6

EDUCATION AND VOCATIONAL TRAINING

6.1 Part Two of the Employment Equality (Age) Regulations 2006[1] prohibits age discrimination in employment and vocational training. Regulation 20 addresses the provision of vocational training and reg 23 covers institutions of further and higher education.

THE PROVISION OF VOCATIONAL TRAINING

6.2 There are five ways in which it is unlawful for any training provider to discriminate against a person seeking or undergoing training, as follows:

(1) in the arrangements he makes for the purpose of determining to whom he should offer training;

(2) in the terms on which the training provider affords him access to any training;

(3) by refusing or deliberately not affording him such access;

(4) by terminating his training; or

(5) by subjecting him to any other detriment during his training.[2]

6.3 Article 3(1)(b) of the Equality Directive[3] states that it applies to: 'access to all types and to all levels of … vocational training'. The Government anticipates that this would be interpreted by the European Court of Justice as including discrimination during the course of training, as such discrimination could deter a person from continuing his access to training or from seeking further access to training. For this reason, reg 20 extends to discriminatory acts taking place during the training itself.

6.4 Regulation 20(1) is subject to objective justification under reg 3(1), so that a discriminatory practice may be justified if it is a proportionate means of achieving a legitimate aim. The exception for genuine occupational requirement[4] applies if the discrimination concerns training that would only fit a person for employment that the employer could lawfully refuse to offer the person seeking training. It is also subject to the exceptions for statutory authority,[5] national security[6] and – more importantly – positive action.[7] The

---

[1] SI 2006/1031.
[2] Reg 20(1).
[3] 2000/78/EC.
[4] Reg 8.
[5] Reg 27.
[6] Reg 28.
[7] Reg 29.

exception for positive action allows any act done in or in connection with either:

(a) affording persons of a particular age or age group access to facilities for training which would help fit them for particular work; or

(b) encouraging persons of a particular age or age group to take advantage of opportunities for doing particular work.

It must reasonably appear to the person doing the act that it prevents or compensates for disadvantages linked to age suffered by persons of that age or age group doing or likely to take up that work.[8]

6.5 The word 'training' is given a broad definition, as follows:

(1) all types and all levels of training which would help fit a person for any employment;

(2) vocational guidance;

(3) facilities for training;

(4) practical work experience provided by an employer to a person whom he does not employ; and

(5) any assessment related to the award of any professional or trade qualification, as defined in reg 19.[9]

6.6 This definition – which widens the parallel definition in the Religion or Belief and Sexual Orientation Regulations[10] – means that an employer offering practical work experience has a potential liability. As such work experience is typically offered to those in secondary or tertiary education, an employer would have to argue that this was positive action or otherwise objectively justified if it was restricted to a particular age group.

6.7   A 'training provider' means anyone who provides, or makes arrangements for the provision of training, with three exceptions. It does not include an employer in relation to training for persons employed by him, since reg 7(2)(b) already makes it unlawful for an employer to discriminate against an employee, 'in the opportunities which he affords him for promotion, a transfer, training, or receiving any other benefit'. Secondly, it does not include a governing body of an educational establishment to which reg 23 (institutions of further and higher education) applies, or would apply but for the operation of any other provision of these Regulations. Again, this is to prevent duplication. Thirdly, the definition of 'training provider' does not include a proprietor of a school in relation to any registered pupil.[11]

6.8 One important aspect of vocational training is its funding, which may therefore affect access. For example, a training provider might run an IT course that receives government funding for participants under 25. Article 3.3 of the Equality Directive[12] states that the Directive does not apply to

---

[8]   The exception for positive action is considered in Chapter 3.
[9]   See Chapter 3.
[10] SIs 2003/1660 and 1661.
[11] 'Registered pupil' has the meaning given by the Education Act 1996, s 434.
[12] 2000/78/EC.

payments of any kind made by state schemes, so the age limits in the funding arrangements are lawful. However, that would not justify the training provider in only admitting people within this age limit and refusing places to anybody 26 or over on grounds of their age. Such a provision would have to be objectively justified. Rather than denying access to people aged 26 or over, the training provider could require them to pay for their own place on the course.

6.9 It is unlawful for a training provider to subject a person seeking or undergoing training to harassment.[13]

INSTITUTIONS OF FURTHER AND HIGHER EDUCATION

6.10 Article 3.1(b) of the Equality Directive[14] extends the scope of the Directive to vocational training, which the European Court of Justice has construed as including:

> 'any form of education which prepares for a qualification for a particular profession, trade or employment or which provides the necessary skills for such a profession, trade or employment is vocational training, whatever the age and the level of training of the pupils or students, even if the training programme includes an element of general education'.[15]

6.11 This definition was endorsed by the Court in *Blaizot v University of Liège*,[16] as follows:

> 'With regard to the issue whether university studies prepare for a qualification for a particular profession, trade or employment or provide the necessary training and skills for such a profession, trade or employment, it must be emphasised that this is the case not only where the final academic examination directly provides the required qualification for a particular profession, trade or employment but also in so far as the studies in question provide specific training and skills, that is to say where a student needs the knowledge so acquired for the pursuit of a profession, trade or employment, even if no legislative or administrative provisions make the acquisition of that knowledge a prerequisite for that purpose.'

In general, university studies fulfil these criteria. The only exceptions are certain courses of study which, because of their particular nature, are intended for persons wishing to improve their general knowledge rather than prepare themselves for an occupation.'[17]

6.12 In a memorandum considering this issue in the context of the Employment Equality (Sexual Orientation) Regulations 2003,[18] the Department of Trade and Industry took the view that the majority of further

---

[13] Reg 19(2).
[14] 2000/78/EC.
[15] *Gravier v City of Liege* C-293/83, [1985] ECR 606.
[16] C-24/86, [1988] ECR 355.
[17] Ibid. paras 19 and 20.
[18] SI 2003/1661.

and higher education courses (but by no means all) would therefore fall within the scope of vocational training. For example, a degree in law or medicine would, while a degree in medieval history or classics might not. A degree in chemistry might, depending upon the circumstances. However, limiting the anti-discrimination provision to those courses falling within the definition of vocational training would create uncertainty both for the institutions and for individuals and there would need to be case law to establish the parameters. Therefore, it was better to apply the provision to all acts by further and higher education institutions, to include courses that might fall outside the definition. The additional obligation in respect of such courses could be justified because it is closely related to the obligations under the Equality Directive.[19] The same approach applies with the Age Regulations.

6.13 Regulation 23 applies to three types of institution in England and Wales: an institution within the further education sector,[20] a university; and an institution within the higher education sector.[21] There are parallel definitions for Scottish educational institutions.[22] 'University' includes a university college and the college, school or hall of a university.[23]

6.14 It is unlawful for the governing bodies of such institutions to discriminate against a person in three ways:

(1) in the terms on which it offers to admit him to the establishment as a student;

(2) by refusing or deliberately not accepting an application for his admission to the establishment as a student; or

(3) where he is a student of the establishment—

   (a) in the way it affords him access to any benefits,

   (b) by refusing or deliberately not affording him access to them, or

   (c) by excluding him from the establishment or subjecting him to any other detriment.[24]

6.15 A 'student' is any person who receives education at an educational establishment to which this regulation applies.[25]

6.16 As with vocational training, the method of funding may be relevant. The grants and loans for tuition fees and maintenance paid to students under the Education (Student Support) Regulations 2006 are from public funds.[26] Student support in the United Kingdom is therefore a 'state scheme' and, as

---

[19]   21st Report of Joint Committee on Statutory Instruments (Session 2002-2003); DTI memorandum 30 May 2003.
[20]   As defined by the Further and Higher Education Act 1992, s 91(3).
[21]   Ibid, s 91(5).
[22]   As defined by the Further and Higher Education (Scotland) Act 1992, ss 1, 36(1); the Education (Scotland) Act 1980, ss 1(5)(b)(ii), 135; together with an institution within the higher education sector within Part Two of that Act.
[23]   Reg 23(6).
[24]   Reg 23(1).
[25]   Reg 23(6).
[26]   SI 2006/955, made under the Teaching and Higher Education Act 1998, s 22.

such, this method of funding falls outside the Equality Directive.[27] As maintenance loans for students affect maintenance during study and not admission to a course of study, they are not related to access. Similarly, bursaries and scholarships are not covered, because they are incentives, as opposed to relating directly to access.[28]

6.17 It is unlawful for the governing body of an educational establishment to which reg 23 applies to subject a student or someone applying for admission as a student to harassment.[29] The exception for genuine occupational requirement also applies if the discrimination concerns training that would only fit a person for employment that the employer could lawfully refuse to offer the person seeking training.[30]

Remedies

6.18 Claims involving institutions of further and higher education are the only claims under the Age Regulations that fall outside the jurisdiction of the employment tribunal, as such claims must be brought in the county court.[31] This is considered further in Chapter 8.

---

[27] 2000/78/EC.
[28] See DTI's, 'A Guide for Providers of Vocational Training'.
[29] Reg 23(2).
[30] Reg 23(3).
[31] Reg 39.

Chapter 7

PENSIONS

INTRODUCTION

7.1 This chapter considers the application of the Age Regulations to occupational pension schemes and their application to personal pension schemes (see reg 11 of and Sch 2 to the Age Regulations). The Department for Trade and Industry has published guidance[1] ('the DTI Guidance') on the impact of the Age Regulations on these schemes and this is also referred to in this chapter where appropriate.

Impact of the Age Regulations on occupational pension schemes

7.2 The Age Regulations create a range of potentially difficult issues for occupational pension schemes. A wide variety of practices and procedures will need to be revised if they cannot be objectively justified. The test for discrimination applies on a case-by-case basis. Though the Age Regulations contain various exemptions, these are narrowly drafted and many common practices could be in breach of the requirements. For example, assume a final salary scheme has a normal retirement age of 65 (the default retirement age under the Regulations) but the employer allows employees to work beyond this age. If an employee working beyond age 65 is not allowed to continue to accrue pensionable service, this is potentially indirect age discrimination.

OVERVIEW OF THE PENSIONS ASPECTS OF THE AGE REGULATIONS

Application to trustees and managers of occupational pension schemes: reg 11

7.3 It is unlawful, except in relation to rights accrued or benefits payable in respect of service prior to the coming into force of the regulations, for the trustees or managers (in this chapter jointly referred to as trustees) to discriminate against a member[2] or a prospective member[3] of a scheme in

---
[1] *The Impact of Age Regulations on Pension Schemes*, DTI Guidance (April 2006).
[2] See 7.10.

carrying out any of their functions in relation to it (including their functions relating to the admission of members to the scheme and the treatment of members in the scheme) (see reg 11(1)).

7.4 It is unlawful for trustees of occupational pension schemes to subject a member or a prospective member to harassment (see reg 11(2)).

7.5 More detailed provisions relating to occupational pension schemes, such as implying a non-discrimination rule into all schemes and exempting various scheme provisions and practices are set out in Sch 2.

Examples of possible discrimination

- Direct discrimination occurs where trustees treat an individual less favourably than another individual on the grounds of age. For example, a scheme pays different rates of pension increases on the basis of the member's age (though see the limited exemption in Sch 2, para 27).

- Indirect discrimination occurs where an apparently age neutral provision disadvantages workers of a particular age. For example, if an employer makes contributions to a scheme which match those made by the employee on a 1:1 basis for employees who have completed up to ten years service and a 2:1 basis for employees who have completed more than ten years service, this may be potentially discriminatory (though see reg 32 for possible exemptions for benefits based on length of service).

DETAILED PROVISIONS: Sch 2

7.6 Schedule 2 is divided into three parts. Part 1 covers general provisions and includes definitions (which also apply to reg 11), the non-discrimination rule, the procedure in employment tribunals and the remedies. Part 2 sets out specific age-related practices and procedures in relation to occupational pension schemes that are exempt (from the non-discrimination rule). The DTI Guidance includes a table of categories of exemptions. This has been adapted and included as the appendix to this chapter for reference. Part 3 of Sch 2 sets out specific age-related practices and procedures in relation to contributions by employers to personal pension schemes. Where a scheme practice or procedure is not covered by a specific exemption, trustees have the option of either objectively justifying it in relation to their own particular circumstances, or amending the rule, practice or provision.

---

[3] Prospective member means any person who under the terms of his employment or the scheme rules, is able at his option to become a scheme member, will become a scheme member after a certain period of employment, will automatically become a member unless he elects otherwise or may be admitted as a member subject to any person's consent (Sch 2, para 1(5)).

PENSION SCHEMES – GENERAL: Part 1 of Sch 2

Definitions

7.7 For the purposes of the Age Regulations, private pensions are divided into two broad categories, occupational pension schemes and personal pension schemes. Occupational schemes are generally trust-based schemes which are established by an employer for the purpose of providing retirement benefits to the workforce. This includes defined benefit, money purchase and hybrid schemes. Personal pension schemes are based on a contractual relationship between the individual and the provider, generally an insurance company.

7.8 The Age Regulations do not cover state pensions, contracted-out national insurance rebates, pension-sharing arrangements on divorce and annuities purchased from insurance companies by individuals.[4]

7.9 In the Age Regulations 'scheme' means an occupational pension scheme as defined in para 1(1)–(3) of Sch 2 (see also Sch 2, para 1(4)). In the majority of provisions in the Age Regulations, occupational pension scheme means a scheme falling within s 1(1) of the Pension Schemes Act 1993[5] (Sch 2, para 1(1)). However this definition is modified for the purposes of specific exemptions.[6] This ensures that occupational pension schemes as defined in the Pension Schemes Act 1993 and the Finance Act 2004 are covered by the Age Regulations. Most death benefit only schemes[7] will not be able to benefit from the majority of the exemptions.

7.10 There are also four other definitions worthy of note (Sch 2, para 1(5)):

- Age-related benefits are defined as a benefit provided by a scheme to a member:

    (a) on, or following, his retirement (including early retirement on grounds of ill health or otherwise),

    (b) on his reaching a particular age, or

    (c) on termination of his service in an employment.

---

[4] See Chapter 3 DTI Guidance.

[5] Section 1(1): occupational pension scheme means a pension scheme that (a)(i) for the purpose of providing benefits to, or in respect of, people with service in employments of a description, or (ii) for that purpose and also for the purpose of providing benefits to, or in respect of, other people, is established by, or by persons who include, a person to whom sub-s (2) applies when the scheme is established or (as the case may be) to whom that subsection would have applied when the scheme was established had that subsection then been in force, and (b) that has its main administration in the United Kingdom or outside the Member States, or a pension scheme that is prescribed or is of a prescribed description.

[6] The definition is modified in relation to the para 7(a), 12, 13 and 30 exemptions in Sch 2 (see 7.25, 7.40, 7.42 and 7.71 respectively).

[7] Most death benefit only schemes do not qualify as occupational pension schemes.

- Member is defined as any active member, deferred member or pensioner member. For the purposes of para 12 (age-related rules and practices) this definition is modified.[8]

- 'Normal pension age' has the meaning given by s 180 of the Pension Schemes Act 1993.[9] 'Normal retirement age'[10] in relation to a member means that age at which workers in the undertaking for which the member worked at the time of his retirement and who held the same kind of position as the member held at his retirement were required to retire. (This should be read in conjunction with the Regulations as a whole which establish a default retirement age of 65.)

7.11   In setting any minimum pension age or normal retirement age employers and trustees should take into account Her Majesty's Revenue and Customs' ('HMRC') requirements in respect of low retirement ages. The minimum retirement age is currently 50. Under the Finance Act 2004 this will increase to 55 with effect from 6 April 2010. There are some exceptions in respect of some professions; for example, footballers have a normal retirement age of 35.[11]

7.12 The Age Regulations apply to sectionalised schemes as if each section of the scheme were a separate scheme.[12] This means that different age-related practices could operate within a single scheme but not fall foul of the Age Regulations.

Non-discrimination rule

7.13 As a result of para 2 of Sch 2 each occupational pension scheme is treated as including a non-discrimination rule. This provides that the trustees must refrain from doing any act which is made unlawful by reg 11. All other scheme provisions have effect subject to the non-discrimination rule.

7.14 If the scheme rules do not give the trustees the power to make alterations to the scheme so as to comply with this requirement, or if they have such a power but the procedure for exercising it is unduly complex or protracted or involves obtaining consents which cannot be obtained or can only be obtained with undue delay or difficulty, the trustees may by resolution amend the scheme in order to comply. If any amendments are made by resolution, they may be retrospective but only to 1 October 2006

---

[8]   See 7.40.
[9]   Section 180: (1) normal pension age, in relation to a scheme and a member's pensionable service under it, means (a) in a case where the scheme provides for the member only a guaranteed minimum pension, the earliest age at which the member is entitled to receive the guaranteed minimum pension on retirement from any employment to which the scheme applies; and (b) in any other case, the earliest age at which the member is entitled to receive benefits (other than a guaranteed minimum pension) on his retirement from such employment. (2) For the purposes of sub-s (1) any scheme rule making special provision as to early retirement on grounds of ill-health or otherwise is to be disregarded.
[10]   Sch 2, para 1(5).
[11]   See Sch 2 to Registered Pension Schemes (Prescribed Schemes and Occupations) Regulations 2005 (SI 2005/3451).
[12]   Para 1(6).

(the date of the coming into force of the Age Regulations). In addition, if employer consent is required for amendments under the scheme's amendment power, the resolution is also subject to employer consent.

7.15 The Age Regulations do not specify whether the alteration should level up (provide all members with the more favourable terms) or level down (provide all members with the less favourable terms). This will be a matter for consideration by the trustees and, if appropriate, with the employer, depending on all the circumstances. Until any amendments are made, the trustees should administer the scheme on a levelled-up basis.[13]

7.16 The use of the resolution power where consents 'cannot be obtained'[14] is potentially confusing. This would seem to cover the situation where the consent cannot be obtained because, for example, the members refuse to give their consent (as opposed to say, simply being untraceable). Further, what may be an unduly complex amendment procedure may depend on the circumstances of the scheme.

7.17 If scheme rules do need to be amended to comply with the Age Regulations, the amendments will be exempt from the statutory consultation procedure set out in the Occupational Pension Schemes (Consultation by Employers and Miscellaneous Amendment) Regulations 2006.[15]

Exceptions: paras 3 and 4

7.18 The exemptions listed in Parts 2[16] and 3[17] of Sch 2 will not constitute age discrimination (Sch 2, paras 3 and 4).

Procedure in employment tribunals and remedies

7.19 Employment tribunals are given jurisdiction to hear a complaint of age discrimination in relation to pensions (see reg 36). Where a member or prospective member presents a complaint to a tribunal that the trustees have committed an act which is unlawful by virtue of reg 11[18] or 24[19] or are treated as having committed such an act against him (under reg 25[20] or 26[21]), the employer is automatically treated as a party to the proceedings and is entitled to appear and to be heard at the tribunal (under para 5 of Sch 2).

7.20 The remedies that may be awarded if a complaint is upheld are also set out in Sch 2 (Sch 2, para 6). If the complaint relates to:

---

[13] See DTI Guidance, Q&A section.
[14] Sch 2, para 2(3)(ii).
[15] Regulation 10(1)(a) of SI 2006/349, which came into force 6 April 2006.
[16] Excepted rules, practices, actions and decisions relating to occupational pension schemes.
[17] Excepted rules, practices, actions and decisions relating to contributions by employers to personal pension schemes.
[18] See 7.3.
[19] Relationships which have come to an end.
[20] Liability of employers and principals.
[21] Aiding unlawful acts.

- the terms on which the individual may be admitted to the scheme, the tribunal may make an order declaring that the person has the right to be admitted to the scheme;

- the terms of membership of the scheme, the tribunal may make an order declaring that the person has the right to membership of the scheme without discrimination.

7.21 An order may be retrospective (but not to a time before 1 October 2006) and may make such other provisions in regard to the terms or capacity of admission or membership as the tribunal considers appropriate (Sch 2, para 6(2)). However, if para 6 of Sch 2 applies, the tribunal may not make an order for compensation under reg 38(1)(b) (whether in relation to arrears of benefits or otherwise) except in relation to injury to feelings or by virtue of reg 38(3). (Regulation 38(1)(b) enables a tribunal to make an order for compensation to be paid to the complainant corresponding to any award of damages that could have been ordered by a county court or sheriff court if the complaint had fallen to be dealt with under reg 39.[22])

7.22 A tribunal will, however, be able to award compensation in relation to a complaint by pensioner members (as para 6 does not apply to such complainants – Sch 2, para 6(1)(b)). If a claim is upheld in respect of a practice that is discriminatory, any award will be made on the basis of levelled-up benefits until such time (if at all) as the trustees implement an amendment levelling down benefits.[23]

7.23 If an employee claims that he has suffered age discrimination it will be necessary for him to show that he has been treated worse than another employee who is in the same position except for their age. If there is in reality no other employee, the complainant can compare himself with a hypothetical comparator.[24]

7.24 An individual may also make a complaint through his scheme's internal dispute resolution procedure. If not satisfied with the result, the individual may bring his complaint to the Pensions Ombudsman (though the Ombudsman will not generally consider a complaint that has been made to an Employment Tribunal).

---

[22] See chapter 8.
[23] DTI Guidance Q&A.
[24] See DTI Guidance.

EXCEPTED RULES, PRACTICES, ACTIONS AND DECISIONS RELATING TO OCCUPATIONAL PENSION SCHEMES: Part 2 of Sch 2

Admission to schemes

7.25 Paragraph 7(a) applies to occupational schemes as defined in para 1(2) of Sch 2. That definition states that occupational pension scheme means a scheme falling within the meaning given by s 1(1) of the Pension Schemes Act 1993[25] under which only retirement benefit activities within the meaning of s 255(4)[26] of the Pensions Act 2004 are carried out.

7.26 Paragraph 7(a) exempts a minimum or a maximum age for admission to a pension scheme, including different ages for admission for different groups or categories of workers. Pension schemes generally have a minimum age for admission. For example, an employee will only be eligible to join the scheme if they are at least 18 years old. They also generally have a maximum age for admission. For example, if a scheme has a retirement date of 65, it is common to find that an individual cannot join the scheme after having reached the age of 64. In setting the minimum age for admission, employers need to take care that they do not fall foul of the stakeholder pension legislation.[27]

7.27 Paragraph 7(b) (which applies to schemes falling within the para 1(1) definition) exempts a minimum level of pensionable pay for admission provided that the level does not exceed the lower earnings limit.[28] The lower earnings limit is set at £4,368 per annum for the year 2006/07. Pensionable pay is defined in para 1(5) as that part of a member's pay which counts as pensionable under the scheme rules. The meaning of the term in any particular case will therefore depend on scheme rules.

The use of age criteria in actuarial calculations

7.28 The operational funding of occupational pension schemes, particularly defined benefit schemes, relies heavily on actuarial calculations and advice involving the use of age criteria. The use of age criteria in actuarial calculations is exempt (Sch 2, para 8). Sub-paragraphs (a)–(c) provide three examples:

---

[25] See n 5.

[26] Section 255(4): retirement benefits means: (a) operations related to retirement benefits, and (b) activities arising from operations related to retirement benefits. Section 255(5) defines 'retirement benefits' as: (a) benefits paid by reference to reaching retirement and (b) benefits which are supplementary to those in para (a) that are provided on an ancillary basis as death or disability benefits or support benefits such as ill health benefits.

[27] Under the Welfare Reform and Pensions Act 1999 an employer is required to provide access for all his employees to a stakeholder pension. There is an exception where the employer provides an occupational scheme to his employees. However, to benefit from this exception the scheme must be offered to all employees aged at least 18 years. So in reality 18 tends to be the minimum age for admission.

[28] See s 5(1) of the Social Security Contributions and Benefits Act 1992.

- the use of age criteria in the actuarial calculation of any age-related benefit[29] commencing before any early retirement pivot age[30] or enhancement of such benefit commencing after any late retirement pivot age[31] (Sch 2, para 8(a)). This exemption will allow the general practice of actuarially reducing a pension which is taken early to continue;

- the use of age criteria in the actuarial calculation of member or employer contributions to a scheme (Sch 2, para 8(b));

- the use of age criteria in the actuarial calculation of any age-related benefit commuted in exchange for a lump sum (Sch 2, para 8(c)). Typically schemes give members the option to take part of their pension as a lump sum on retirement. This is generally viewed favourably by members as it is tax free. It may also be advantageous for a scheme itself as a means of removing the longevity risk associated with the amount of pension which has been commuted. (The longevity risk is the risk that the pension will have to be provided for a longer period as mortality rates improve.) As a result of the provisions of the Finance Act 2004 the maximum amount an individual may commute is now 25% of their total pension benefits in exchange for a lump sum. If a member does exercise this option (on the basis that the scheme rules provide this option) the amount of their annual pension will be reduced. The size of the lump sum received will depend on a range of factors including the commutation factors used. (These determine the rate at which the pension will be commuted.) Under some schemes, the relevant provisions simply state that the rate of commutation will be actuarially determined. Such provisions will be able to benefit from this exemption. However, under other schemes, the commutation factors are expressly stated in the scheme rules. If that is the case, there is a risk that such provisions will be discriminatory on the grounds of age.

7.29 These are simply examples and are not an exhaustive list. The DTI Guidance explains that any other use of age criteria in making actuarial calculations in relation to a scheme is exempt. Other examples include the use of age criteria in the actuarial calculation of transfer values and in the 'purchase' of a dependant's pension.

Contributions

7.30 Differences in the rate of member or employer contributions paid to the extent that such differences relate to differences in pensionable pay are exempt (Sch 2, para 9). For example, a contribution rate of 4% for individuals earning up to £40,000 and a contribution rate of 5% for individuals earning more than £40,000 would remain lawful.

---

[29] See 7.10.
[30] Early retirement pivot age is the minimum age specified in the scheme rules at which an individual can take his full pension without reduction (disregarding any provisions applying to ill health early retirement benefits) (Sch 2, para 1(5)).
[31] Late retirement pivot age is the age specified in the scheme rules above which benefit becomes payable with an actuarial enhancement (Sch 2, para 1(5)).

Contributions under money purchase arrangements

Age-related contribution rates

7.31 Money purchase arrangements are defined in para 1(5) by reference to s 152(2) of the Finance Act 2004.[32]

7.32 Age-related contributions made by members or employers under a money purchase arrangement are exempt where the aim in setting different rates is:

- to equalise the amount of benefits to which members of different ages who are otherwise in a comparable situation will become entitled under the arrangement; or

- to make the amount of benefit to which such members will become entitled under the arrangement more nearly equal.

7.33 The practice of setting increasing contributions rates (paid by either or both the employer and the employee) according to the age profile of the member is not discriminatory (Sch 2, para 10(a)). However this only applies where the aim is to equalise benefits or to provide benefits which are more nearly equal to members of different ages under the arrangement.

7.34 How flexibly this provision will be interpreted by the courts is not yet clear. A rigid interpretation would make the exemption difficult to utilise. Contribution rates under many schemes may be set so as to meet this aim in a general way. The DTI Guidance suggests that the provision should be interpreted flexibly as it states that it will apply where the contributions are intended 'to provide (more or less) comparable target pensions at retirement'.

7.35 Multiple age-related contributions bands, for example where the rate of contribution is increased each year, would benefit from the exemption. However, schemes which have just two or three bands are likely to be considered to be discriminatory. The DTI Guidance suggests that 10 bands are likely to be sufficient to satisfy the more nearly equal test but the position is less clear if there are five bands. The number of bands required to be able to satisfy this test will also depend on the particular scheme's circumstances.

Equal contribution rates

7.36 The converse situation is also not discriminatory (Sch 2, para 10(b)). Equal rates of member or employer contributions, regardless of the age of

---

[32] A money purchase arrangement is an arrangement under which all the benefits that are provided are cash balance benefits or other money purchase benefits. Money purchase benefits are benefits the rate or amount of which is calculated by reference to an amount available for the provision of benefits to or in respect of the member (s 152(4)). Cash balance benefits are benefits the rate or amount of which is calculated by reference to amount available for the provision of benefits to or in respect of the member otherwise than wholly by reference to payments made under the arrangement by or in respect of the member (s 152(5)).

the member by or in respect of whom the contributions are made, are also exempt.

Contributions under defined benefits arrangements

Age-related contributions

7.37 The term 'defined benefits arrangements' is defined in para 1(5) by reference to s 152(6) of the Finance Act 2004.[33]

7.38 Age-related member or employer contributions are exempt (Sch 2, para 11) to the extent that:

- each year of pensionable service entitles members in a comparable situation to accrue a right to defined benefits based on the same fraction of pensionable pay; and

- the aim in setting the rates is to reflect the increasing cost of providing the defined benefits in respect of members as they get older.

7.39 It is less common for employee contributions in defined benefit arrangements to be expressly age related. If employee contributions are increased in bands according to the age of the member, provided there is no change in the accrual rate (for example, the fraction of pensionable pay accrued each year remained at say an 80th) and the aim of the banding is to reflect the increasing cost of pensions, this practice would be exempt. If there were just two bands this exemption would be more difficult to utilise. It would be difficult to show that the bands were intended to reflect the additional costs in anything other than the most general manner. A number of bands would fit more easily under this exemption. Its application will depend on the extent to which the aim in setting the contribution rates is interpreted flexibly and practically.

Age related rules, practices, actions and decisions relating to benefit

Minimum age for entitlement to benefit

7.40 Setting a minimum age of entitlement to, or payment of, any age-related benefit to a member[34] is exempt (Sch 2, para 12). However, payment of an age-related benefit under a defined benefits arrangement before an early retirement pivot age[35] where that benefit is subject to actuarial

---

[33] A defined benefits arrangement is an arrangement under which all of the benefits that may be provided to or in respect of a member are defined benefits. Defined benefits are benefits which are not money purchase benefits but which are calculated by reference to earnings or service of the member or any other factor other than an amount available for their provision (s 152(7)).

[34] In para 12 members includes any active, deferred or pensioner member within the meaning of s 151(2)–(4) of the Finance Act 2004.

[35] See n 30.

reduction to take account of the early payment and the member is not credited with additional years of service, is also exempt. (The definition of 'scheme' is modified for the purposes of para 12.)[36]

7.41 The DTI Guidance includes an example relating to this paragraph. This refers to benefits being taken from age 50. This minimum retirement age will be exempt provided the benefits are not enhanced. (However, if age 50 were the early retirement pivot age, benefits could be enhanced.)

Transitional provisions

7.42 There are transitional provisions in relation to individuals who are active[37] or prospective members[38] of a scheme on 1 October 2006. Under para 13[39] a minimum age for entitlement to or payment of any age-related benefit to such members under a defined benefits arrangement before an early retirement pivot age where the benefit is not subject to actuarial reduction for early receipt or the benefit results from the crediting of additional years of service is exempt. As these transitional provisions apply to active members of a scheme (as well as prospective members) they may have wide-ranging application.

7.43 This transitional protection is likely to be lost if the member transfers his active membership from one scheme to another.

7.44 These provisions are intended to enable the practice of offering early retirement redundancy packages to members who are in active service when the Age Regulations come into force to continue. Similarly prospective members have the same protection. Such individuals may have an expectation or a contractual entitlement to such benefits or may be unable to remedy any shortfall in any early retirement pension at this stage in their working lives.

Pivot ages

7.45 An early retirement pivot age[40] or a late retirement pivot age,[41] including different ages for different groups or categories of members, is exempt (Sch 2, para 14). This will enable schemes to continue to set different ages at which different groups may take their benefits early without

---

[36] In paras 12, 13 and 30 occupational pension scheme is defined as such a scheme falling within the definition in s 1(1) of the Pension Schemes Act 1993 (see n 5) or s 150(5) of the Finance Act 2004. Under s 150(5) such a scheme is defined as a scheme established by an employer and having effect or capable of having effect to provide benefits for the employees of that employer or any other employer.

[37] Active member has the same meaning as in s 124(1) of the Pensions Act 1995 and for the purposes of para 13 includes an active member as defined in s 151(2) of the Finance Act 2004 – a person is an active member if there are arrangements made under the scheme for the accrual of benefits to or in respect of that person.

[38] See n 3.

[39] In para 13 the definition of occupational pension scheme is modified – see n 36.

[40] See n 30.

[41] See n 31.

actuarial reduction (for example, senior executives might be entitled to take unreduced benefits from an earlier age).

In service pensions and flexible retirement

7.46 The exemption for late retirement pivot ages does not go so far as to enable schemes to prevent members who have reached a certain age from continuing to accrue pensionable service if they continue working. Most defined benefits schemes include late retirement provisions. These make provision for members who reach normal retirement age (say 65) but continue working after that age. In some schemes, if members continue in active service they cease to accrue pensionable service. Their benefits are actuarially enhanced to take account of the fact that they have ceased to accrue pensionable service and to take account of the fact that their benefits, when taken, will be received for a shorter period. The late retirement pivot age exemption would exempt both practices but does not provide an exemption which enables a scheme to prevent the accrual of future pensionable service. This is likely to be a significant issue for trustees of many defined benefit schemes.

7.47 This issue is considered in the Q&A and Case Studies section of the DTI Guidance. The Guidance states that a rule which stops members who are already drawing a pension from continuing to accrue benefits may be indirectly discriminatory. For example, if proportionately more 55-year-old members than, say, 64-year-old members would like to continue working while drawing benefits rather than having to make the choice between drawing a pension and accruing benefits, it will disadvantage the 55-year-old members as compared to the 64-year-old members. However, such a provision would be lawful if it could be objectively justified.

7.48 A similar problem affects the practice of requiring members to switch sections of a scheme if they wish to continue pensionable service after reaching normal retirement age. For example, being required to switch from a defined benefits section to a money purchase section. This is likely to be discriminatory.

7.49 As a result of the provisions of the Finance Act 2004, the traditional restrictions preventing employers with occupational schemes from providing a pension to employees who continue to work for the company have been removed. This (so the government claims) is to encourage flexible retirement. Some scheme rules however reflect this traditional practice. This practice may amount to indirect discrimination unless it can be objectively justified.

Ill health early retirement

7.50 Some schemes provide an enhancement of any age-related benefit paid to members who retire early on ill health grounds. This practice will continue to be lawful (Sch 2, para 15) where the enhancement is by reference to the number of years of pensionable service which the member would have completed if he had continued in pensionable service up to the age specified in the rules for that purpose. (This is likely to be normal retirement age.)

7.51 Without such an exemption, schemes may face claims by older members who take ill health early retirement on the grounds that such members have not received the same enhancement of their benefit as a younger ill health retiree with the same length service. For example, a member aged 55 who takes ill health early retirement receives the same pension that he would have received had he retired at normal retirement age. A member aged 40 who takes ill health early retirement also receives the same pension that he would have received had he worked until normal retirement age. Assuming both members have the same number of years of pensionable service at the point at which they take ill health retirement, the older worker could claim indirect discrimination.

Bridging pensions

7.52 Bridging pensions are also known as variable pensions and even level pensions. The term refers to an additional pension paid to male members who are receiving a pension from a contracted-out scheme between the ages of 60 and 65. On reaching state pension age the scheme pension is reduced to take account of the additional pension received during the preceding five years. For the individual concerned, their total amount of pension received does not vary. On reaching state pension age their scheme pension and their state pension together are equivalent to the pension they received before state pension age. This practice will not be discriminatory (Sch 2, para 16). The exemption will prevent male members from making a complaint that post age 65 they do not continue to receive the additional pension.

7.53 This exemption is narrow. It only applies in the circumstances prescribed for the purposes of s 64(2) of the Pensions Act 1995 by reg 13 of the Occupational Pension Schemes (Equal Treatment) Regulations 1995.[42] Some schemes have a more flexible level pension or variable pension provisions. For example, it may be an option which applies to both male and female members who retire before state pension age. Such wider bridging pension provisions are not exempt and are likely to be discriminatory unless they can be objectively justified.

Reduction in pension for young dependants

7.54 The reduction of any pension for a dependant who is more than a specified number of years younger than the member is exempt (Sch 2,

---

[42] Regulation 13 of SI 1995/3183: The first situation to which the regulation applies is if the man is in receipt of a pension from the scheme and has not attained pensionable age but would have attained pensionable age if he were a woman. The second circumstance described in the regulations is if an additional amount of pension is paid to the man which does not exceed the amount of Category A retirement pension that would be payable to a woman with earnings the same as the man's earnings in respect of his period of pensionable service under the scheme (assuming that the requirements for entitlement to Category A retirement pension were satisfied and a claim made).

para 17). For example, under many schemes, if a pensioner dies any pension payable to his spouse is reduced if that spouse is more than 10 years younger than the member. This reduction is to reflect the length of time the spouse will receive the pension. As a result of this exemption, a 'young spouse' will not be able to claim discrimination on these grounds.

Life assurance on ill health early retirement

7.55 For pensioner members[43] who have taken ill health early retirement, the discontinuance of life assurance on their reaching normal retirement age (or if no normal retirement age applies, age 65) is exempt (Sch 2, para 18).

Other rules, practices, actions and decisions relating to benefit

Differences in pensionable service

7.56 Any difference in the amount of any age related benefit or death benefit where that difference relates to the number of years of pensionable service[44] is not discriminatory (Sch 2, para 19). However, this exemption only applies if, for members in a comparable situation, there is no difference in the accrual rate (ie the members accrue a benefit based on the same fraction of pensionable pay). This is an important exemption for defined benefit schemes where members' pensions are generally directly related to the number of years of pensionable service.

7.57 However the exemption will not apply where there is a change in accrual rate after a certain period of pensionable service (for example from 80th to 60th after 10 years' service).

Differences in pensionable pay

7.58 Any difference in any age related benefits or death benefit payable to a member to the extent that the difference is attributable to differences over time in pensionable pay is exempt (Sch 2, para 20). For example, in a final salary scheme a member's pension will relate to the member's final pensionable salary. A member with 10 years' service whose salary on retiring was £55,000 would (all other things being equal) receive a larger pension than a member with the same number of years of pensionable service, whose final pensionable salary was £50,000.[45]

---

[43] Defined as having the meaning given by s 124(1) of the Pensions Act 1995 (Sch 2, para 1(5)).
[44] Defined in s 124(1) of the Pensions Act 1995. Pensionable service, in relation to a member of an occupational pension scheme, means service in any description or category of employment to which the scheme relates which qualifies the member for payment of pension or other benefits.
[45] For example, 20/80th x £55,000 as opposed to 10/80ths x £50,000.

Maximum number of years of pensionable service

7.59 Under the pre 6 April 2006 tax regime for pensions, HMRC imposed a maximum number of years of pensionable service which could be accrued by a member. Consequently many schemes include an express limitation on the number of years of pensionable service. As a result of the changes to the taxation of pensions made by Part IV of the Finance Act 2004 (which came into force on 6 April 2006) this limitation is no longer a requirement. Paragraph 21 however provides an exemption for the continuation of this practice. For example, pensionable service could be limited to a maximum of 40 years.

7.60 There are other target benefits which may or may not be exempt under the Regulations. For example, assume a company's occupational pension scheme aims to provide a pension of two-thirds of final salary to all executives who have completed 20 years' service. There is no specific exemption for this type of practice under the Age Regulations. The length of service condition may be indirectly discriminatory and, if so, will need to be objectively justified.

Minimum period of pensionable service

7.61 Imposing a minimum period of pensionable service before age-related benefits or death benefits are payable is exempt (Sch 2, para 22). However this only applies if the minimum period does not exceed two years. (As a result of the changes made by the Finance Act 2004, schemes are now required to offer members with service of between three months and two years the option on leaving of either a return of their contributions or a transfer to another scheme.)

Minimum earnings level

7.62 Some schemes impose a minimum earnings level for the provision of benefits. This is exempt provided the minimum level is not above the limit referred to in s 5(1) of the Social Security Contributions and Benefits Act 1992 (Sch 2, para 23) (the lower earnings level[46]).

Maximum level of pensionable pay

7.63 Imposing a maximum level of pensionable pay for the calculation of any age-related benefits or death benefits is exempt (Sch 2, para 24). Before Part IV of the Finance Act 2004 came into force (on 6 April 2006) regulations made under s 590C of the Income and Corporation Taxes Act 1988 imposed a maximum level of pay which could be pensionable (the earnings cap). So, for example, if an individual had earnings of say £150,000 in the tax year ending April 2006, his pensionable earnings (for tax exempt approved occupational schemes) were limited to £105,600 (ie the earnings cap figure for 2005/06). Though s 590C has been repealed by the Finance

---

[46] Set at £4,368 per annum for 2006/07.

Act 2004, schemes will continue to be able to impose a maximum level of pay which is pensionable from an age discrimination perspective.

Closure of schemes

Closing a scheme to new members

7.64 Closing a scheme to new joiners will not be discriminatory as a result of the exemption in para 25. A defined benefit scheme may remain open to existing members (in other words existing members will continue to accrue benefits under the scheme), even though the scheme may be closed to new joiners. Closure of defined benefit occupational schemes to new hires is an increasingly common business practice. This can lead to the development of a two-tier workforce with new, and therefore typically younger, workers being excluded from an employer's occupational scheme. This exemption is intended to prevent age discrimination claims being made by the younger workers.

7.65 This exemption does not apply to the related business practice of closing a scheme to future accrual (as well as to new members). This practice may be potentially indirectly discriminatory. There is a risk that an older employee who may not have the same opportunity to build up a reasonable pension may claim indirect discrimination in comparison with a younger employee who has more time before retirement to build up pension benefits. In addition, younger employees may claim that their pension is reduced if they have not had the opportunity to build up benefits in a final salary scheme.

Other rules, practices, actions and decisions

Indexation of pensions

7.66 There are three exemptions which are related to or have the same objective as s 52 of the Pensions Act 1995 (Sch 2, paras 26–28). These are discussed below. Section 52 provides for the statutory indexation of pensions in payment.

7.67 Increases to pensions in payment which are made to members aged over 55 but not below that age are not discriminatory (Sch 2, para 26).

7.68 Differences in the rate of increase in pensions in payment for members of different ages to the extent that the aim in setting the different rates is to maintain the relative value of members' pensions is exempt (Sch 2, para 27). For example, a scheme may pay higher increases to pensioners who have reached a certain age (generally 75) if these older pensioners have been more seriously affected by cost of living increases than younger pensioners since their retirement began.

7.69 There is also a similar exemption for any difference in the rate of increase in pensions in payment for members whose pensions have been in payment for different periods of time. However this exemption only applies to the extent that the aim in setting the different rates is to maintain the relative value of members' pensions (Sch 2, para 28).

Age limit for transfers

7.70 Provisions which set an age limit for transfers into or out of the scheme are exempt (Sch 2, para 29). However this exemption only applies if the age limit is no more than one year below the normal retirement age (such as 64 where the normal retirement age is 65).

Registered pension schemes

7.71 Any rule, practice, action or decision relating to entitlement to, or payment of, benefits under a registered pension scheme[47] is exempt under para 30(1).[48] This applies if that rule, practice, action or decision is necessary to ensure tax relief or exemption under Part IV of the Finance Act 2004, or to prevent any tax charge arising, whoever may be liable in relation that charge. For example, a provision that lump sums will not be payable to members who first draw their benefits aged at least 75, would not be discriminatory under the Age Regulations. This restriction is one which schemes may impose to avoid tax charges under the 2004 Act. Similarly a provision that members cannot continue to accrue pensionable service after age 75 would not be discriminatory. Tax charges would arise if continuing accrual occurred.

7.72 Sub-paragraph (2) of para 30 excludes from the general exemption in sub-para (1) any rules, practices, actions or decisions setting a minimum age for entitlement to or payment of any age related benefit. Paragraphs 12 and 13 relate to the setting of minimum ages for the receipt of benefits.

PERSONAL PENSION SCHEMES: Part 3 of Sch 2

Contributions to personal pension schemes

7.73 There are limited exemptions in relation personal pension schemes. These apply to contributions to these schemes.[49] Different rates of contributions by an employer according to the age of the workers in respect

---

[47] Defined in para 1(7) as having the meaning given by s 150(2) of the Finance Act 2004. Section 150(2): a scheme which is registered under Chapter 2 of Part 4 of that Act.

[48] The definition of occupational pension scheme is modified for this paragraph – see n 36 for modification.

[49] Defined in para 1(7) has having the meaning given by s 1(1) of the Pension Schemes Act 1993 (see n 5).

of whom the contribution is made are exempt where the aim in setting different rates is:

- to equalise the amount of benefits to which members of different ages who are otherwise in a comparable situation will become entitled under their personal pension schemes; or

- to make the amount of benefit to which such members will become entitled under their personal pension schemes more nearly equal.

7.74 This exemption mirrors that in para 10 for occupational pension schemes. The same problems and issues will apply. The DTI Guidance expressly refers to Group Personal Pension Schemes ('GPPS') in their example of how to make use of these exemptions. For example, employer contributions to a GPPS at the rate of 6% for employees earning up to £30,000 and at the rate of 6% for employees earning more than that amount would be exempt.

7.75 Differences in the rate of contributions by an employer in respect of different workers to the extent that this relates to differences in remuneration are exempt (Sch 2, para 32). For example, an employer may make a 5% contribution for employees earning up to £35,000 and a 6% contribution for employees earning more than that sum.

OBJECTIVE JUSTIFICATION AND REG 32

7.76 Schedule 2 details specific exemptions which apply in relation to occupational pension schemes and also, to a limited extent, to personal pension schemes. If these exemptions cannot be utilised, scheme practices or provisions may continue to be lawful if they can be objectively justified. Objective justification is considered in detail in chapter 2.

7.77 In addition employers may be able to make use of the exemption for benefits based on length of service under reg 32. For example, if two years' service has to be undertaken before an individual can join a final salary section of a scheme this may be permitted under reg 32. Though employers may be able to use reg 32 this is not an option for trustees. Trustee will need to objectively justify this practice if it is indirectly discriminatory against younger workers.

TRUSTEE ISSUES

7.78 The Age Regulations impose an extra burden on trustees of occupational pension schemes. When determining whether a practice or provision is objectively justified, the trustees must ensure proper records are kept. In addition, trustees should not rely on assertions but should seek professional independent advice where appropriate. This in turn should be recorded as evidence of the objective justification.

APPENDIX[50]
OCCUPATIONAL PENSION SCHEMES – BROAD OVERVIEW OF EXEMPTIONS

EVENT	JOIN	CONTRIBUTIONS	TRANSFER	CLOSE SCHEME	RETIRE	AFTER RETIREMENT	DIE
TYPES OF DISCRIMINATION	Rules on admission	Different contribution rates	Different values on leaving service and age limit for transfer of benefits in or out	Closing a scheme to new entrants but keeping it open to existing members	Differences in pension benefits based on early/late retirement pivot ages, years of service/pay, enhanced pension for ill health retirees and bridging pensions	Pension increases dependent on age, or time since retirement	Different treatment for dependants
EXEMPTIONS TO CONSIDER	Para 7, reg 32	Paras 8, 9, 10 and 11, reg 32	Paras 8 and 26–29	Para 25	Paras 8, 12–24 and 30	Paras 26–29	Paras 12–24 and 30

The exemptions relating to age-related contributions to personal pension schemes are not included in this table.

[50] Derived from *The Impact of Age Regulations on Pension Schemes*, DTI Guidance (April 2006).

Chapter 8

LIABILITIES AND REMEDIES

LIABILITY

8.1 The Age Regulations establish the potential liability of employers, principals and a wide range of others, such as the trustees or managers of occupational pension schemes, those who appoint office holders and the chief officer of police. They also establish the principle of vicarious liability and the liability of those aiding unlawful acts.

Liability of employers

8.2 Just as an employer may be primarily liable for its unlawful discriminatory acts, so anything done by a person in the course of his employment shall be treated for the purposes of the Age Regulations as done by his employer as well as by him, whether or not it was done with the employer's knowledge or approval.[1] This principle of vicarious liability reflects similar provisions in other discrimination legislation and derives from the relationship between the employee and the employer and the latter's right, and theoretical obligation, to control the relevant activity of the employee. Dual vicarious liability is also permissible, where an employee is lent by one employer to work for another, but both share responsibility for an employee's acts.[2] The employee may also have knowingly aided the employer to do the unlawful act.[3]

8.3 The common law principles as to the meaning of 'in the course of employment' have been replaced by a more flexible test of fairness and justice for the purpose of establishing vicarious liability, turning, in the circumstances of each case, on the closeness of the connection between the employee's wrongdoing and the nature of the employment and/or whether the risk of such wrongdoing was one reasonably incidental to it.[4]

8.4 The employer has a potential defence if it can show that it took such steps as were reasonably practicable to prevent the employee from doing the discriminatory act or from doing in the course of his employment acts of that description.[5] Case law in respect of the analogous provision in the Sex Discrimination Act 1975 establishes that the proper approach is, first, to

---

[1]   Reg 25(1).
[2]   *Viasystems (Tyneside) Ltd v Thermal Transfer (Northern) Ltd* [2005] IRLR 983, CA.
[3]   See 10.6 below.
[4]   *Majrowski v Guy's and St Thomas's NHS Trust* [2005] IRLR 340, CA.
[5]   Reg 25(3).

identify whether the employer took any steps at all to prevent the employee from doing the act or acts complained of; and, secondly, to consider whether there were any further steps that it could have taken which were reasonably practicable.[6] It is permissible to take into account the extent of the difference, if any, which the action is likely to make in considering whether an action which the employer should have taken is reasonably practicable, although whether or not taking those steps would have prevented the discrimination is not determinative. The concept of reasonable practicability entitles the employer in this context to consider whether the time, effort and expense of the suggested measures are disproportionate to the result likely to be achieved.[7]

Liability of principals

8.5 The principle of vicarious liability also applies to the relationship of principal and agent.[8] Anything done by a person as agent for another person with the authority of that person (express or implied and whether precedent or subsequent) shall be treated for the purposes of the Age Regulations as done by that other person as well as by him. Therefore, the principal is vicariously liable for the discriminatory acts of the agent and jointly liable with the agent. There is no defence that the principal took steps to prevent the discrimination at the hands of the agent.

Aiding unlawful acts

8.6 A person who knowingly aids another person to do an act made unlawful by the Age Regulations is treated as having done the same kind of unlawful act in his own right.[9] For example, if an HR manager discriminates against applicants for employment by shortlisting on the basis of age, the employer will be liable, but the HR manager might also be liable having knowingly aided the company to discriminate. The expression 'aids' bears no technical or special meaning in this context. A person aids another if he helps or assists, or cooperates or collaborates with him. He does so whether or not his help is substantial and productive, provided the help is not so insignificant as to be negligible. It does not matter who instigates or initiates the relationship.[10]

8.7 There is a defence where a person acts in reliance upon a statement made to him by the other person that the particular act would not be unlawful by reason of any provision of the Age Regulations and it must be reasonable to rely upon that statement.[11] The other person who knowingly or

---

6   *Canniffe v East Riding of Yorkshire Council* [2000] IRLR 555, EAT.
7   *Croft v Royal Mail Group* [2003] 592, CA.
8   Reg 25(2).
9   Reg 26(1).
10   *Anyanwu v South Bank Students' Union et al* [2001] IRLR 305, HL.
11   Reg 26(2).

recklessly makes such a statement, which in a material respect is false or misleading, commits an offence.[12]

CLAIMS IN THE EMPLOYMENT TRIBUNAL

8.8 The employment tribunal has jurisdiction to hear a complaint by any person that another person has committed against the complainant an act of unlawful discrimination or is to be treated as having committed such an act by virtue of regs 25 (liability of employers and principals) or 26 (aiding unlawful acts).[13]

8.9 The employment tribunal's jurisdiction does not include: first, qualifications bodies (reg 19), where the act is one in respect of which an appeal or proceedings in the nature of an appeal may be brought under any enactment; secondly, where the act of discrimination is by an institute of further or higher education (reg 23); and thirdly, where the relationship between institute and student has come to an end (reg 24).[14] Jurisdiction for complaints in respect of an institute of further or higher education lies with the county or sheriff court.[15]

Employment Tribunal proceedings

8.10 It is not the purpose of this chapter to provide a detailed guide to the practice and procedure of the employment tribunal, but only to deal with points that are of particular relevance to an age discrimination claim.

The statutory questionnaire

8.11 Under reg 41, a person who considers that he may have been discriminated against or subjected to harassment may serve on the respondent a questionnaire. This is a parallel provision to the statutory questionnaires for other forms of discrimination and the regulation is entitled 'Help for persons in obtaining information etc'. Forms for request and reply are set out in Schs 3 and 4, although these are optional so long as a form to the like effect is used 'with such variation as the circumstances require'.[16]

8.12 It is important for the potential claimant to formulate the questions with care and equally important for the respondent to consider how it replies. Where the claimant questions the respondent, whether or not in accordance with the statutory questionnaire procedure, the questions and replies are admissible as evidence (subject to reg 41). Further, if it appears to the tribunal that the respondent deliberately and without reasonable excuse

---

12   Reg 26(3).
13   Reg 36(1).
14   Reg 36(2).
15   See 8.44 below.
16   Reg 41(1).

failed to reply within eight weeks of service of the questions or gave evasive or equivocal replies, the tribunal can draw any inference that it considers just and equitable, including an inference that the respondent committed an unlawful act.[17] The drawing of inferences is not limited to the statutory form for reply; the EAT has held that the tribunal is not precluded from drawing an inference from any written explanation.[18]

8.13 As well as dealing with issues specific to the particular act of discrimination, it would make sense for the complainant to focus questions upon a respondent's knowledge of and experience in implementing the Code of Practice on Age Diversity at Work (originally issued in 1999 and revised in 2002) and the ACAS Guide, *Age and the Workplace*, given that adverse inferences may also be drawn from any failure to comply with any relevant code of practice.[19] Statistical information is also useful material from which a tribunal could draw inferences, such as the average age of a workforce or of particular employees and applicants.

8.14 For the question to be admissible as evidence, there are rules as to the timing of the questionnaire. It can be served before a complaint has been presented so long as it is served within a period of three months beginning with when the act complained of was done. If it is served after the complaint has been presented, then it must be within the period of 21 days beginning with the day on which the complaint was presented. Alternatively leave can be sought to serve out of time within a period specified. The power to extend any time limit is included under the employment tribunal's general power to manage proceedings.[20] An application to extend time must be made in compliance with r 11 of the Employment Tribunal Rules, so that, for example, details of the application must also be sent to the respondent.

8.15 The questionnaire and any reply can be served by delivering it to the respondent or person aggrieved or by posting it to the usual or last-known residence or place of business. Where solicitors are instructed, service can be upon them; where the person to be served is a body corporate or a trade union or employer's association, then service can be upon the secretary or clerk of the body, union or association at its registered or principal office.

Time for bringing a complaint

8.16 A complaint must be presented to the tribunal before the end of the period of three months beginning when the act complained of was done.[21] There are three qualifications to that rule:

---

[17] Reg 41(2).
[18] *Dattani v Chief Constable of West Mercia Police* [2005] IRLR 327.
[19] See, for example, *Igen Ltd v Wong* [2005] IRLR 258, CA.
[20] Employment Tribunals (Constitution and Rules of Procedure) Regulations 2004, SI 2004/1861, Sch 1, r 10(2)(e).
[21] Reg 42(1).

(1) where the making of a contract is, by reason of the inclusion of any term, an unlawful act, that act shall be treated as extending through the duration of the contract;

(2) any act extending over a period shall be treated as done at the end of that period;

(3) a deliberate omission is treated as done when the person in question decided upon it. A person is taken as deciding upon an omission when he does an act inconsistent with doing the omitted act or, in the absence of such inconsistent behaviour, when the period expires within which he might reasonably have been expected to do the omitted act if it was to be done.[22]

8.17 Where it is out of time, the tribunal may nevertheless consider the complaint if, in all the circumstances of the case, it is just and equitable to do so. This discretion must be exercised alongside the stringent rules for acceptance of claims and – where relevant – the statutory dispute resolution procedures. As the burden is on the claimant to convince the tribunal that it is just and equitable to extend time to consider a complaint, 'the exercise of discretion is the exception rather than the rule'.[23] The discretion is broader than that given to tribunals under the 'not reasonably practicable' formula[24] and there is a body of case law covering those factual situations in which the discretion is more likely to be exercised.[25]

8.18 One particular situation is where the employee must first raise a grievance under the statutory dispute resolution before a claim to the tribunal of unlawful discrimination can be accepted.[26] Under s 32 of the Employment Act 2002, an employee 'shall not present a complaint to an employment tribunal' if it concerns a grievance in respect of which the statutory grievance procedure applies, the employee has not completed the first step in the procedure and more than one month has elapsed after the end of 'the original time limit for making the complaint'. However, the EAT has held that this requirement does not override the discretion of an employment tribunal to extend time on just and equitable grounds.[27]

Dispute resolution procedures

8.19 Discrimination in the employment field on the grounds of age is added to Schs 3, 4 and 5 to the Employment Act 2002.[28] Schedule 4 lists the tribunal jurisdictions to which s 32 of the 2002 Act ('Complaints about grievances') applies. If an employee wishes to bring a complaint to the

---

[22] Reg 42(4).
[23] *Robertson v Bexley Community Centre* [2003] IRLR 434, at para 25, per Auld LJ.
[24] *British Coal Corpn v Keeble* [1997] IRLR 336, EAT.
[25] See, for example, *Apelogun-Gabriels v London Borough of Lambeth* [2002] IRLR 116; *Southwark London Borough v Afolabi* [2003] IRLR 220; *Chohan v Derby Law Centre* [2004] IRLR 685, EAT.
[26] See 10.19 below.
[27] *BUPA Care Homes (BNH) Ltd v Spillett* and *Cann v Tesco Stores Ltd* [2006] IRLR 248.
[28] Sch 8.

employment tribunal, he must first raise a grievance.[29] The tribunal will not accept the complaint unless: (1) the employee has set out his grievance in writing and sent a copy to his employer; and (2) 28 days have passed since the day on which the grievance was sent.

8.20 A 'grievance' is defined as 'a complaint by an employee about action which his employer has taken or is contemplating taking against him'.[30] The statutory grievance procedure applies in relation to any grievance that could form the basis of a complaint to an employment tribunal. There are two sets of grievance procedures: the standard procedure and the modified procedure. The standard procedure will apply to most grievances and is a three-step process.

8.21 Step 1 is the written statement setting out the grievance. The employee is not obliged to set out the 'basis' for the grievance at this stage, since that requirement is triggered by the employer's invitation to attend a meeting to discuss the grievance: 'What is necessary ... is that the employer should understand the general nature of the complaint being made ...'.[31] Step 2 is a meeting to discuss the grievance. This meeting must not take place unless the employee has informed the employer of the basis for the grievance and the employer has had a reasonable opportunity to consider its response. Step 3 is an appeal against a decision, if the employee is not satisfied with it.

8.22 The modified procedure omits the meeting and any appeal and it only applies where: (1) the employee has ceased to be employed by the employer; (2) the employer was either unaware of the grievance before the employment ceased, or was aware but the standard procedure was not commenced or not completed before the last day of the employee's employment; and (3) the parties have agreed in writing in relation to the grievance (after the employer became aware of the grievance) that the modified procedure should apply.

8.23 Neither grievance procedure applies in a number of circumstances.

First, is where the employment has ended and neither the standard nor the modified procedure has been commenced and it has ceased to be reasonably practicable to raise a grievance.

Second, is where the grievance is that the employer has dismissed or is contemplating dismissing the employee. As the word 'dismissed' has the meaning given to it by the Employment Rights Act 1996 s 95(1)(a) and (b), the grievance procedure does apply where an employee is alleging constructive dismissal.

Third, neither grievance procedure applies where the grievance is that the employer has taken or is contemplating taking relevant disciplinary action against the employee, unless the reason for the grievance is one of the following:

---

[29]   See *Shergold v Fieldway Medical Centre* [2006] IRLR 76,EAT, *Galaxy Showers Ltd v Wilson* [2006] IRLR 83, EAT, and *Mark Warner Ltd v Aspland* [2006] IRLR 87, EAT.

[30]   Employment Act 2002 (Dispute Resolution) Regulations 2004, SI 2004/752, reg 2(1).

[31]   *Shergold v Fieldway Medical Centre* [2006] IRLR 76.

(1) the relevant disciplinary action amounted to or, if it took place, would amount to, unlawful discrimination, or

(2) the grounds on which the employer took, or is contemplating taking, the action are unrelated to the grounds on which he asserted that he took, or was contemplating taking, the action.

8.24 In both of those instances, the standard grievance procedure applies (or the modified procedure, as the case may be), but the parties are treated as having complied with the procedure so long as the employee has set out the grievance in a written statement and sent it to the employer either before any meeting under the dismissal and disciplinary procedures or (where these do not apply) before presenting a complaint to the employment tribunal.

8.25 Finally, the grievance procedures do not apply in three further situations:

(1) where the employee has reasonable grounds for believing that commencing the grievance procedure or complying with the subsequent requirement would result in a significant threat to himself, his property, any other person or the property of another person;

(2) where the employee has been subjected to harassment and has reasonable grounds to believe that commencing the grievance procedure or complying with the subsequent requirement would result in his being subjected to further harassment;

(3) where it is not practicable to commence the grievance procedure or comply with the subsequent requirement within a reasonable period.

ACAS conciliation and arbitration

8.26 The Employment Tribunals Act 1996 is amended to allow a copy of a complaint of age discrimination to be sent to a conciliation officer of the Advisory, Conciliation and Arbitration Service ('ACAS').[32] It is the duty of the conciliation officer to try and promote a settlement of the proceedings without a tribunal hearing, either if he is requested to do so by both parties or if, in the absence of any such request, the conciliation officer considers that there is a reasonable prospect of a successful outcome. Where a complaint has yet to be brought to the tribunal, the potential parties can also ask the conciliation officer to try and promote a settlement. Consistent with other anti-discrimination legislation, age discrimination proceedings are likely to be excluded from provisions for fixed periods of conciliation during tribunal proceedings.[33]

8.27 Any conciliated settlement will usually be recorded in writing using form COT3. The signing of a COT3 then precludes a claimant from bringing proceedings in an employment tribunal on a subject within the scope of the

---

[32] S 18(1)(r).
[33] Employment Tribunals Rules of Procedure, r 22 (as yet unamended).

settlement. There is no duty on an ACAS officer to advise on the merits of a claim before an employee enters into any binding settlement agreement.[34]

Compromise

8.28   A compromise contract will also act to prevent the initiation or continuation of employment tribunal proceedings, subject to a number of conditions.[35] The contract must be in writing and must relate to the particular complaint. The claimant must have received advice from a relevant independent adviser – who must be identified in the contract – as to the terms and effect of the compromise contract and, in particular, its effect on his ability to pursue a complaint before an employment tribunal. That adviser must be covered by a contract of insurance. The compromise contract must also state that the conditions regulating compromise contracts are satisfied. The term 'relevant legal adviser' is defined to include: a qualified lawyer; an officer, official, employee or member of an independent trade union who has been certified by the trade union as competent to give such advice and authorised to do so; a person working at an advice centre who is certified as competent and authorised to give advice. However, the adviser must not be employed by, acting for or connected with the other party, nor must the trade union or advice centre be the other party. An adviser from an advice centre is also not a relevant independent adviser if the claimant makes a payment for the advice.

8.29   In *Hinton v University of East London*,[36] the Court of Appeal considered that:

> 'If actual proceedings are compromised it is good practice for the particulars of the proceedings and of the particular allegations made in them to be inserted in the compromise agreement in the form of a brief factual and legal description. If the compromise is of a particular claim which is not yet the subject of proceedings, it is good practice for the particulars of the nature of the allegations and of the statute under which they are made or the common law basis of the alleged claim to be inserted in the compromise agreement in the form of a brief factual and legal description.'

The burden of proof

8.30   Where the claimant proves facts from which the tribunal could conclude, in the absence of an adequate explanation, that the respondent has committed an act of unlawful discrimination, the tribunal shall uphold the complaint unless the respondent proves that it did not commit, or is not to be treated as having committed that act.[37] This 'reversed' burden of proof is central to discrimination law and derives from European law,[38] having first

---

34   *Clarke v Redcar & Cleveland Borough Council* [2006] IRLR 324.
35   Sch 5, para 2.
36   [2005] IRLR 552.
37   Reg 37.
38   Burden of Proof Directive 1997/80/EC.

been introduced in the United Kingdom through amendments to the Sex Discrimination Act 1975.[39]

8.31 The Court of Appeal has given recent and detailed guidance on the reversal of the burden of proof in *Igen Ltd v Wong*[40] and it is helpful to set out the annex to that decision:

'(1) Pursuant to s 63A of the SDA, it is for the claimant who complains of sex discrimination to prove on the balance of probabilities facts from which the tribunal could conclude, in the absence of an adequate explanation, that the respondent has committed an act of discrimination against the claimant which is unlawful by virtue of Part II or which by virtue of s 41 or s 42 of the SDA is to be treated as having been committed against the claimant. These are referred to below as "such facts".

(2) If the claimant does not prove such facts he or she will fail.

(3) It is important to bear in mind in deciding whether the claimant has proved such facts that it is unusual to find direct evidence of sex discrimination. Few employers would be prepared to admit such discrimination, even to themselves. In some cases the discrimination will not be an intention but merely based on the assumption that "he or she would not have fitted in".

(4) In deciding whether the claimant has proved such facts, it is important to remember that the outcome at this stage of the analysis by the tribunal will therefore usually depend on what inferences it is proper to draw from the primary facts found by the tribunal.

(5) It is important to note the word "could" in s 63A(2). At this stage the tribunal does not have to reach a definitive determination that such facts would lead it to the conclusion that there was an act of unlawful discrimination. At this stage a tribunal is looking at the primary facts before it to see what inferences of secondary fact could be drawn from them.

(6) In considering what inferences or conclusions can be drawn from the primary facts, the tribunal must assume that there is no adequate explanation for those facts.

(7) These inferences can include, in appropriate cases, any inferences that it is just and equitable to draw in accordance with s 74(2)(b) of the SDA from an evasive or equivocal reply to a questionnaire or any other questions that fall within s 74(2) of the SDA.

(8) Likewise, the tribunal must decide whether any provision of any relevant code of practice is relevant and if so, take it into account in determining, such facts pursuant to s 56A(10) of the SDA. This means that inferences may also be drawn from any failure to comply with any relevant code of practice.

---

[39] S 63A, amended by the Sex Discrimination (Indirect Discrimination and Burden of Proof) Regulations 2001, SI 2001/2660.

[40] [2005] IRLR 258; revising the guidance in *Barton v Investec Henderson Crosthwaite Securities Ltd* [2003] IRLR 332, EAT.

(9) Where the claimant has proved facts from which conclusions could be drawn that the respondent has treated the claimant less favourably on the ground of sex, then the burden of proof moves to the respondent.

(10) It is then for the respondent to prove that he did not commit, or as the case may be, is not to be treated as having committed, that act.

(11) To discharge that burden it is necessary for the respondent to prove, on the balance of probabilities, that the treatment was in no sense whatsoever on the grounds of sex, since "no discrimination whatsoever" is compatible with the Burden of Proof Directive.

(12) That requires a tribunal to assess not merely whether the respondent has proved an explanation for the facts from which such inferences can be drawn, but further that it is adequate to discharge the burden of proof on the balance of probabilities that sex was not a ground for the treatment in question.

(13) Since the facts necessary to prove an explanation would normally be in the possession of the respondent, a tribunal would normally expect cogent evidence to discharge that burden of proof. In particular, the tribunal will need to examine carefully explanations for failure to deal with the questionnaire procedure and/or code of practice.'

8.32 The Court is describing a two-stage process and the claimant must first prove facts from which conclusions could be drawn that the respondent has treated the claimant less favourably on the ground of sex. This means more than just the possibility of discrimination. For example, if an applicant aged 50 unsuccessfully applies for a position which is given to an applicant aged 30, then it is possible that age was a reason for the older applicant not being selected, but that is not enough to establish primary facts from which the tribunal could infer age discrimination. If the older applicant was better qualified – or had the same qualifications – then those would be primary facts from which conclusions could be drawn that the employer has treated the older applicant less favourably on the ground of age and the evidential burden will then move to the respondent employer.[41]

8.33 Applicants for any position are likely to be of different ages and will frequently have the same experience and/or qualifications, so it may not be difficult to establish primary facts from which an inference could be drawn. The tribunal should take a broad view of the surrounding circumstances,[42] therefore other factors, such as the average age of a particular workforce compared with the industry average, may also allow the tribunal to draw an inference that age was the reason for different treatment. The evidential burden on the respondent is to prove, on the balance of probabilities, that the treatment was 'in no sense whatsoever' on the grounds of age, which may be a difficult task, as there may not be 'cogent evidence' to discharge that burden.

---

[41]   *Dresdner Kleinwort Wasserstein Ltd v Adebayo* [2005] IRLR 514.
[42]   *Anya v University of Oxford* [2001] IRLR 377.

Remedies

8.34 Where a tribunal finds that a complaint is well-founded, it shall provide one or more of three different remedies as it considers just and equitable.[43]

Declaration of rights

8.35 Where a complaint of age discrimination has succeeded, the claimant is entitled to an order declaring the rights of the claimant and respondent in relation to the act to which the complaint relates.

Compensation

8.36 The second potential remedy is an order requiring the respondent to pay compensation of an amount corresponding to any damages that could have been ordered by a county court; in other words, compensation for age discrimination is assessed in the same way as damages for a statutory tort. The question for the tribunal is what loss flowed from the unlawful act and there is no upper limit on compensation. Where the complaint is of indirect discrimination, then a tribunal may not award compensation if the respondent proves that the provision, criterion or practice was not applied with the intention of treating the claimant unfavourably on the grounds of age, unless it would not be just and equitable only to make a declaration or recommendation.[44]

8.37 Schedule 3 to the Employment Act 2002 is amended by the Age Regulations, which means that the adjustment of awards under s 31 of that Act applies to complaints of age discrimination. Therefore, where an employer or employee has failed to complete the statutory grievance procedure, the tribunal must increase or decrease the award by 10% and may do so by up to 50%, subject to a discretion where exceptional circumstances apply. There is also provision for the award of interest on any compensation under the Employment Tribunals (Interest on Awards in Discrimination Cases) Regulations 1996.[45]

8.38 Where a dismissal is both unfair and an act of age discrimination or harassment, a tribunal cannot compensate for the same loss under more than one provision.[46] This is to prevent double recovery. However, the position is not always straightforward. In unfair dismissal cases the compensatory award shall be such amount as the tribunal considers 'just and equitable'.[47] Compensation for unfair dismissal is capped,[48] whereas there is no statutory limit to compensation for a dismissal is compensatory. The recoupment

---

[43] Reg 38(1).
[44] Reg 38(2).
[45] SI 1996/2803, as amended by Sch 8, para 56.
[46] Employment Rights Act 1996, s 126, as amended by Sch 8, para 29.
[47] Ibid, s 123(1).
[48] Ibid, s 124.

provisions apply to compensation for unfair dismissal, but do not apply where the award is made in respect of discrimination.[49]

8.39 Compensation for discrimination can include an award for injury to feelings and, in a case where the unlawful conduct has caused no actual financial loss, that will frequently be the only remedy awarded. The Court of Appeal has provided guidelines on the appropriate brackets for such awards: in the most serious cases, such as where there has been a lengthy campaign of discriminatory harassment, the bracket should normally be between £15,000 and £25,000; the middle bracket between £5,000 and £15,000 should be used for serious cases, which do not merit an award in the highest band; awards of between £500 and £5,000 are appropriate for less serious cases, such as where the act of discrimination is an isolated or one-off occurrence. In general, awards of less than £500 are to be avoided altogether, as they risk being regarded as so low as not to be a proper recognition of injury to feelings.[50]

8.40 Aggravated damages can be awarded for an act of discrimination,[51] as can exemplary damages in some circumstances.[52]

Recommendations

8.41 The third remedy open to a tribunal is to make a recommendation that the respondent take, within a specified period, action appearing to the tribunal to be practicable for the purpose of obviating or reducing the adverse effect on the complainant of any act of discrimination or harassment to which the complaint relates. This gives the tribunal 'an extremely wide discretion',[53] although it is a discretion directed at the adverse effect on the claimant, rather than at obtaining broad-based changes for a wider class of persons.

8.42 A tribunal would go too far if it recommended that a claimant who has been the victim of discrimination in selection for employment should be appointed to the next available, suitable job or should be promoted, as that would be unfair to the other applicants for that post,[54] but it might recommend that the claimant be considered for the post. The provision allowing recommendations does not permit positive discrimination and to appoint or promote a claimant without considering other applicants who might have superior qualifications for the vacancy could amount to direct discrimination against those other applicants on the grounds of age.[55]

---

[49]   Employment Protection (Recoupment of Jobseeker's Allowance and Income Support) Regulations 1996, SI 1996/2349.

[50]   *Vento v Chief Constable of West Yorkshire Police* [2003] IRLR 102; see also *Virgo Fidelis Senior School v Boyle* [2004] IRLR 268, EAT.

[51]   *Armitage, Marsden and HM Prison Service v Johnson* [1997] IRLR 162, EAT.

[52]   *Kuddus v Chief Constable of Leicestershire Constabulary* [2002] 2 AC 122, HL.

[53]   *Chief Constable of West Yorkshire Police v Vento (No 2)* [2002] IRLR 177, EAT; the issue of recommendations was not considered by the Court of Appeal: [2003] IRLR 102.

[54]   *Noone v North West Thames Regional Health Authority (No 2)* [1988] IRLR 530, CA.

[55]   *British Gas plc v Sharma* [1991] IRLR 101, EAT.

8.43 If a respondent fails without reasonable justification to comply with a recommendation made by the tribunal, then the tribunal may – if it thinks it just and equitable – increase any award of compensation or, if no order was previously made, make an order for compensation.[56]

PROCEEDINGS IN THE COUNTY OR SHERIFF COURT

8.44 Under reg 39, the county court (and sheriff court in Scotland) has a limited jurisdiction to hear complaints of age discrimination which is unlawful by virtue of reg 23 (institutions of further and higher education), including where the relationship has come to an end (under reg 24). A county or sheriff court shall not consider a claim unless proceedings are instituted before the end of the period of six months beginning when the act complained of was done.[57] The same qualifications apply to this rule as to the three-month time limit in the employment tribunal.[58] There is a discretion to extend time where it is just and equitable to do so.[59]

8.45 The complaint may be made the subject of civil proceedings in the like manner as any other claim in tort (or, in Scotland, reparation for breach of statutory duty), which means that the remedies will be damages, including compensation for injury to feelings,[60] a declaration and an injunction. The questionnaire procedure under reg 41 also applies to county or sheriff court claims, with service required within six months of the act complained of where it is served before proceedings are commenced; where proceedings have been started, service is with the leave of the court and within a period specified by the court.

---

[56] Reg 38(3).
[57] Reg 42(2).
[58] Reg 42(4).
[59] Reg 42(3).
[60] Reg 39(3).

Appendix 1

THE EMPLOYMENT EQUALITY (AGE) REGULATIONS 2006, SI 2006/1031

Made   3rd April 2006

Coming into force   1st October 2006

CONTENTS

PART 1
GENERAL

PART 2
DISCRIMINATION IN EMPLOYMENT AND VOCATIONAL TRAINING

PART 3
OTHER UNLAWFUL ACTS

PART 4
GENERAL EXCEPTIONS FROM PARTS 2 AND 3

PART 5
ENFORCEMENT

PART 6
SUPPLEMENTAL

A draft of these Regulations was laid before Parliament in accordance with paragraph 2 of Schedule 2 to the European Communities Act 1972(**a**), and was approved by resolution of each House of Parliament;

The Secretary of State, who is a Minister designated for the purposes of section 2(2) of the European Communities Act 1972 in relation to discrimination(**b**), makes the following Regulations in exercise of the powers conferred by section 2(2):—

PART 1

GENERAL

Citation, commencement and extent

1.—(1) These Regulations may be cited as the Employment Equality (Age) Regulations 2006, and shall come into force on 1st October 2006.

(**a**) 1972 c 68.

(**b**) See the European Communities (Designation) (No 3) Order 2002 (SI 2002/1819).

(2) Any amendment, repeal or revocation made by these Regulations has the same extent as the provision to which it relates.

(3) Subject to that, these Regulations do not extend to Northern Ireland.

Interpretation

2.—(1) In these Regulations, references to discrimination are to any discrimination falling within regulation 3 (discrimination on grounds of age), regulation 4 (discrimination by way of victimisation) or regulation 5 (instructions to discriminate) and related expressions shall be construed accordingly, and references to harassment shall be construed in accordance with regulation 6 (harassment on grounds of age).

(2) In these Regulations—

'1996 Act' means the Employment Rights Act 1996(**a**);

'act' includes a deliberate omission;

'benefit', except in regulation 11 and Schedule 2 (pension schemes), includes facilities and services;

'commencement date' means 1st October 2006;

'Crown employment' means —

(a)   service for purposes of a Minister of the Crown or government department, other than service of a person holding a statutory office; or

(b)   service on behalf of the Crown for purposes of a person holding a statutory office or purposes of a statutory body;

'detriment' does not include harassment within the meaning of regulation 6;

'employment' means employment under a contract of service or of apprenticeship or a contract personally to do any work, and related expressions (such as 'employee' and 'employer') shall be construed accordingly, but this definition does not apply in relation to regulation 30 (exception for retirement) or to Schedules 2, 6, 7 and 8;

'Great Britain' includes such of the territorial waters of the United Kingdom as are adjacent to Great Britain;

'Minister of the Crown' includes the Treasury and the Defence Council;

'proprietor', in relation to a school, has the meaning given by section 579 of the Education Act 1996(**b**);

'relevant member of the House of Commons staff' means any person who was appointed by the House of Commons Commission or who is a member of the Speaker's personal staff;

'relevant member of the House of Lords staff' means any person who is employed under a contract of employment with the Corporate Officer of the

---

(**a**) 1996 c 18.
(**b**) 1996 c 56; section 579 has been amended on a number of occasions. The relevant amendments for the purposes of these Regulations were those made by section 140(1) of, and paragraph 183(a)(iii) of Schedule 30 to, the School Standards and Framework Act 1998 (c 31) and regulation 3 of SI 2003/2045.

House of Lords;

'school', in England and Wales, has the meaning given by section 4 of the Education Act 1996(**a**), and, in Scotland, has the meaning given by section 135(1) of the Education (Scotland) Act 1980(**b**), and references to a school are to an institution in so far as it is engaged in the provision of education under those sections;

'service for purposes of a Minister of the Crown or government department' does not include service in any office mentioned in Schedule 2 (Ministerial offices) to the House of Commons Disqualification Act 1975(**c**);

'statutory body' means a body set up by or in pursuance of an enactment, and 'statutory office' means an office so set up; and

'worker' in relation to regulations 32 and 34 and to Schedule 2, means, as the case may be—

(a) an employee;

(b) a person holding an office or post to which regulation 12 (office-holders etc) applies;

(c) a person holding the office of constable;

(d) a partner within the meaning of regulation 17 (partnerships);

(e) a member of a limited liability partnership within the meaning of that regulation;

(f) a person in Crown employment;

(g) a relevant member of the House of Commons staff;

(h) a relevant member of the House of Lords staff.

(3) In these Regulations references to 'employer', in their application to a person at any time seeking to employ another, include a person who has no employees at that time.

Discrimination on grounds of age

3.—(1) For the purposes of these Regulations, a person ('A') discriminates against another person ('B') if—

(a) on grounds of B's age, A treats B less favourably than he treats or would treat other persons, or

(b) A applies to B a provision, criterion or practice which he applies or would apply equally to persons not of the same age group as B, but—

(i) which puts or would put persons of the same age group as B at a particular disadvantage when compared with other persons, and

(ii) which puts B at that disadvantage,

(**a**) Section 4 was amended by section 51 of the Education Act 1997 (c 44) and Part 3 of Schedule 22 to the Education Act 2002 (c 32).
(**b**) 1980 c 44.
(**c**) 1975 c 24; Schedule 2 was amended by the Scotland Act 1998 (c 46), sections 48(6) and 87(1) and Schedule 9, and by SI 2002/794.

and A cannot show the treatment or, as the case may be, provision, criterion or practice to be a proportionate means of achieving a legitimate aim.

(2) A comparison of B's case with that of another person under paragraph (1) must be such that the relevant circumstances in the one case are the same, or not materially different, in the other.

(3) In this regulation—

(a) 'age group' means a group of persons defined by reference to age, whether by reference to a particular age or a range of ages; and

(b) the reference in paragraph (1)(a) to B's age includes B's apparent age.

Discrimination by way of victimisation

4.—(1) For the purposes of these Regulations, a person ('A') discriminates against another person ('B') if he treats B less favourably than he treats or would treat other persons in the same circumstances, and does so by reason that B has—

(a) brought proceedings against A or any other person under or by virtue of these Regulations;

(b) given evidence or information in connection with proceedings brought by any person against A or any other person under or by virtue of these Regulations;

(c) otherwise done anything under or by reference to these Regulations in relation to A or any other person; or

(d) alleged that A or any other person has committed an act which (whether or not the allegation so states) would amount to a contravention of these Regulations,

or by reason that A knows that B intends to do any of those things, or suspects that B has done or intends to do any of them.

(2) Paragraph (1) does not apply to treatment of B by reason of any allegation made by him, or evidence or information given by him, if the allegation, evidence or information was false and not made (or, as the case may be, given) in good faith.

Instructions to discriminate

5. For the purposes of these Regulations, a person ('A') discriminates against another person ('B') if he treats B less favourably than he treats or would treat other persons in the same circumstances, and does so by reason that—

(a) B has not carried out (in whole or in part) an instruction to do an act which is unlawful by virtue of these Regulations, or

(b) B, having been given an instruction to do such an act, complains to A or to any other person about that instruction.

Harassment on grounds of age

6.—(1) For the purposes of these Regulations, a person ('A') subjects another person ('B') to harassment where, on grounds of age, A engages in unwanted conduct which has the purpose or effect of—

(a) violating B's dignity; or

(b) creating an intimidating, hostile, degrading, humiliating or offensive environment for B.

(2) Conduct shall be regarded as having the effect specified in paragraph (1)(a) or (b) only if, having regard to all the circumstances, including in particular the perception of B, it should reasonably be considered as having that effect.

PART 2

DISCRIMINATION IN EMPLOYMENT AND VOCATIONAL TRAINING

Applicants and employees

7.—(1) It is unlawful for an employer, in relation to employment by him at an establishment in Great Britain, to discriminate against a person—

(a) in the arrangements he makes for the purpose of determining to whom he should offer employment;

(b) in the terms on which he offers that person employment; or

(c) by refusing to offer, or deliberately not offering, him employment.

(2) It is unlawful for an employer, in relation to a person whom he employs at an establishment in Great Britain, to discriminate against that person—

(a) in the terms of employment which he affords him;

(b) in the opportunities which he affords him for promotion, a transfer, training, or receiving any other benefit;

(c) by refusing to afford him, or deliberately not affording him, any such opportunity; or

(d) by dismissing him, or subjecting him to any other detriment.

(3) It is unlawful for an employer, in relation to employment by him at an establishment in Great Britain, to subject to harassment a person whom he employs or who has applied to him for employment.

(4) Subject to paragraph (5), paragraph (1)(a) and (c) does not apply in relation to a person—

(a) whose age is greater than the employer's normal retirement age or, if the employer does not have a normal retirement age, the age of 65; or

(b) who would, within a period of six months from the date of his application to the employer, reach the employer's normal retirement age or, if the employer does not have a normal retirement age, the age of 65.

(5) Paragraph (4) only applies to a person to whom, if he was recruited by the employer, regulation 30 (exception for retirement) could apply.

(6) Paragraph (2) does not apply to benefits of any description if the employer is concerned with the provision (for payment or not) of benefits of that description to the public, or to a section of the public which includes the employee in question,

unless—

(a) that provision differs in a material respect from the provision of the benefits by the employer to his employees; or

(b) the provision of the benefits to the employee in question is regulated by his contract of employment; or

(c) the benefits relate to training.

(7) In paragraph (2)(d) reference to the dismissal of a person from employment includes reference—

(a) to the termination of that person's employment by the expiration of any period (including a period expiring by reference to an event or circumstance), not being a termination immediately after which the employment is renewed on the same terms; and

(b) to the termination of that person's employment by any act of his (including the giving of notice) in circumstances such that he is entitled to terminate it without notice by reason of the conduct of the employer.

(8) In paragraph (4) 'normal retirement age' is an age of 65 or more which meets the requirements of section 98ZH of the 1996 Act(**a**).

Exception for genuine occupational requirement etc

8.—(1) In relation to discrimination falling within regulation 3 (discrimination on grounds of age)—

(a) regulation 7(1)(a) or (c) does not apply to any employment;

(b) regulation 7(2)(b) or (c) does not apply to promotion or transfer to, or training for, any employment; and

(c) regulation 7(2)(d) does not apply to dismissal from any employment,

where paragraph (2) applies.

(2) This paragraph applies where, having regard to the nature of the employment or the context in which it is carried out—

(a) possessing a characteristic related to age is a genuine and determining occupational requirement;

(b) it is proportionate to apply that requirement in the particular case; and

(c) either—

(i) the person to whom that requirement is applied does not meet it, or

(ii) the employer is not satisfied, and in all the circumstances it is reasonable for him not to be satisfied, that that person meets it.

Contract workers

9.—(1) It is unlawful for a principal, in relation to contract work at an establishment in Great Britain, to discriminate against a contract worker—

(**a**) Section 98ZH of the 1996 Act is inserted into that Act by regulation 49 of, and paragraph 23 of Schedule 8 to, these Regulations.

    (a)   in the terms on which he allows him to do that work;

    (b)   by not allowing him to do it or continue to do it;

    (c)   in the way he affords him access to any benefits or by refusing or deliberately not affording him access to them; or

    (d)   by subjecting him to any other detriment.

(2) It is unlawful for a principal, in relation to contract work at an establishment in Great Britain, to subject a contract worker to harassment.

(3) A principal does not contravene paragraph (1)(b) by doing any act in relation to a contract worker where, if the work were to be done by a person taken into the principal's employment, that act would be lawful by virtue of regulation 8 (exception for genuine occupational requirement etc).

(4) Paragraph (1) does not apply to benefits of any description if the principal is concerned with the provision (for payment or not) of benefits of that description to the public, or to a section of the public to which the contract worker in question belongs, unless that provision differs in a material respect from the provision of the benefits by the principal to his contract workers.

(5) In this regulation—

'principal' means a person ('A') who makes work available for doing by individuals who are employed by another person who supplies them under a contract made with A;

'contract work' means work so made available; and

'contract worker' means any individual who is supplied to the principal under such a contract.

Meaning of employment and contract work at establishment in Great Britain

10.—(1) For the purposes of this Part ('the relevant purposes'), employment is to be regarded as being at an establishment in Great Britain if the employee—

    (a)   does his work wholly or partly in Great Britain; or

    (b)   does his work wholly outside Great Britain and paragraph (2) applies.

(2) This paragraph applies if—

    (a)   the employer has a place of business at an establishment in Great Britain;

    (b)   the work is for the purposes of the business carried on at that establishment; and

    (c)   the employee is ordinarily resident in Great Britain—

        (i)   at the time when he applies for or is offered the employment, or

        (ii) at any time during the course of the employment.

(3) The reference to 'employment' in paragraph (1) includes—

    (a)   employment on board a ship only if the ship is registered at a port of registry in Great Britain, and

    (b)   employment on an aircraft or hovercraft only if the aircraft or hovercraft is registered in the United Kingdom and operated by a person who has his principal place of business, or is ordinarily resident, in Great Britain.

(4) Subject to paragraph (5), for the purposes of determining if employment concerned with the exploration of the sea bed or sub-soil or the exploitation of their natural resources is outside Great Britain, this regulation has effect as if references to Great Britain included—

    (a) any area designated under section 1(7) of the Continental Shelf Act 1964(**a**) except an area or part of an area in which the law of Northern Ireland applies; and

    (b) in relation to employment concerned with the exploration or exploitation of the Frigg Gas Field, the part of the Norwegian sector of the Continental Shelf described in Schedule 1.

(5) Paragraph (4) shall not apply to employment which is concerned with the exploration or exploitation of the Frigg Gas Field unless the employer is—

    (a) a company registered under the Companies Act 1985(**b**);

    (b) an oversea company which has established a place of business within Great Britain from which it directs the exploration or exploitation in question; or

    (c) any other person who has a place of business within Great Britain from which he directs the exploration or exploitation in question.

(6) In this regulation—

'the Frigg Gas Field' means the naturally occurring gas-bearing sand formations of the lower Eocene age located in the vicinity of the intersection of the line of latitude 59 degrees 53 minutes North and of the dividing line between the sectors of the Continental Shelf of the United Kingdom and the Kingdom of Norway and includes all other gas-bearing strata from which gas at the start of production is capable of flowing into the above-mentioned gas-bearing sand formations;

'oversea company' has the same meaning as in section 744 of the Companies Act 1985.

(7) This regulation applies in relation to contract work within the meaning of regulation 9 as it applies in relation to employment; and, in its application to contract work, references to 'employee', 'employer' and 'employment' are references to (respectively) 'contract worker', 'principal' and 'contract work' within the meaning of regulation 9.

Pension schemes

11.—(1) It is unlawful, except in relation to rights accrued or benefits payable in respect of periods of service prior to the coming into force of these Regulations, for the trustees or managers of an occupational pension scheme to discriminate against a member or prospective member of the scheme in carrying out any of their functions in relation to it (including in particular their functions relating to the admission of members to the scheme and the treatment of members of it).

(**a**) 1964 c 29.
(**b**) 1985 c 6.

(2) It is unlawful for the trustees or managers of an occupational pension scheme, in relation to the scheme, to subject to harassment a member or prospective member of it.

(3) Schedule 2 (pension schemes) shall have effect for the purposes of—

    (a)   defining terms used in this regulation and in that Schedule;

    (b)   exempting certain rules and practices in or relating to pension schemes from Parts 2 and 3 of these Regulations;

    (c)   treating every occupational pension scheme as including a non-discrimination rule;

    (d)   giving trustees or managers of an occupational pension scheme power to alter the scheme so as to secure conformity with the non-discrimination rule;

    (e)   making provision in relation to the procedures, and remedies which may be granted, on certain complaints relating to occupational pension schemes presented to an employment tribunal under regulation 36 (jurisdiction of employment tribunals).

Office-holders etc

12.—(1) It is unlawful for a relevant person, in relation to an appointment to an office or post to which this regulation applies, to discriminate against a person—

    (a)   in the arrangements which he makes for the purpose of determining to whom the appointment should be offered;

    (b)   in the terms on which he offers him the appointment; or

    (c)   by refusing to offer him the appointment.

(2) It is unlawful, in relation to an appointment to an office or post to which this regulation applies and which is an office or post referred to in paragraph (8)(b), for a relevant person on whose recommendation (or subject to whose approval) appointments to the office or post are made, to discriminate against a person—

    (a)   in the arrangements which he makes for the purpose of determining who should be recommended or approved in relation to the appointment; or

    (b)   in making or refusing to make a recommendation, or giving or refusing to give an approval, in relation to the appointment.

(3) It is unlawful for a relevant person, in relation to a person who has been appointed to an office or post to which this regulation applies, to discriminate against him—

    (a)   in the terms of the appointment;

    (b)   in the opportunities which he affords him for promotion, a transfer, training or receiving any other benefit, or by refusing to afford him any such opportunity;

    (c)   by terminating the appointment; or

    (d)   by subjecting him to any other detriment in relation to the appointment.

(4) It is unlawful for a relevant person, in relation to an office or post to which this regulation applies, to subject to harassment a person—

(a)   who has been appointed to the office or post;

(b)   who is seeking or being considered for appointment to the office or post; or

(c)   who is seeking or being considered for a recommendation or approval in relation to an appointment to an office or post referred to in paragraph (8)(b).

(5) Paragraphs (1) and (3) do not apply to any act in relation to an office or post where, if the office or post constituted employment, that act would be lawful by virtue of regulation 8 (exception for genuine occupational requirement etc); and paragraph (2) does not apply to any act in relation to an office or post where, if the office or post constituted employment, it would be lawful by virtue of regulation 8 to refuse to offer the person such employment.

(6) Paragraph (3) does not apply to benefits of any description if the relevant person is concerned with the provision (for payment or not) of benefits of that description to the public, or a section of the public to which the person appointed belongs, unless—

(a)   that provision differs in a material respect from the provision of the benefits by the relevant person to persons appointed to offices or posts which are the same as, or not materially different from, that which the person appointed holds; or

(b)   the provision of the benefits to the person appointed is regulated by the terms and conditions of his appointment; or

(c)   the benefits relate to training.

(7) In paragraph (3)(c) the reference to the termination of the appointment includes a reference—

(a)   to the termination of the appointment by the expiration of any period (including a period expiring by reference to an event or circumstance), not being a termination immediately after which the appointment is renewed on the same terms and conditions; and

(b)   to the termination of the appointment by any act of the person appointed (including the giving of notice) in circumstances such that he is entitled to terminate the appointment without notice by reason of the conduct of the relevant person.

(8) This regulation applies to—

(a)   any office or post to which persons are appointed to discharge functions personally under the direction of another person, and in respect of which they are entitled to remuneration; and

(b)   any office or post to which appointments are made by (or on the recommendation of or subject to the approval of) a Minister of the Crown, a government department, the National Assembly for Wales or any part of the Scottish Administration,

but not to a political office or a case where regulation 7 (applicants and employees), 9 (contract workers), 15 (barristers), 16 (advocates) or 17 (partnerships) applies, or would apply but for the operation of any other provision of these Regulations.

(9) For the purposes of paragraph (8)(a) the holder of an office or post—

(a)   is to be regarded as discharging his functions under the direction of another person if that other person is entitled to direct him as to when and where he discharges those functions;

(b) is not to be regarded as entitled to remuneration merely because he is entitled to payments—

(i) in respect of expenses incurred by him in carrying out the function of the office or post; or

(ii) by way of compensation for the loss of income or benefits he would or might have received from any person had he not been carrying out the functions of the office or post.

(10) In this regulation—

(a) appointment to an office or post does not include election to an office or post;

(b) 'political office' means—

(i) any office of the House of Commons held by a member of it;

(ii) a life peerage within the meaning of the Life Peerages Act 1958(**a**), or any office of the House of Lords held by a member of it;

(iii) any office mentioned in Schedule 2 (Ministerial offices) to the House of Commons Disqualification Act 1975(**b**);

(iv) the offices of Leader of the Opposition, Chief Opposition Whip or Assistant Opposition Whip within the meaning of the Ministerial and other Salaries Act 1975(**c**);

(v) any office of the Scottish Parliament held by a member of it;

(vi) a member of the Scottish Executive within the meaning of section 44 of the Scotland Act 1998(**d**), or a junior Scottish Minister within the meaning of section 49 of that Act;

(vii) any office of the National Assembly for Wales held by a member of it;

(viii) in England, any office of a county council, a London borough council, a district council, or a parish council held by a member of it;

(ix) in Wales, any office of a county council, a county borough council, or a community council held by a member of it;

(x) in relation to a council constituted under section 2 of the Local Government etc (Scotland) Act 1994(**e**) or a community council established under section 51 of the Local Government (Scotland) Act 1973(**f**), any office of such a council held by a member of it;

(**a**) 1958 c 21.
(**b**) 1975 c 24; Schedule 2 was amended by the Scotland Act 1998 (c 46), sections 48(6) and 87(1) and Schedule 9, and by SI 2002/794.
(**c**) 1975 c 27.
(**d**) 1998 c 46.
(**e**) 1994 c 39; section 2 was amended by the Environment Act 1995 (c 25), Schedule 22, paragraph 232(1).
(**f**) 1973 c 65; section 51 was amended by the Local Government etc (Scotland) Act 1994 (c 39), Schedule 14, paragraph 1.

> (xi) any office of the Greater London Authority held by a member of it;
>
> (xii) any office of the Common Council of the City of London held by a member of it;
>
> (xiii) any office of the Council of the Isles of Scilly held by a member of it;
>
> (xiv) any office of a political party;

(c) 'relevant person', in relation to an office or post, means—

> (i) any person with power to make or terminate appointments to the office or post, or to determine the terms of appointment,
>
> (ii) any person with power to determine the working conditions of a person appointed to the office or post in relation to opportunities for promotion, a transfer, training or for receiving any other benefit, and
>
> (iii) any person or body referred to in paragraph (8)(b) on whose recommendation or subject to whose approval appointments are made to the office or post;

(d) references to making a recommendation include references to making a negative recommendation; and

(e) references to refusal include references to deliberate omission.

Police

13.—(1) For the purposes of this Part, the holding of the office of constable shall be treated as employment—

(a) by the chief officer of police as respects any act done by him in relation to a constable or that office;

(b) by the police authority as respects any act done by it in relation to a constable or that office.

(2) For the purposes of regulation 25 (liability of employers and principals)—

(a) the holding of the office of constable shall be treated as employment by the chief officer of police (and as not being employment by any other person); and

(b) anything done by a person holding such an office in the performance, or purported performance, of his functions shall be treated as done in the course of that employment.

(3) There shall be paid out of the police fund—

(a) any compensation, costs or expenses awarded against a chief officer of police in any proceedings brought against him under these Regulations, and any costs or expenses incurred by him in any such proceedings so far as not recovered by him in the proceedings; and

(b) any sum required by a chief officer of police for the settlement of any claim made against him under these Regulations if the settlement is approved by the police authority.

(4) Any proceedings under these Regulations which, by virtue of paragraph (1), would lie against a chief officer of police shall be brought against the chief officer of police for the time being or in the case of a vacancy in that office, against the person for the time being performing the functions of that office; and references in paragraph (3) to the chief officer of police shall be construed accordingly.

(5) A police authority may, in such cases and to such extent as appear to it to be appropriate, pay out of the police fund—

(a) any compensation, costs or expenses awarded in proceedings under these Regulations against a person under the direction and control of the chief officer of police;

(b) any costs or expenses incurred and not recovered by such a person in such proceedings; and

(c) any sum required in connection with the settlement of a claim that has or might have given rise to such proceedings.

(6) Paragraphs (1) and (2) apply to a police cadet and appointment as a police cadet as they apply to a constable and the office of constable.

(7) Subject to paragraph (8), in this regulation—

'chief officer of police'—

(a) in relation to a person appointed, or an appointment falling to be made, under a specified Act, has the same meaning as in the Police Act 1996(**a**);

(b) in relation to a person appointed, or an appointment falling to be made, under the Police (Scotland) Act 1967(**b**), means the chief constable of the relevant police force;

(c) in relation to any other person or appointment means the officer or other person who has the direction and control of the body of constables or cadets in question;

'police authority'—

(a) in relation to a person appointed, or an appointment falling to be made, under a specified Act, has the same meaning as in the Police Act 1996;

(b) in relation to a person appointed, or an appointment falling to be made, under the Police (Scotland) Act 1967, has the meaning given in that Act;

(c) in relation to any other person or appointment, means the authority by whom the person in question is or on appointment would be paid;

'police cadet' means any person appointed to undergo training with a view to becoming a constable;

'police fund'—

(a) in relation to a chief officer of police within sub-paragraph (a) of the above definition of that term, has the same meaning as in the Police Act 1996;

(b) in any other case means money provided by the police authority; and

---

(**a**) 1996 c 16.
(**b**) 1967 c 77.

'specified Act' means the Metropolitan Police Act 1829(**a**), the City of London Police Act 1839(**b**) or the Police Act 1996.

(8) In relation to a constable of a force who is not under the direction and control of the chief officer of police for that force, references in this regulation to the chief officer of police are references to the chief officer of the force under whose direction and control he is, and references in this regulation to the police authority are references to the relevant police authority for that force.

(9) This regulation is subject to regulation 14.

Serious Organised Crime Agency

14.—(1) For the purposes of this Part, any constable or other person who has been seconded to SOCA to serve as a member of its staff shall be treated as employed by SOCA.

(2) For the purposes of regulation 25 (liability of employers and principals)—

    (a)   the secondment of any constable or other person to SOCA to serve as a member of its staff shall be treated as employment by SOCA (and not as employment by any other person); and

    (b)   anything done by a person so seconded in the performance, or purported performance, of his functions shall be treated as done in the course of that employment.

(3) In this regulation 'SOCA' means the Serious Organised Crime Agency established under section 1 of, and Schedule 1 to, the Serious Organised Crime and Police Act 2005(**c**).

Barristers

15.—(1) It is unlawful for a barrister or barrister's clerk, in relation to any offer of a pupillage or tenancy, to discriminate against a person—

    (a)   in the arrangements which are made for the purpose of determining to whom the pupillage or tenancy should be offered;

    (b)   in respect of any terms on which it is offered; or

    (c)   by refusing, or deliberately not offering, it to him.

(2) It is unlawful for a barrister or barrister's clerk, in relation to a pupil or tenant in the set of chambers in question, to discriminate against him—

    (a)   in respect of any terms applicable to him as a pupil or tenant;

    (b)   in the opportunities for training, or gaining experience, which are afforded or denied to him;

    (c)   in the benefits which are afforded or denied to him; or

    (d)   by terminating his pupillage, or by subjecting him to any pressure to leave the chambers or other detriment.

(**a**) 1829 c 44.
(**b**) 2 & 3 Vict c xciv.
(**c**) 2005 c 15.

(3) It is unlawful for a barrister or barrister's clerk, in relation to a pupillage or tenancy in the set of chambers in question, to subject to harassment a person who is, or has applied to be, a pupil or tenant.

(4) It is unlawful for any person, in relation to the giving, withholding or acceptance of instructions to a barrister, to discriminate against any person by subjecting him to a detriment, or to subject him to harassment.

(5) In this regulation—

'barrister's clerk' includes any person carrying out any of the functions of a barrister's clerk;

'pupil', 'pupillage' and 'set of chambers' have the meanings commonly associated with their use in the context of barristers practising in independent practice; and

'tenancy' and 'tenant' have the meanings commonly associated with their use in the context of barristers practising in independent practice, but also include reference to any barrister permitted to work in a set of chambers who is not a tenant.

(6) This regulation extends to England and Wales only.

Advocates

16.—(1) It is unlawful for an advocate, in relation to taking any person as his pupil, to discriminate against a person—

(a)   in the arrangements which he makes for the purpose of determining whom he will take as his pupil;

(b)   in respect of any terms on which he offers to take any person as his pupil; or

(c)   by refusing to take, or deliberately not taking, a person as his pupil.

(2) It is unlawful for an advocate, in relation to a person who is his pupil, to discriminate against him—

(a)   in respect of any terms applicable to him as a pupil;

(b)   in the opportunities for training, or gaining experience, which are afforded or denied to him;

(c)   in the benefits which are afforded or denied to him; or

(d)   by terminating the relationship, or by subjecting him to any pressure to terminate the relationship or other detriment.

(3) It is unlawful for an advocate, in relation to a person who is his pupil or taking any person as his pupil, to subject such a person to harassment.

(4) It is unlawful for any person, in relation to the giving, withholding or acceptance of instructions to an advocate, to discriminate against any person by subjecting him to a detriment, or to subject him to harassment.

(5) In this regulation—

'advocate' means a member of the Faculty of Advocates practising as such; and

'pupil' has the meaning commonly associated with its use in the context of a person training to be an advocate.

(6) This regulation extends to Scotland only.

Partnerships

17.—(1) It is unlawful for a firm, in relation to a position as partner in the firm, to discriminate against a person—

    (a) in the arrangements they make for the purpose of determining to whom they should offer that position;

    (b) in the terms on which they offer him that position;

    (c) by refusing to offer, or deliberately not offering, him that position; or

    (d) in a case where the person already holds that position—

        (i) in the way they afford him access to any benefits or by refusing to afford, or deliberately not affording, him access to them; or

        (ii) by expelling him from that position, or subjecting him to any other detriment.

(2) It is unlawful for a firm, in relation to a position as partner in the firm, to subject to harassment a person who holds or has applied for that position.

(3) Paragraphs (1)(a) to (c) and (2) apply in relation to persons proposing to form themselves into a partnership as they apply in relation to a firm.

(4) Paragraph (1) does not apply to any act in relation to a position as partner where, if the position were employment, that act would be lawful by virtue of regulation 8 (exception for genuine occupational requirement etc).

(5) In the case of a limited partnership references in this regulation to a partner shall be construed as references to a general partner as defined in section 3 of the Limited Partnerships Act 1907(**a**).

(6) This regulation applies to a limited liability partnership as it applies to a firm; and, in its application to a limited liability partnership, references to a partner in a firm are references to a member of the limited liability partnership.

(7) In this regulation, 'firm' has the meaning given by section 4 of the Partnership Act 1890(**b**).

(8) In paragraph (1)(d) reference to the expulsion of a person from a position as partner includes reference—

    (a) to the termination of that person's partnership by the expiration of any period (including a period expiring by reference to an event or circumstance), not being a termination immediately after which the partnership is renewed on the same terms; and

    (b) to the termination of that person's partnership by any act of his (including the giving of notice) in circumstances such that he is entitled to terminate it without notice by reason of the conduct of the other partners.

(**a**) 1907 c 24.
(**b**) 1890 c 39.

Trade organisations

18.—(1) It is unlawful for a trade organisation to discriminate against a person—

(a) in the terms on which it is prepared to admit him to membership of the organisation; or

(b) by refusing to accept, or deliberately not accepting, his application for membership.

(2) It is unlawful for a trade organisation, in relation to a member of the organisation, to discriminate against him—

(a) in the way it affords him access to any benefits or by refusing or deliberately omitting to afford him access to them;

(b) by depriving him of membership, or varying the terms on which he is a member; or

(c) by subjecting him to any other detriment.

(3) It is unlawful for a trade organisation, in relation to a person's membership or application for membership of that organisation, to subject that person to harassment.

(4) In this regulation—

'trade organisation' means an organisation of workers, an organisation of employers, or any other organisation whose members carry on a particular profession or trade for the purposes of which the organisation exists;

'profession' includes any vocation or occupation; and

'trade' includes any business.

Qualifications bodies

19.—(1) It is unlawful for a qualifications body to discriminate against a person—

(a) in the terms on which it is prepared to confer a professional or trade qualification on him;

(b) by refusing or deliberately not granting any application by him for such a qualification; or

(c) by withdrawing such a qualification from him or varying the terms on which he holds it.

(2) It is unlawful for a qualifications body, in relation to a professional or trade qualification conferred by it, to subject to harassment a person who holds or applies for such a qualification.

(3) In this regulation—

'qualifications body' means any authority or body which can confer a professional or trade qualification, but it does not include—

(a) a governing body of an educational establishment to which regulation 23 (institutions of further and higher education) applies, or would apply but for the operation of any other provision of these Regulations, or

(b) a proprietor of a school;

'confer' includes renew or extend;

'professional or trade qualification' means any authorisation, qualification, recognition, registration, enrolment, approval or certification which is needed for, or facilitates engagement in, a particular profession or trade;

'profession' and 'trade' have the same meaning as in regulation 18.

The provision of vocational training

20.—(1) It is unlawful, in relation to a person seeking or undergoing training, for any training provider to discriminate against him—

  (a) in the arrangements he makes for the purpose of determining to whom he should offer training;

  (b) in the terms on which the training provider affords him access to any training;

  (c) by refusing or deliberately not affording him such access;

  (d) by terminating his training; or

  (e) by subjecting him to any other detriment during his training.

(2) It is unlawful for a training provider, in relation to a person seeking or undergoing training, to subject him to harassment.

(3) Paragraph (1) does not apply if the discrimination concerns training that would only fit a person for employment which, by virtue of regulation 8 (exception for genuine occupational requirement etc), the employer could lawfully refuse to offer the person seeking training.

(4) In this regulation—

'professional or trade qualification' has the same meaning as in regulation 19;

'registered pupil' has the meaning given by section 434 of the Education Act 1996(**a**);

'training' means—

  (a) all types and all levels of training which would help fit a person for any employment;

  (b) vocational guidance;

  (c) facilities for training;

  (d) practical work experience provided by an employer to a person whom he does not employ; and

  (e) any assessment related to the award of any professional or trade qualification;

'training provider' means any person who provides, or makes arrangements for the provision of, training, but it does not include—

  (a) an employer in relation to training for persons employed by him;

  (b) a governing body of an educational establishment to which regulation 23 (institutions of further and higher education) applies, or would apply but for the operation of any other provision of these Regulations; or

---

(**a**) 1996 c 56.

(c)   a proprietor of a school in relation to any registered pupil.

Employment agencies, careers guidance etc

21.—(1) It is unlawful for an employment agency to discriminate against a person—

(a)   in the terms on which the agency offers to provide any of its services;

(b)   by refusing or deliberately not providing any of its services; or

(c)   in the way it provides any of its services.

(2) It is unlawful for an employment agency, in relation to a person to whom it provides its services, or who has requested it to provide its services, to subject that person to harassment.

(3) Paragraph (1) does not apply to discrimination if it only concerns employment which, by virtue of regulation 8 (exception for genuine occupational requirement etc), the employer could lawfully refuse to offer the person in question.

(4) An employment agency shall not be subject to any liability under this regulation if it proves that—

(a)   it acted in reliance on a statement made to it by the employer to the effect that, by reason of the operation of paragraph (3), its action would not be unlawful; and

(b)   it was reasonable for it to rely on the statement.

(5) A person who knowingly or recklessly makes a statement such as is referred to in paragraph (4)(a) which in a material respect is false or misleading commits an offence, and shall be liable on summary conviction to a fine not exceeding level 5 on the standard scale.

(6) For the purposes of this regulation—

(a)   'employment agency' means a person who, for profit or not, provides services for the purpose of finding employment for workers or supplying employers with workers, but it does not include—

(i)   a governing body of an educational establishment to which regulation 23 (institutions of further and higher education) applies, or would apply but for the operation of any other provision of these Regulations; or

(ii)   a proprietor of a school; and

(b)   references to the services of an employment agency include guidance on careers and any other services related to employment.

Assisting persons to obtain employment etc

22.—(1) It is unlawful for the Secretary of State to discriminate against any person by subjecting him to a detriment, or to subject a person to harassment, in the provision of facilities or services under section 2 of the Employment and Training Act 1973(**a**) (arrangements for assisting persons to obtain employment).

(**a**) 1973 c 50; section 2 was substituted by section 25(1) of the Employment Act 1988 (c 19), and

(2) It is unlawful for Scottish Enterprise or Highlands and Islands Enterprise to discriminate against any person by subjecting him to a detriment, or to subject a person to harassment, in the provision of facilities or services under such arrangements as are mentioned in section 2(3) of the Enterprise and New Towns (Scotland) Act 1990(**a**) (arrangements analogous to arrangements in pursuance of the said Act of 1973).

(3) This regulation does not apply in a case where—

   (a) regulation 20 (the provision of vocational training) applies or would apply but for the operation of any other provision of these Regulations, or

   (b) the Secretary of State is acting as an employment agency within the meaning of regulation 21 (employment agencies, careers guidance etc).

Institutions of further and higher education

23.—(1) It is unlawful, in relation to an educational establishment to which this regulation applies, for the governing body of that establishment to discriminate against a person—

   (a) in the terms on which it offers to admit him to the establishment as a student;

   (b) by refusing or deliberately not accepting an application for his admission to the establishment as a student; or

   (c) where he is a student of the establishment—

      (i) in the way it affords him access to any benefits,

      (ii) by refusing or deliberately not affording him access to them, or

      (iii) by excluding him from the establishment or subjecting him to any other detriment.

(2) It is unlawful, in relation to an educational establishment to which this regulation applies, for the governing body of that establishment to subject to harassment a person who is a student at the establishment, or who has applied for admission to the establishment as a student.

(3) Paragraph (1) does not apply if the discrimination concerns training that would only fit a person for employment which, by virtue of regulation 8 (exception for genuine occupational requirement etc), the employer could lawfully refuse to offer the person in question.

(4) This regulation applies to the following educational establishments in England and Wales, namely—

   (a) an institution within the further education sector (within the meaning of section 91(3) of the Further and Higher Education Act 1992(**b**));

   (b) a university;

---

amended by the Employment Act 1989 (c 38), Schedule 7, Part 1, and by section 47(1) of the Trade Union Reform and Employment Rights Act 1993 (c 19).

(**a**) 1990 c 35.

(**b**) 1992 c 13.

(c) an institution, other than a university, within the higher education sector (within the meaning of section 91(5) of the Further and Higher Education Act 1992).

(5) This regulation applies to the following educational establishments in Scotland, namely—

(a) a college of further education within the meaning of section 36(1) of the Further and Higher Education (Scotland) Act 1992(**a**) under the management of a board of management within the meaning of Part I of that Act;

(b) a college of further education maintained by an education authority in the exercise of its further education functions in providing courses of further education within the meaning of section 1(5)(b)(ii) of the Education (Scotland) Act 1980(**b**);

(c) any other educational establishment (not being a school) which provides further education within the meaning of section 1 of the Further and Higher Education (Scotland) Act 1992;

(d) an institution within the higher education sector (within the meaning of Part 2 of the Further and Higher Education (Scotland) Act 1992);

(e) a central institution (within the meaning of section 135 of the Education (Scotland) Act 1980).

(6) In this regulation—

'education authority' has the meaning given by section 135(1) of the Education (Scotland) Act 1980;

'governing body' includes—

(a) the board of management of a college referred to in paragraph (5)(a), and

(b) the managers of a college or institution referred to in paragraph (5)(b) or (e);

'student' means any person who receives education at an educational establishment to which this regulation applies; and

'university' includes a university college and the college, school or hall of a university.

Relationships which have come to an end

24.—(1) In this regulation a 'relevant relationship' is a relationship during the course of which an act of discrimination against, or harassment of, one party to the relationship ('B') by the other party to it ('A') is unlawful by virtue of any preceding provision of this Part.

(2) Where a relevant relationship has come to an end, it is unlawful for A—

(a) to discriminate against B by subjecting him to a detriment; or

(b) to subject B to harassment;

(**a**) 1992 c 37.
(**b**) 1980 c 44.

where the discrimination or harassment arises out of and is closely connected to that relationship.

(3) In paragraph (1), reference to an act of discrimination or harassment which is unlawful includes, in the case of a relationship which has come to an end before the coming into force of these Regulations, reference to an act of discrimination or harassment which would, after the coming into force of these Regulations, be unlawful.

PART 3

OTHER UNLAWFUL ACTS

Liability of employers and principals

25.—(1) Anything done by a person in the course of his employment shall be treated for the purposes of these Regulations as done by his employer as well as by him, whether or not it was done with the employer's knowledge or approval.

(2) Anything done by a person as agent for another person with the authority (whether express or implied, and whether precedent or subsequent) of that other person shall be treated for the purposes of these Regulations as done by that other person as well as by him.

(3) In proceedings brought under these Regulations against any person in respect of an act alleged to have been done by an employee of his it shall be a defence for that person to prove that he took such steps as were reasonably practicable to prevent the employee from doing that act, or from doing in the course of his employment acts of that description.

Aiding unlawful acts

26.—(1) A person who knowingly aids another person to do an act made unlawful by these Regulations shall be treated for the purpose of these Regulations as himself doing an unlawful act of the like description.

(2) For the purposes of paragraph (1) an employee or agent for whose act the employer or principal is liable under regulation 25 (or would be so liable but for regulation 25(3)) shall be deemed to aid the doing of the act by the employer or principal.

(3) A person does not under this regulation knowingly aid another to do an unlawful act if—

    (a)   he acts in reliance on a statement made to him by that other person that, by reason of any provision of these Regulations, the act which he aids would not be unlawful; and

    (b)   it is reasonable for him to rely on the statement.

(4) A person who knowingly or recklessly makes a statement such as is referred to in paragraph (3)(a) which in a material respect is false or misleading commits an offence, and shall be liable on summary conviction to a fine not exceeding level 5 on the standard scale.

PART 4

GENERAL EXCEPTIONS FROM PARTS 2 AND 3

Exception for statutory authority

27.—(1) Nothing in Part 2 or 3 shall render unlawful any act done in order to comply with a requirement of any statutory provision.

(2) In this regulation 'statutory provision' means any provision (whenever enacted) of—

(a) an Act or an Act of the Scottish Parliament;

(b) an instrument made by a Minister of the Crown under an Act;

(c) an instrument made under an Act or an Act of the Scottish Parliament by the Scottish Ministers or a member of the Scottish Executive.

Exception for national security

28. Nothing in Part 2 or 3 shall render unlawful an act done for the purpose of safeguarding national security, if the doing of the act was justified by that purpose.

Exceptions for positive action

29.—(1) Nothing in Part 2 or 3 shall render unlawful any act done in or in connection with—

(a) affording persons of a particular age or age group access to facilities for training which would help fit them for particular work; or

(b) encouraging persons of a particular age or age group to take advantage of opportunities for doing particular work;

where it reasonably appears to the person doing the act that it prevents or compensates for disadvantages linked to age suffered by persons of that age or age group doing that work or likely to take up that work.

(2) Nothing in Part 2 or 3 shall render unlawful any act done by a trade organisation within the meaning of regulation 18 in or in connection with—

(a) affording only members of the organisation who are of a particular age or age group access to facilities for training which would help fit them for holding a post of any kind in the organisation; or

(b) encouraging only members of the organisation who are of a particular age or age group to take advantage of opportunities for holding such posts in the organisation,

where it reasonably appears to the organisation that the act prevents or compensates for disadvantages linked to age suffered by those of that age or age group holding such posts or likely to hold such posts.

(3) Nothing in Part 2 or 3 shall render unlawful any act done by a trade organisation within the meaning of regulation 18 in or in connection with encouraging only persons of a particular age or age group to become members of the

organisation where it reasonably appears to the organisation that the act prevents or compensates for disadvantages linked to age suffered by persons of that age or age group who are, or are eligible to become, members.

Exception for retirement

30.—(1) This regulation applies in relation to an employee within the meaning of section 230(1) of the 1996 Act, a person in Crown employment, a relevant member of the House of Commons staff, and a relevant member of the House of Lords staff.

(2) Nothing in Part 2 or 3 shall render unlawful the dismissal of a person to whom this regulation applies at or over the age of 65 where the reason for the dismissal is retirement.

(3) For the purposes of this regulation, whether or not the reason for a dismissal is retirement shall be determined in accordance with sections 98ZA to 98ZF of the 1996 Act(**a**).

Exception for the national minimum wage

31.—(1) Nothing in Part 2 or 3 shall render it unlawful for a relevant person ('A') to be remunerated in respect of his work at a rate which is lower than the rate at which another such person ('B') is remunerated for his work where—

    (a)   the hourly rate of the national minimum wage for a person of A's age is lower than that for a person of B's age, and

    (b)   the rate at which A is remunerated is below the single hourly rate for the national minimum wage prescribed by the Secretary of State under section 1(3) of the National Minimum Wage Act 1998(**b**).

(2) Nothing in Part 2 or 3 shall render it unlawful for an apprentice who is not a relevant person to be remunerated in respect of his work at a rate which is lower than the rate at which an apprentice who is a relevant person is remunerated for his work.

(3) In this regulation—

    'apprentice' means a person who is employed under a contract of apprenticeship or, in accordance with regulation 12(3) of the National Minimum Wage Regulations 1999(**c**), is to be treated as employed under such a contract;

    'relevant person' means a person who qualifies for the national minimum wage(**d**) (whether at the single hourly rate for the national minimum wage prescribed by the Secretary of State under section 1(3) of the National Minimum Wage Act 1998 or at a different rate).

(**a**) Employment Rights Act 1996 (c 18); sections 98ZA to 98ZF are inserted by paragraph 23 of Schedule 8 to these Regulations.

(**b**) 1998 c 39. The hourly rate is prescribed in regulation 11 of the National Minimum Wage Regulations 1999 (SI 1999/584) and that rate has most recently been amended by regulation 2 of the National Minimum Wage Regulations 1999 (Amendment) Regulations 2005 (SI 2005/2019).

(**c**) SI 1999/584, to which relevant amendments have been made by SI 2000/1989 and SI 2004/1930.

(**d**) A person qualifies for the national minimum wage if he is a person who – (a) is a worker; (b) is working, or ordinarily works, in the UK under a contract; and (c) has ceased to be of compulsory school age: see s.1(2) of the National Minimum Wage Act 1998.

Exception for provision of certain benefits based on length of service

32.—(1) Subject to paragraph (2), nothing in Part 2 or 3 shall render it unlawful for a person ('A'), in relation to the award of any benefit by him, to put a worker ('B') at a disadvantage when compared with another worker ('C'), if and to the extent that the disadvantage suffered by B is because B's length of service is less than that of C.

(2) Where B's length of service exceeds 5 years, it must reasonably appear to A that the way in which he uses the criterion of length of service, in relation to the award in respect of which B is put at a disadvantage, fulfils a business need of his undertaking (for example, by encouraging the loyalty or motivation, or rewarding the experience, of some or all of his workers).

(3) In calculating a worker's length of service for these purposes, A shall calculate—

(a) the length of time the worker has been working for him doing work which he reasonably considers to be at or above a particular level (assessed by reference to the demands made on the worker, for example, in terms of effort, skills and decision making); or

(b) the length of time the worker has been working for him in total;

and on each occasion on which he decides to use the criterion of length of service in relation to the award of a benefit to workers, it is for him to decide which of these definitions to use to calculate their lengths of service.

(4) For the purposes of paragraph (3), in calculating the length of time a worker has been working for him—

(a) A shall calculate the length of time in terms of the number of weeks during the whole or part of which the worker was working for him;

(b) A may discount any period during which the worker was absent from work (including any period of absence which at the time it occurred was thought by A or the worker to be permanent) unless in all the circumstances (including the way in which other workers' absences occurring in similar circumstances are treated by A in calculating their lengths of service) it would not be reasonable for him to do so;

(c) A may discount any period of time during which the worker was present at work ('the relevant period') where—

(i) the relevant period preceded a period during which the worker was absent from work, and

(ii) in all the circumstances (including the length of the worker's absence, the reason for his absence, the effect his absence has had on his ability to discharge the duties of his work, and the way in which other workers are treated by A in similar circumstances) it is reasonable for A to discount the relevant period.

(5) For the purposes of paragraph (3)(b), a worker shall be treated as having worked for A during any period during which he worked for another if—

(a) that period is treated as a period of employment with A for the purposes of the 1996 Act by virtue of the operation of section 218 of that Act; or

(b) were the worker to be made redundant by A, that period and the period he has worked for A would amount to 'relevant service' within the meaning of section 155 of that Act.

(6) In paragraph (5)—

    (a) the reference to being made redundant is a reference to being dismissed by reason of redundancy for the purposes of the 1996 Act;

    (b) the reference to section 155 of that Act is a reference to that section as modified by the Redundancy Payments (Continuity of Employment in Local Government, etc.) (Modification) Order 1999(**a**).

(7) In this regulation—

'benefit' does not include any benefit awarded to a worker by virtue of his ceasing to work for A; and

'year' means a year of 12 calendar months.

Exception for provision of enhanced redundancy payments to employees

33.—(1) Nothing in Part 2 or 3 shall render it unlawful for an employer—

    (a) to give a qualifying employee an enhanced redundancy payment which is less in amount than the enhanced redundancy payment which he gives to another such employee if both amounts are calculated in the same way;

    (b) to give enhanced redundancy payments only to those who are qualifying employees by virtue of sub-paragraph (a) or (c)(i) of the definition of qualifying employee below.

(2) In this regulation—

'the appropriate amount', 'a redundancy payment' and 'a week's pay' have the same meaning as they have in section 162 of the 1996 Act(**b**);

'enhanced redundancy payment' means a payment of an amount calculated in accordance with paragraph (3) or (4);

'qualifying employee' means—

    (a) an employee who is entitled to a redundancy payment by virtue of section 135 of the 1996 Act;

    (b) an employee who would have been so entitled but for the operation of section 155 of that Act;

    (c) an employee who agrees to the termination of his employment in circumstances where, had he been dismissed—

        (i) he would have been a qualifying employee by virtue of sub-paragraph (a) of this definition; or

        (ii) he would have been a qualifying employee by virtue of sub-paragraph (b).

(**a**) SI 1999/2277. See Schedule 2, Part 1, paragraph 2.
(**b**) Subsections (4), (5) and (8) of section 162 of the 1996 Act have been repealed by regulation 49 of, and paragraph 32 of Schedule 8 to, these Regulations. Subsection (6) was amended by the Employment Rights (Dispute Resolution) Act 1998 (c 8), section 1(2)(a). Subsection (7) was repealed by the Employment Relations Act 1999 (c 26), sections 9 and 44 and Schedule 4, Part 3, paragraphs 5 and 30.

(3) For an amount to be calculated in accordance with this paragraph it must be calculated in accordance with section 162(1) to (3) of the 1996 Act.

(4) For an amount to be calculated in accordance with this paragraph—

(a)   it must be calculated as in paragraph (3);

(b)   however, in making that calculation, the employer may do one or both of the following things—

(i)   he may treat a week's pay as not being subject to a maximum amount or as being subject to a maximum amount above the amount laid down in section 227 of the 1996 Act(**a**);

(ii)   he may multiply the appropriate amount allowed for each year of employment by a figure of more than one;

(c)   having made the calculation as in paragraph (3) (whether or not in making that calculation he has done anything mentioned in sub-paragraph (b)) the employer may increase the amount thus calculated by multiplying it by a figure of more than one.

(5) For the purposes of paragraphs (3) and (4), the reference to 'the relevant date' in section 162(1)(a) of the 1996 Act is to be read, in the case of a qualifying employee who agrees to the termination of his employment, as a reference to the date on which that termination takes effect.

Exception for provision of life assurance cover to retired workers

34.—(1) Where a person ('A') arranges for workers to be provided with life assurance cover after their early retirement on grounds of ill health, nothing in Part 2 or 3 shall render it unlawful—

(a)   where a normal retirement age applied in relation to any such workers at the time they took early retirement, for A to arrange for such cover to cease when such workers reach that age;

(b)   in relation to any other workers, for A to arrange for such cover to cease when the workers reach the age of 65.

(2) In this regulation, 'normal retirement age', in relation to a worker who has taken early retirement, means the age at which workers in A's undertaking who held the same kind of position as the worker held at the time of his retirement were normally required to retire.

(**a**)   The amount laid down in section 227 may be increased or decreased by Order made by the Secretary of State under section 34 of the Employment Relations Act 1999. The amount laid down in section 227 is currently £290: see SI 2005/3352.

PART 5

ENFORCEMENT

Restriction of proceedings for breach of Regulations

35.—(1) Except as provided by these Regulations no proceedings, whether civil or criminal, shall lie against any person in respect of an act by reason that the act is unlawful by virtue of a provision of these Regulations.

(2) Paragraph (1) does not prevent the making of an application for judicial review or the investigation or determination of any matter in accordance with Part 10 (investigations: the Pensions Ombudsman) of the Pension Schemes Act 1993(**a**) by the Pensions Ombudsman.

Jurisdiction of employment tribunals

36.—(1) A complaint by any person ('the complainant') that another person ('the respondent')—

-   (a)   has committed against the complainant an act to which this regulation applies; or

-   (b)   is by virtue of regulation 25 (liability of employers and principals) or 26 (aiding unlawful acts) to be treated as having committed against the complainant such an act;

may be presented to an employment tribunal.

(2) This regulation applies to any act of discrimination or harassment which is unlawful by virtue of any provision of Part 2 other than—

-   (a)   where the act is one in respect of which an appeal or proceedings in the nature of an appeal may be brought under any enactment, regulation 19 (qualifications bodies);

-   (b)   regulation 23 (institutions of further and higher education); or

-   (c)   where the act arises out of and is closely connected to a relationship between the complainant and the respondent which has come to an end but during the course of which an act of discrimination against, or harassment of, the complainant by the respondent would have been unlawful by virtue of regulation 23, regulation 24 (relationships which have come to an end).

(3) In paragraph (2)(c), reference to an act of discrimination or harassment which would have been unlawful includes, in the case of a relationship which has come to an end before the coming into force of these Regulations, reference to an act of discrimination or harassment which would, after the coming into force of these Regulations, have been unlawful.

(4) In this regulation, 'enactment' includes an enactment comprised in, or in an instrument made under, an Act of the Scottish Parliament.

(**a**) 1993 c 48.

Burden of proof: employment tribunals

37.—(1) This regulation applies to any complaint presented under regulation 36 to an employment tribunal.

(2) Where, on the hearing of the complaint, the complainant proves facts from which the tribunal could, apart from this regulation, conclude in the absence of an adequate explanation that the respondent—

(a) has committed against the complainant an act to which regulation 36 applies; or

(b) is by virtue of regulation 25 (liability of employers and principals) or 26 (aiding unlawful acts) to be treated as having committed against the complainant such an act,

the tribunal shall uphold the complaint unless the respondent proves that he did not commit, or as the case may be, is not to be treated as having committed, that act.

Remedies on complaints in employment tribunals

38.—(1) Where an employment tribunal finds that a complaint presented to it under regulation 36 is well-founded, the tribunal shall make such of the following as it considers just and equitable—

(a) an order declaring the rights of the complainant and the respondent in relation to the act to which the complaint relates;

(b) an order requiring the respondent to pay to the complainant compensation of an amount corresponding to any damages he could have been ordered by a county court or by a sheriff court to pay to the complainant if the complaint had fallen to be dealt with under regulation 39 (jurisdiction of county and sheriff courts);

(c) a recommendation that the respondent take within a specified period action appearing to the tribunal to be practicable for the purpose of obviating or reducing the adverse effect on the complainant of any act of discrimination or harassment to which the complaint relates.

(2) As respects an unlawful act of discrimination falling within regulation 3(1)(b) (discrimination on the grounds of age), if the respondent proves that the provision, criterion or practice was not applied with the intention of treating the complainant unfavourably on grounds of age, an order may be made under paragraph (1)(b) only if the employment tribunal—

(a) makes such order under paragraph (1)(a) (if any) and such recommendation under paragraph (1)(c) (if any) as it would have made if it had no power to make an order under paragraph (1)(b); and

(b) (where it makes an order under paragraph (1)(a) or a recommendation under paragraph (1)(c) or both) considers that it is just and equitable to make an order under paragraph (1)(b) as well.

(3) If without reasonable justification the respondent to a complaint fails to comply with a recommendation made by an employment tribunal under paragraph (1)(c), then, if it thinks it just and equitable to do so—

(a) the tribunal may increase the amount of compensation required to be paid to the complainant in respect of the complaint by an order made under paragraph (1)(b); or

(b)   if an order under paragraph (1)(b) was not made, the tribunal may make such an order.

(4) Where an amount of compensation falls to be awarded under paragraph (1)(b), the tribunal may include in the award interest on that amount subject to, and in accordance with, the provisions of the Employment Tribunals (Interest on Awards in Discrimination Cases) Regulations 1996(**a**).

(5) This regulation has effect subject to paragraph 6 of Schedule 2 (pension schemes).

Jurisdiction of county and sheriff courts

39.—(1) A claim by any person ('the claimant') that another person ('the respondent')—

(a)   has committed against the claimant an act to which this regulation applies; or

(b)   is by virtue of regulation 25 (liability of employers and principals) or 26 (aiding unlawful acts) to be treated as having committed against the claimant such an act,

may be made the subject of civil proceedings in like manner as any other claim in tort or (in Scotland) in reparation for breach of statutory duty.

(2) Proceedings brought under paragraph (1) shall—

(a)   in England and Wales, be brought only in a county court; and

(b)   in Scotland, be brought only in a sheriff court.

(3) For the avoidance of doubt it is hereby declared that damages in respect of an unlawful act to which this regulation applies may include compensation for injury to feelings whether or not they include compensation under any other head.

(4) This regulation applies to any act of discrimination or harassment which is unlawful by virtue of—

(a)   regulation 23 (institutions of further and higher education); or

(b)   where the act arises out of and is closely connected to a relationship between the claimant and the respondent which has come to an end but during the course of which an act of discrimination against, or harassment of, the claimant by the respondent would have been unlawful by virtue of regulation 23, regulation 24 (relationships which have come to an end).

(5) In paragraph (4)(b), reference to an act of discrimination or harassment which would have been unlawful includes, in the case of a relationship which has come to an end before the coming into force of these Regulations, reference to an act of discrimination or harassment which would, after the coming into force of these Regulations, have been unlawful.

(**a**) SI 1996/2803. Regulation 1(2) of those Regulations is amended by paragraph 56 of, and Schedule 8 to, these Regulations.

Burden of proof: county and sheriff courts

40.—(1) This regulation applies to any claim brought under regulation 39 in a county court in England and Wales or a sheriff court in Scotland.

(2) Where, on the hearing of the claim, the claimant proves facts from which the court could, apart from this regulation, conclude in the absence of an adequate explanation that the respondent—

    (a) has committed against the claimant an act to which regulation 39 applies; or

    (b) is by virtue of regulation 25 (liability of employers and principals) or 26 (aiding unlawful acts) to be treated as having committed against the claimant such an act,

the court shall uphold the claim unless the respondent proves that he did not commit, or as the case may be, is not to be treated as having committed, that act.

Help for persons in obtaining information etc

41.—(1) In accordance with this regulation, a person ('the person aggrieved') who considers he may have been discriminated against, or subjected to harassment, in contravention of these Regulations may serve on the respondent to a complaint presented under regulation 36 (jurisdiction of employment tribunals) or a claim brought under regulation 39 (jurisdiction of county and sheriff courts) questions in the form set out in Schedule 3 or forms to the like effect with such variation as the circumstances require; and the respondent may if he so wishes reply to such questions by way of the form set out in Schedule 4 or forms to the like effect with such variation as the circumstances require.

(2) Where the person aggrieved questions the respondent (whether in accordance with paragraph (1) or not)—

    (a) the questions, and any reply by the respondent (whether in accordance with paragraph (1) or not) shall, subject to the following provisions of this regulation, be admissible as evidence in the proceedings;

    (b) if it appears to the court or tribunal that the respondent deliberately, and without reasonable excuse, omitted to reply within eight weeks of service of the questions or that his reply is evasive or equivocal, the court or tribunal may draw any inference from that fact that it considers it just and equitable to draw, including an inference that he committed an unlawful act.

(3) In proceedings before a county court in England or Wales or a sheriff court in Scotland, a question shall only be admissible as evidence in pursuance of paragraph (2)(a)—

    (a) where it was served before those proceedings had been instituted, if it was so served within the period of six months beginning when the act complained of was done;

    (b) where it was served when those proceedings had been instituted, if it was served with the leave of, and within a period specified by, the court in question.

(4) In proceedings before an employment tribunal, a question shall only be admissible as evidence in pursuance of paragraph (2)(a)—

    (a) where it was served before a complaint had been presented to the tribunal, if it was so served within the period of three months beginning when the act complained of was done;

    (b) where it was so served when a complaint had been presented to the tribunal, either—

        (i) if it was served within the period of twenty-one days beginning with the day on which the complaint was presented, or

        (ii) if it was so served later with leave given, and within a period specified, by a direction of the tribunal.

(5) A question and any reply thereto may be served on the respondent or, as the case may be, on the person aggrieved—

    (a) by delivering it to him;

    (b) by sending it by post to him at his usual or last-known residence or place of business;

    (c) where the person to be served is a body corporate or is a trade union or employers' association within the meaning of the Trade Union and Labour Relations (Consolidation) Act 1992(**a**), by delivering it to the secretary or clerk of the body, union or association at its registered or principal office or by sending it by post to the secretary or clerk at that office;

    (d) where the person to be served is acting by a solicitor, by delivering it at, or by sending it by post to, the solicitor's address for service; or

    (e) where the person to be served is the person aggrieved, by delivering the reply, or sending it by post, to him at his address for reply as stated by him in the document containing the questions.

(6) This regulation is without prejudice to any other enactment or rule of law regulating interlocutory and preliminary matters in proceedings before a county court, sheriff court or employment tribunal, and has effect subject to any enactment or rule of law regulating the admissibility of evidence in such proceedings.

(7) In this regulation 'respondent' includes a prospective respondent.

Period within which proceedings to be brought

42.—(1) An employment tribunal shall not consider a complaint under regulation 36 unless it is presented to the tribunal before the end of the period of three months beginning when the act complained of was done.

(2) A county court or a sheriff court shall not consider a claim brought under regulation 39 unless proceedings in respect of the claim are instituted before the end of the period of six months beginning when the act complained of was done.

(3) A court or tribunal may nevertheless consider any such complaint or claim which is out of time if, in all the circumstances of the case, it considers that it is just and equitable to do so.

(**a**) 1992 c 52.

(4) For the purposes of this regulation and regulation 41 (help for persons in obtaining information etc)—

(a) when the making of a contract is, by reason of the inclusion of any term, an unlawful act, that act shall be treated as extending throughout the duration of the contract; and

(b) any act extending over a period shall be treated as done at the end of that period; and

(c) a deliberate omission shall be treated as done when the person in question decided upon it,

and in the absence of evidence establishing the contrary a person shall be taken for the purposes of this regulation to decide upon an omission when he does an act inconsistent with doing the omitted act or, if he has done no such inconsistent act, when the period expires within which he might reasonably have been expected to do the omitted act if it was to be done.

PART 6

SUPPLEMENTAL

Validity of contracts, collective agreements and rules of undertakings

43. Schedule 5 (validity of contracts, collective agreements and rules of undertakings) shall have effect.

Application to the Crown etc

44.—(1) These Regulations apply—

(a) to an act done by or for purposes of a Minister of the Crown or government department; or

(b) to an act done on behalf of the Crown by a statutory body, or a person holding a statutory office,

as they apply to an act done by a private person.

(2) These Regulations apply to Crown employment as they apply to employment by a private person, and shall so apply as if references to a contract of employment included references to the terms of service and references to dismissal included references to termination of Crown employment.

(3) Paragraphs (1) and (2) have effect subject to paragraph (4) and regulations 13 (police) and 14 (Serious Organised Crime Agency).

(4) These regulations do not apply to service in any of the naval, military or air forces of the Crown.

(5) Regulation 10(3) (meaning of employment and contract work at establishment in Great Britain) shall have effect in relation to any ship, aircraft or hovercraft belonging to or possessed by Her Majesty in right of the government of the United Kingdom as it has effect in relation to a ship, aircraft or hovercraft specified in regulation 10(3)(a) or (b).

(6) The provisions of Parts 2 to 4 of the Crown Proceedings Act 1947(**a**) shall apply to proceedings against the Crown under these Regulations as they apply to proceedings in England and Wales which by virtue of section 23 of that Act are treated for the purposes of Part 2 of that Act as civil proceedings by or against the Crown, except that in their application to proceedings under these Regulations section 20 of that Act (removal and transfer of proceedings) shall not apply.

(7) The provisions of Part 5 of the Crown Proceedings Act 1947 shall apply to proceedings against the Crown under these Regulations as they apply to proceedings in Scotland which by virtue of the said Part are treated as civil proceedings by or against the Crown, except that in their application to proceedings under these Regulations the proviso to section 44 of that Act (proceedings against the Crown in the Sheriff Court) shall not apply.

Application to House of Commons staff

45.—(1) Subject to paragraphs (2) and (3), these Regulations apply in relation to employment as a relevant member of the House of Commons staff as they apply in relation to other employment.

(2) These Regulations apply to employment as such a member as they apply to employment by a private person, and shall so apply as if references to a contract of employment included references to the terms of employment of such a member and references to dismissal included references to termination of such employment.

(3) In relation to employment as such a member, subsections (6) to (12) of section 195 of the 1996 Act(**b**) (person to be treated as employer of House of Commons staff) apply, with any necessary modifications, for the purposes of these Regulations.

Application to House of Lords staff

46.—(1) These Regulations apply in relation to employment as a relevant member of the House of Lords staff as they apply in relation to other employment.

(2) Section 194(7) of the 1996 Act (continuity of employment) applies for the purposes of this regulation.

Duty to consider working beyond retirement

47. Schedule 6, which sets out the procedure to be followed if an employee (within the meaning of that Schedule) is to be retired, shall have effect.

Duty to consider working beyond retirement – transitional provisions

48. Schedule 7, which sets out transitional provisions in relation to the duty to consider working beyond retirement, shall have effect.

(**a**) 1947 c 44.
(**b**) Employment Rights Act 1996 (c 18); subsection (8) was amended by the Employment Rights (Dispute Resolution) Act 1998 (c 8), section 1(2)(a).

Amendments, transitionals, repeals and revocations

49.—a) Schedule 8, which contains amendments to and repeals of legislation and related transitional provisions, shall have effect.

(2) Schedule 9, which contains repeals and revocations, shall have effect.

SCHEDULE 1

Regulation 10(4)

Norwegian part of the Frigg Gas Field

1. The part of the Norwegian sector of the Continental Shelf described in this Schedule is the area defined by—

(a) the sets of lines of latitude and longitude joining the following surface co-ordinates—

Longitude	Latitude
02 degrees 05 minutes 30 seconds E	60 degrees 00 minutes 45 seconds N
02 degrees 05 minutes 30 seconds E	59 degrees 58 minutes 45 seconds N
02 degrees 06 minutes 00 seconds E	59 degrees 58 minutes 45 seconds N
02 degrees 06 minutes 00 seconds E	59 degrees 57 minutes 45 seconds N
02 degrees 07 minutes 00 seconds E	59 degrees 57 minutes 45 seconds N
02 degrees 07 minutes 00 seconds E	59 degrees 57 minutes 30 seconds N
02 degrees 07 minutes 30 seconds E	59 degrees 57 minutes 30 seconds N
02 degrees 07 minutes 30 seconds E	59 degrees 55 minutes 30 seconds N
02 degrees 10 minutes 30 seconds E	59 degrees 55 minutes 30 seconds N
02 degrees 10 minutes 30 seconds E	59 degrees 54 minutes 45 seconds N
02 degrees 11 minutes 00 seconds E	59 degrees 54 minutes 45 seconds N
02 degrees 11 minutes 00 seconds E	59 degrees 54 minutes 15 seconds N
02 degrees 12 minutes 30 seconds E	59 degrees 54 minutes 15 seconds N
02 degrees 12 minutes 30 seconds E	59 degrees 54 minutes 00 seconds N
02 degrees 13 minutes 30 seconds E	59 degrees 54 minutes 00 seconds N
02 degrees 13 minutes 30 seconds E	59 degrees 54 minutes 30 seconds N
02 degrees 15 minutes 30 seconds E	59 degrees 54 minutes 30 seconds N
02 degrees 15 minutes 30 seconds E	59 degrees 53 minutes 15 seconds N
02 degrees 10 minutes 30 seconds E	59 degrees 53 minutes 15 seconds N
02 degrees 10 minutes 30 seconds E	59 degrees 52 minutes 45 seconds N
02 degrees 09 minutes 30 seconds E	59 degrees 52 minutes 45 seconds N
02 degrees 09 minutes 30 seconds E	59 degrees 52 minutes 15 seconds N
02 degrees 08 minutes 30 seconds E	59 degrees 52 minutes 15 seconds N
02 degrees 08 minutes 30 seconds E	59 degrees 52 minutes 00 seconds N
02 degrees 07 minutes 30 seconds E	59 degrees 52 minutes 00 seconds N
02 degrees 07 minutes 30 seconds E	59 degrees 51 minutes 30 seconds N
02 degrees 05 minutes 30 seconds E	59 degrees 51 minutes 30 seconds N
02 degrees 05 minutes 30 seconds E	59 degrees 51 minutes 00 seconds N
02 degrees 04 minutes 00 seconds E	59 degrees 51 minutes 00 seconds N
02 degrees 04 minutes 00 seconds E	59 degrees 50 minutes 30 seconds N
02 degrees 03 minutes 00 seconds E	59 degrees 50 minutes 30 seconds N
02 degrees 03 minutes 00 seconds E	59 degrees 50 minutes 00 seconds N

(b)   a line from the point 02 degrees 03 minutes 00 seconds E 59 degrees 50 minutes 00 seconds N west along the parallel of latitude 59 degrees 50 minutes 00 seconds N until its intersection with the Dividing Line;

(c)   a line from the point of intersection specified in sub-paragraph (b) along the Dividing Line until its intersection with the parallel of latitude 60 degrees 00 minutes 45 seconds N;

(d)   a line from the point of intersection specified in sub-paragraph (c) east along the parallel of latitude 60 degrees 00 minutes 45 degrees N until its intersection with the meridian 02 degrees 05 minutes 30 seconds E.

2. In this Schedule, the 'Dividing Line' means the dividing line as defined in an Agreement dated 10th March 1965 and made between the government of the United Kingdom of Great Britain and Northern Ireland and the government of the Kingdom of Norway as supplemented by a Protocol dated 22nd December 1978.

SCHEDULE 2

Regulation 11(3)

Pension schemes

Part 1

Pension schemes – general

Interpretation

1.—(1) In this Schedule, subject to sub-paragraphs (2) and (3), 'occupational pension scheme' means an occupational pension scheme within the meaning of section 1(1) of the Pension Schemes Act 1993(**a**).

(2) In relation to rules, practices, actions and decisions identified at paragraph 7(a), 'occupational pension scheme' means an occupational pension scheme within the meaning of section 1(1) of the Pension Schemes Act 1993 under which only retirement-benefit activities within the meaning of section 255(4) of the Pensions Act 2004(**b**) are carried out.

(3) In relation to rules, practices, actions and decisions identified at paragraphs 12, 13 and 30, 'occupational pension scheme' means an occupational pension scheme within the meaning of either section 1(1) of the Pension Schemes Act 1993 or section 150(5) of the Finance Act 2004(**c**).

(4) In this Schedule, 'scheme' means an occupational pension scheme, construed in accordance with sub-paragraphs (1) to (3).

(**a**)   1993 c 48; relevant amendments have been made to section 1(1) by the Pensions Act 2004 (c 35), section 239.
(**b**)   2004 c 35.
(**c**)   2004 c 12.

(5) In this Schedule, in relation to a scheme—

'active member' has the meaning given by section 124(1) of the Pensions Act 1995(**a**), but in paragraph 13 also includes an active member within the meaning of section 151(2) of the Finance Act 2004;

'age related benefit' means benefit provided from a scheme to a member—

(a)   on or following his retirement (including early retirement on grounds of ill health or otherwise),

(b)   on his reaching a particular age, or

(c)   on termination of his service in an employment;

'death benefit' means benefit payable from a pension scheme, in respect of a member, in consequence of his death;

'deferred member' has the meaning given by section 124(1) of the Pensions Act 1995;

'defined benefits arrangement' has the meaning given by section 152(6) of the Finance Act 2004(**b**), but the reference in that section to an arrangement shall be read as referring to an arrangement in respect of a member under a scheme as defined in section 1(1) of the Pension Schemes Act 1993(**c**) rather than in respect of a member under a pension scheme as defined in section 150(1) of the Finance Act 2004;

'dependant' means dependant as defined in the scheme rules;

'early retirement pivot age' means an age specified in the scheme rules as the earliest age at which age related benefit becomes payable without actuarial reduction (disregarding any special provision as to early payment on grounds of ill health or otherwise);

'employer' has the meaning given by section 318(1) of the Pensions Act 2004(**d**);

'employer contribution' means any contribution to a scheme by an employer in respect of a member;

'employment' includes any trade, business, profession, office or vocation, whether or not a person is employed in it under a contract of employment or is self employed;

'late retirement pivot age' means an age specified in the scheme rules above which benefit becomes payable with actuarial enhancement;

'managers' has the meaning given by section 124(1) of the Pensions Act 1995(**e**);

'member' means any active member, deferred member or pensioner member, but in paragraph 12 includes any active, deferred or pensioner member within the meaning of section 151(2) to (4) of the Finance Act 2004;

(**a**)   1995 c 26.
(**b**)   2004 c 12.
(**c**)   1993 c 48; relevant amendments to section 1(1) have been made by the Pensions Act 2004 (c 35), section 239.
(**d**)   2004 c 35.
(**e**)   1995 c 26.

'member contribution' means any contribution to a scheme by a member;

'money purchase arrangement' has the meaning given by section 152(2) of the Finance Act 2004, but the reference in that section to an arrangement shall be read as referring to an arrangement in respect of a member under a scheme as defined in section 1(1) of the Pension Schemes Act 1993 rather than in respect of a member under a pension scheme as defined in section 150(1) of the Finance Act 2004;

'non-discrimination rule' means the rule in paragraph 2(1);

'normal pension age' has the meaning given by section 180 of the Pension Schemes Act 1993;

'normal retirement age', in relation to a member, means the age at which workers in the undertaking for which the member worked at the time of his retirement, and who held the same kind of position as the member held at his retirement, were normally required to retire;

'pensionable age' has the meaning given by section 122(1) of the Social Security Contributions and Benefits Act 1992(**a**);

'pensionable pay' means that part of a member's pay which counts as pensionable pay under the scheme rules;

'pensionable service' has the meaning given by section 124(1) of the Pensions Act 1995(**b**);

'pensioner member' has the meaning given by section 124(1) of the Pensions Act 1995(**c**); and

'prospective member' means any person who, under the terms of his employment or the scheme rules or both—

(a) is able, at his own option, to become a member of the scheme,

(b) shall become so able if he continues in the same employment for a sufficient period of time,

(c) shall be so admitted to it automatically unless he makes an election not to become a member, or

(d) may be admitted to it subject to the consent of any person.

(6) In their application to a scheme which is divided into two or more sections, the provisions of this Schedule shall apply as if each section of the scheme was a separate scheme.

(7) In this Schedule—

'personal pension scheme' has the meaning given by section 1(1) of the Pension Schemes Act 1993(**d**);

(**a**) 1992 c 4; relevant amendments have been made to section 122(1) by the Pensions Act 1995 (c 26), section 126 and Schedule 4 paragraph 13(a).
(**b**) 1995 c 26; relevant amendments have been made to section 124(1) by the Pensions Act 2004 (c 35), section 320 and Schedule 13, Part 1.
(**c**) 1995 c 26; relevant amendments have been made to section 124(1) by the Child Support, Pensions and Social Security Act 2000 (c 19), section 56 and Schedule 5, Part 1, paragraph 8(3).
(**d**) 1993 c 48; relevant amendments have been made to section 1(1) by the Pensions Act 2004 (c 35), section 239.

'registered pension scheme' has the meaning given by section 150(2) of the Finance Act 2004(**a**); and

references to contributions under a money purchase arrangement shall be construed as including amounts credited to a member's account whether or not they reflect payments actually made under the scheme.

(8) Any term used in regulation 11 (pension schemes) shall have the same meaning in that regulation as it has in this Schedule.

Non-discrimination rule

2.—(1) Every scheme shall be treated as including a provision ('the non-discrimination rule') containing a requirement that the trustees or managers of the scheme refrain from doing any act which is unlawful by virtue of regulation 11.

(2) The other provisions of the scheme are to have effect subject to the non-discrimination rule.

(3) The trustees or managers of a scheme may—

(a)   if they do not (apart from this sub-paragraph) have power to make such alterations to the scheme as may be required to secure conformity with the non-discrimination rule, or

(b)   if they have such power but the procedure for doing so—

(i)   is liable to be unduly complex or protracted, or

(ii) involves the obtaining of consents which cannot be obtained, or can only be obtained with undue delay or difficulty,

by resolution make such alterations to the scheme.

(4) Alterations made by a resolution such as is referred to in sub-paragraph (3)—

(a)   may have effect in relation to a period before the alterations are made (but may not have effect in relation to any time before the coming into force of these Regulations), and

(b)   shall be subject to the consent of any employer in relation to the scheme whose consent would be required for such a modification if it were to be made under the scheme rules.

Exception for rules, practices, actions and decisions relating to occupational pension schemes

3. Nothing in Part 2 or 3 of these Regulations shall render it unlawful for an employer, or for trustees or managers, to maintain or use, in relation to a scheme, any of the rules, practices, actions or decisions set out in Part 2 of this Schedule.

Exception for rules, practices, actions and decisions relating to contributions by employers to personal pension schemes

4. Nothing in Part 2 or 3 of these Regulations shall render it unlawful for an

---

(**a**) 2004 c 12.

employer, in relation to the payment of contributions to any personal pension scheme in respect of a worker, to maintain or use any of the rules, practices, actions or decisions set out in Part 3 of this Schedule.

Procedure in employment tribunals

5. Where under regulation 36 (jurisdiction of employment tribunals) a member or prospective member of a scheme presents to an employment tribunal a complaint that the trustees or managers of the scheme—

(a) have committed against him an act which is unlawful by virtue of regulation 11 (pension schemes) or 24 (relationships which have come to an end); or

(b) are by virtue of regulation 25 (liability of employers and principals) or 26 (aiding unlawful acts) to be treated as having committed against him such an act,

the employer in relation to the scheme shall, for the purposes of the rules governing procedure, be treated as a party and be entitled to appear and be heard in accordance with those rules.

Remedies in employment tribunals

6.—(1) This paragraph applies where—

(a) under regulation 36 (jurisdiction of employment tribunals) a member or prospective member of a scheme ('the complainant') presents to an employment tribunal a complaint against the trustees or managers of the scheme or an employer;

(b) the complainant is not a pensioner member of the scheme;

(c) the complaint relates to the terms on which persons become members of the scheme, or the terms on which members of the scheme are treated; and

(d) the tribunal finds the complaint to be well-founded.

(2) Where this paragraph applies, the employment tribunal may, without prejudice to the generality of its power under regulation 38(1)(a) (power to make order declaring rights of complainant and respondent), make an order declaring that the complainant has a right—

(a) where the complaint relates to the terms on which persons become members of the scheme, to be admitted to the scheme;

(b) where the complaint relates to the terms on which members of the scheme are treated, to membership of the scheme without discrimination.

(3) An order under sub-paragraph (2)—

(a) may be made in respect of such period as is specified in the order (but may not be made in respect of any time before the coming into force of these Regulations);

(b) may make such provision as the employment tribunal considers appropriate as to the terms on which, or the capacity in which, the complainant is to enjoy such admission or membership.

(4) Where this paragraph applies, the employment tribunal may not make an order for compensation under regulation 38(1)(b), whether in relation to arrears of benefits or otherwise, except—

(a)   for injury to feelings;

(b)   by virtue of regulation 38(3).

Part 2

Excepted rules, practices, actions and decisions relating to occupational pension schemes

Admission to schemes

7. In relation to admission to a scheme—

(a)   a minimum or maximum age for admission, including different ages for admission for different groups or categories of worker;

(b)   a minimum level of pensionable pay for admission, provided that such a minimum is not above the lower earnings limit referred to in section 5(1) of the Social Security Contributions and Benefits Act 1992(**a**).

The use of age criteria in actuarial calculations

8. The use of age criteria in actuarial calculations, for example in the actuarial calculation of—

(a)   any age related benefit commencing before any early retirement pivot age or enhancement of such benefit commencing after any late retirement pivot age;

(b)   member or employer contributions to a scheme; or

(c)   any age related benefit commuted in exchange for the payment of any lump sum.

Contributions

9. Any difference in the rate of member or employer contributions by or in respect of different members to the extent that this is attributable to any differences in the pensionable pay of those members.

Contributions under money purchase arrangements

10. Under a money purchase arrangement—

(**a**) 1992 c 4; relevant amendments have been made to section 5(1) by the Welfare Reform and Pensions Act 1999 (c 30), section 73, Schedule 9, Part 1, paragraph 1.

(a) different rates of member or employer contributions according to the age of the members by or in respect of whom contributions are made where the aim in setting the different rates is—

   (i) to equalise the amount of benefit to which members of different ages who are otherwise in a comparable situation will become entitled under the arrangement, or

   (ii) to make the amount of benefit to which such members will become entitled under the arrangement more nearly equal;

(b) equal rates of member or employer contributions irrespective of the age of the members by or in respect of whom contributions are made.

Contributions under defined benefits arrangements

11. Under a defined benefits arrangement, different rates of member or employer contributions according to the age of the members by or in respect of whom contributions are made, to the extent that—

(a) each year of pensionable service entitles members in a comparable situation to accrue a right to defined benefits based on the same fraction of pensionable pay, and

(b) the aim in setting the different rates is to reflect the increasing cost of providing the defined benefits in respect of members as they get older.

Age related rules, practices, actions and decisions relating to benefit

12. A minimum age for entitlement to or payment of any age related benefit to a member, provided that, in the case of any age related benefit paid under a defined benefits arrangement before any early retirement pivot age—

(a) such benefit is subject to actuarial reduction for early receipt, and

(b) the member is not credited with additional periods of pensionable service.

13. In relation to workers who are active or prospective members of a scheme on the date on which these Regulations come into force, a minimum age for entitlement to or payment of any age related benefit to such members under defined benefit arrangements before any early retirement pivot age, where such benefit is calculated in one or both of the following ways—

(a) it is not made subject to actuarial reduction for early receipt;

(b) it results from crediting the member with additional periods of pensionable service.

14. An early retirement pivot age or a late retirement pivot age, including different such ages for different groups or categories of member.

15. The enhancement of any age related benefit in the event of a member's retirement before any early retirement pivot age on ill health grounds, where that enhancement is calculated by reference to the years of pensionable service which that member would have completed if he had continued in pensionable service up to the age specified for that purpose in the scheme rules.

16. Any rule, practice, action or decision whereby a male member who reaches pensionable age is not entitled or is no longer entitled to any additional amount of pension which would have been payable to such a member before pensionable age in the circumstances prescribed for the purposes of section 64(2) of the Pensions Act 1995(**a**) by regulation 13 of the Occupational Pension Schemes (Equal Treatment) Regulations 1995(**b**).

17. The reduction of any pension payable in consequence of a member's death to any dependant of the member where that dependant is more than a specified number of years younger than the member.

18. In relation to pensioner members who have retired on ill health grounds before any early retirement pivot age, discontinuation of any life assurance cover once any such members reach the normal retirement age which applied to them at the time they retired, or in relation to members to whom no such normal retirement age applied, once such members reach the age of 65.

Other rules, practices, actions and decisions relating to benefit

19. Any difference in the amount of any age related benefit or death benefit payable under a defined benefits arrangement to or in respect of members with different lengths of pensionable service to the extent that the difference in amount is attributable to their differing lengths of service, provided that, for each year of pensionable service, members in a comparable situation are entitled to accrue a right to benefit based upon the same fraction of pensionable pay.

20. Any difference in the amount of any age related benefit or death benefit payable from a scheme to or in respect of different members to the extent that the difference in amount is attributable to differences over time in the pensionable pay of those members.

21. Any limitation of the amount of any age related benefit or death benefit payable from a scheme where the limitation results from imposing a maximum number of years of service by reference to which such benefit may be calculated.

22. Any rule, practice, action or decision whereby any age related benefit or death benefit is only payable to or in respect of members who have completed a minimum period of service, provided that such a minimum period is not longer than 2 years qualifying service within the meaning of section 71(7) of the Pension Schemes Act 1993(**c**).

23. Any limitation on the amount of any age related benefit or death benefit payable from a scheme where the limitation results from imposing a minimum level of pensionable pay by reference to which any such benefit may be calculated, provided that such a minimum is not above the lower earnings limit referred to in section 5(1) of the Social Security Contributions and Benefits Act 1992(**d**).

(**a**) 1995 c 26.
(**b**) SI 1995/3183.
(**c**) 1993 c 48.
(**d**) 1992 c 4; relevant amendments have been made by the Welfare Reform and Pensions Act 1999, c 30, section 73 and Schedule 9, Part 1, paragraph 1.

24. Any limitation on the amount of any age related benefit or death benefit payable from a scheme where the limitation results from imposing a maximum level of pensionable pay by reference to which such benefit may be calculated.

Closure of schemes

25. The closure of a scheme, from a particular date, to workers who have not already joined it.

Other rules, practices, actions and decisions

26. Increases of pensions in payment which are made to members over 55 but not to members below that age.

27. Any difference in the rate of increase of pensions in payment for members of different ages to the extent that the aim in setting the different rates is to maintain the relative value of members' pensions.

28. Any difference in the rate of increase of pensions in payment for members whose pensions have been in payment for different lengths of time to the extent that the aim in setting the different rates is to maintain the relative value of members' pensions.

29. The application of an age limit for transfer of the value of a member's accrued rights into or out of a scheme, provided that any such age limit is not more than one year before the member's normal pension age.

Registered pension schemes

30.—(1) Subject to sub-paragraph (2), any rules, practices, actions or decisions relating to entitlement to or payment of benefits under a registered pension scheme insofar as compliance is necessary to secure any tax relief or exemption available under Part 4 of the Finance Act 2004(**a**) or to prevent any charge to tax arising under that Part of that Act, whoever is liable in relation to such charge.

(2) Sub-paragraph (1) does not apply to any rules, practices, actions or decisions setting a minimum age for entitlement to or payment of any age related benefit.

Part 3

Excepted rules, practices, actions and decisions relating to contributions by employers to personal pension schemes

Contributions by employers

31. Different rates of contributions by an employer according to the age of the workers in respect of whom the contributions are made where the aim in setting the different rates is—

(**a**) 2004 c 12.

(a) to equalise the amount of benefit to which workers of different ages who are otherwise in a comparable situation will become entitled under their personal pension schemes, or

(b) to make the amount of benefit to which such workers will become entitled under their personal pension schemes more nearly equal.

32. Any difference in the rate of contributions by an employer in respect of different workers to the extent that this is attributable to any differences in remuneration payable to those workers.

SCHEDULE 3

Regulation 41(1)

Questionnaire of person aggrieved

To................................*(name of person to be questioned)* of.................................. *(address)*

1.—(1) I..............*(name of questioner)* of.............*(address)* consider that you may have discriminated against me [subjected me to harassment] contrary to the Employment Equality (Age) Regulations 2006.

(2) *(Give date, approximate time and a factual description of the treatment received and of the circumstances leading up to the treatment.)*

(3) I consider that this treatment may have been unlawful because.......................... *(complete if you wish to give reasons, otherwise delete).*

2. Do you agree that the statement in paragraph 1(2) above is an accurate description of what happened? If not, in what respect do you disagree or what is your version of what happened?

3. Do you accept that your treatment of me was unlawful discrimination [harassment]?

If not—

(a) why not,

(b) for what reason did I receive the treatment accorded to me, and

(c) how far did considerations of age affect your treatment of me?

4. *(Any other questions you wish to ask.)*

5. My address for any reply you may wish to give to the questions raised above is [that set out in paragraph 1(1) above] [the following address..]

....*(signature of questioner)*

....*(date)*

N.B.—By virtue of regulation 41 of the Employment Equality (Age) Regulations 2006 this questionnaire and any reply are (subject to the provisions of that regulation) admissible in proceedings under the Regulations. A court or tribunal may draw any such inference as is just and equitable from a failure without reasonable excuse to reply within eight weeks of service of this questionnaire, or from an evasive or equivocal reply, including an inference that the person questioned has committed an unlawful act.

SCHEDULE 4

Regulation 41(1)

Reply by respondent

To……………………….*(name of questioner)* of……………………...…………………..*(address)*

1. I…………………….*(name of person questioned)* of………………………...…...*(address)* hereby acknowledge receipt of the questionnaire signed by you and dated…………...which was served on me on……………….*(date)*.

2. [I agree that the statement in paragraph 1(2) of the questionnaire is an accurate description of what happened.]

[I disagree with the statement in paragraph 1(2) of the questionnaire in that……………………..……]

3. I accept/dispute that my treatment of you was unlawful discrimination [harassment].

[My reasons for so disputing are…………………………………………… The reason why you received the treatment accorded to you and the answers to the other questions in paragraph 3 of the questionnaire are……………………]

4. *(Replies to questions in paragraph 4 of the questionnaire.)*

5. [I have deleted (in whole or in part). the paragraph(s) numbered………………….above, since I am unable/unwilling to reply to the relevant questions in the correspondingly numbered paragraph(s) of the questionnaire for the following reasons……………………….]

…………………………………….*(signature of person questioned)*

…………………………….*(date)*

SCHEDULE 5

Regulation 43

Validity of contracts, collective agreements and rules of undertakings

Part 1

Validity and revision of contracts

1.—(1) A term of a contract is void where—

    (a) the making of the contract is, by reason of the inclusion of the term, unlawful by virtue of these Regulations;

    (b) it is included in furtherance of an act which is unlawful by virtue of these Regulations; or

    (c) it provides for the doing of an act which is unlawful by virtue of these Regulations.

(2) Sub-paragraph (1) does not apply to a term the inclusion of which constitutes, or is in furtherance of, or provides for, unlawful discrimination against, or harassment of, a party to the contract, but the term shall be unenforceable against that party.

(3) A term in a contract which purports to exclude or limit any provision of these Regulations is unenforceable by any person in whose favour the term would operate apart from this paragraph.

(4) Sub-paragraphs (1), (2) and (3) shall apply whether the contract was entered into before or after the date on which these Regulations come into force, but in the case of a contract made before that date, those sub-paragraphs do not apply in relation to any period before that date.

2.—(1) Paragraph 1(3) does not apply—

    (a) to a contract settling a complaint to which regulation 36(1) (jurisdiction of employment tribunals) applies where the contract is made with the assistance of a conciliation officer within the meaning of section 211 of the Trade Union and Labour Relations (Consolidation) Act 1992(**a**);

    (b) to a contract settling a complaint to which regulation 36(1) applies if the conditions regulating compromise contracts under this Schedule are satisfied in relation to the contract; or

    (c) to a contract settling a claim to which regulation 39 (jurisdiction of county or sheriff courts) applies.

(2) The conditions regulating compromise contracts under this Schedule are that—

    (a) the contract must be in writing;

(**a**) 1992 c 52.

(b)   the contract must relate to the particular complaint;

(c)   the complainant must have received advice from a relevant independent adviser as to the terms and effect of the proposed contract and in particular its effect on his ability to pursue a complaint before an employment tribunal;

(d)   there must be in force, when the adviser gives the advice, a contract of insurance, or an indemnity provided for members of a profession or professional body, covering the risk of a claim by the complainant in respect of loss arising in consequence of the advice;

(e)   the contract must identify the adviser; and

(f)   the contract must state that the conditions regulating compromise contracts under this Schedule are satisfied.

(3) A person is a relevant independent adviser for the purposes of sub-paragraph (2)(c)—

(a)   if he is a qualified lawyer;

(b)   if he is an officer, official, employee or member of an independent trade union who has been certified in writing by the trade union as competent to give advice and as authorised to do so on behalf of the trade union; or

(c)   if he works at an advice centre (whether as an employee or a volunteer) and has been certified in writing by the centre as competent to give advice and as authorised to do so on behalf of the centre.

(4) But a person is not a relevant independent adviser for the purposes of sub-paragraph (2)(c) in relation to the complainant—

(a)   if he is employed by, or is acting in the matter for the other party, or is a person who is connected with the other party;

(b)   in the case of a person within sub-paragraph (3)(b) or (c), if the trade union or advice centre is the other party or a person who is connected with the other party; or

(c)   in the case of a person within sub-paragraph (3)(c), if the complainant makes a payment for the advice received from him.

(5) In sub-paragraph (3)(a) 'qualified lawyer' means—

(a)   as respects England and Wales, a barrister (whether in practice as such or employed to give legal advice), a solicitor who holds a practising certificate, or a person other than a barrister or solicitor who is an authorised advocate or authorised litigator (within the meaning of the Courts and Legal Services Act 1990(**a**); and

(b)   as respects Scotland, an advocate (whether in practice as such or employed to give legal advice), or a solicitor who holds a practising certificate.

(6) A person shall be treated as being a qualified lawyer within sub-paragraph (5)(a) if he is a Fellow of the Institute of Legal Executives employed by a solicitors' practice.

(**a**) 1990 c 41.

(7) In sub-paragraph (3)(b) 'independent trade union' has the same meaning as in the Trade Union and Labour Relations (Consolidation) Act 1992.

(8) For the purposes of sub-paragraph (4)(a) any two persons are to be treated as connected—

   (a) if one is a company of which the other (directly or indirectly) has control; or

   (b) if both are companies of which a third person (directly or indirectly) has control.

(9) An agreement under which the parties agree to submit a dispute to arbitration—

   (a) shall be regarded for the purposes of sub-paragraphs (1)(a) and (b) as being a contract settling a complaint if—

      (i) the dispute is covered by a scheme having effect by virtue of an order under section 212A of the Trade Union and Labour Relations (Consolidation) Act 1992, and

      (ii) the agreement is to submit it to arbitration in accordance with the scheme, but

   (b) shall be regarded as neither being nor including such a contract in any other case.

3.—(1) On the application of a person interested in a contract to which paragraph 1(1) or (2) applies, a county court or a sheriff court may make such order as it thinks fit for—

   (a) removing or modifying any term rendered void by paragraph 1(1), or

   (b) removing or modifying any term made unenforceable by paragraph 1(2);

but such an order shall not be made unless all persons affected have been given notice in writing of the application (except where under rules of court notice may be dispensed with) and have been afforded an opportunity to make representations to the court.

(2) An order under sub-paragraph (1) may include provision as respects any period before the making of the order (but after the coming into force of these Regulations).

Part 2

Collective agreements and rules of undertakings

4.—(1) This Part of this Schedule applies to—

   (a) any term of a collective agreement, including an agreement which was not intended, or is presumed not to have been intended, to be a legally enforceable contract;

   (b) any rule made by an employer for application to all or any of the persons who are employed by him or who apply to be, or are, considered by him for employment;

   (c) any rule made by a trade organisation (within the meaning of regulation 18) or a qualifications body (within the meaning of regulation 19) for application to—

(i) all or any of its members or prospective members; or

(ii) all or any of the persons on whom it has conferred professional or trade qualifications (within the meaning of regulation 19) or who are seeking the professional or trade qualifications which it has power to confer.

(2) Any term or rule to which this Part of this Schedule applies is void where—

(a) the making of the collective agreement is, by reason of the inclusion of the term, unlawful by virtue of these Regulations;

(b) the term or rule is included or made in furtherance of an act which is unlawful by virtue of these Regulations; or

(c) the term or rule provides for the doing of an act which is unlawful by virtue of these Regulations.

(3) Sub-paragraph (2) shall apply whether the agreement was entered into, or the rule made, before or after the date on which these Regulations come into force; but in the case of an agreement entered into, or a rule made, before the date on which these Regulations come into force, that sub-paragraph does not apply in relation to any period before that date.

5. A person to whom this paragraph applies may present a complaint to an employment tribunal that a term or rule is void by virtue of paragraph 4 if he has reason to believe—

(a) that the term or rule may at some future time have effect in relation to him; and

(b) where he alleges that it is void by virtue of paragraph 4(2)(c), that—

(i) an act for the doing of which it provides, may at some such time be done in relation to him, and

(ii) the act would be unlawful by virtue of these Regulations if done in relation to him in present circumstances.

6. In the case of a complaint about—

(a) a term of a collective agreement made by or on behalf of—

(i) an employer,

(ii) an organisation of employers of which an employer is a member, or

(iii) an association of such organisations of one of which an employer is a member, or

(b) a rule made by an employer within the meaning of paragraph 4(1)(b),

paragraph 5 applies to any person who is, or is genuinely and actively seeking to become, one of his employees.

7. In the case of a complaint about a rule made by an organisation or body to which paragraph 4(1)(c) applies, paragraph 5 applies to any person—

(a) who is, or is genuinely and actively seeking to become, a member of the organisation or body;

(b) on whom the organisation or body has conferred a professional or trade qualification (within the meaning of regulation 19) which the organisation or body has power to confer; or

(c) who is genuinely and actively seeking such a professional or trade qualification which the organisation or body has power to confer.

8.—(1) When an employment tribunal finds that a complaint presented to it under paragraph 5 is well-founded the tribunal shall make an order declaring that the term or rule is void.

(2) An order under sub-paragraph (1) may include provision as respects any period before the making of the order (but after the coming into force of these Regulations).

9. The avoidance by virtue of paragraph 4(2) of any term or rule which provides for any person to be discriminated against shall be without prejudice to the following rights (except in so far as they enable any person to require another person to be treated less favourably than himself), namely—

(a) such of the rights of the person to be discriminated against; and

(b) such of the rights of any person who will be treated more favourably in direct or indirect consequence of the discrimination,

as are conferred by or in respect of a contract made or modified wholly or partly in pursuance of, or by reference to, that term or rule.

10. In this Schedule 'collective agreement' means any agreement relating to one or more of the matters mentioned in section 178(2) of the Trade Union and Labour Relations (Consolidation) Act 1992 (collective agreements and collective bargaining), being an agreement made by or on behalf of one or more employers or one or more organisations of employers or associations of such organisations with one or more organisations of workers or associations of such organisations.

SCHEDULE 6

Regulation 47

Duty to consider working beyond retirement

Interpretation

1.—(1) In this Schedule—

'dismissal' means a dismissal within the meaning of section 95 of the 1996 Act(**a**);

'employee' means a person to whom regulation 30 (exception for retirement) applies and references to 'employer' shall be construed accordingly;

(a) Employment Rights Act 1996 (c 18); section 95 has been amended by section 57 of, and by Schedule 1, paragraph 29, and Schedule 2 to, the Employment Relations Act 2004 (c 24), and by regulation 11 of, and paragraph 3(1) and (7) of Part 1 of Schedule 2 to, SI 2002/2034.

'intended date of retirement' has the meaning given by sub-paragraph (2);

'operative date of termination' means (subject to paragraph 10(3))—

(a) where the employer terminates the employee's contract of employment by notice, the date on which the notice expires, or

(b) where the employer terminates the contract of employment without notice, the date on which the termination takes effect;

'request' means a request made under paragraph 5; and

'worker' has the same meaning as in section 230(3) of the 1996 Act.

(2) In this Schedule 'intended date of retirement' means—

(a) where the employer notifies a date in accordance with paragraph 2, that date;

(b) where the employer notifies a date in accordance with paragraph 4 and either no request is made or a request is made after the notification, that date;

(c) where,

    (i) the employer has not notified a date in accordance with paragraph 2,

    (ii) a request is made before the employer has notified a date in accordance with paragraph 4 (including where no notification in accordance with that paragraph is given),

    (iii) the request is made by an employee who has reasonable grounds for believing that the employer intends to retire him on a certain date, and,

    (iv) the request identifies that date,

the date so identified;

(d) in a case to which paragraph 3 has applied, any earlier or later date that has superseded the date mentioned in paragraph (a), (b) or (c) as the intended date of retirement by virtue of paragraph 3(3);

(e) in a case to which paragraph 10 has applied, the later date that has superseded the date mentioned in paragraph (a), (b) or (c) as the intended date of retirement by virtue of paragraph 10(3)(b).

Duty of employer to inform employee

2.—(1) An employer who intends to retire an employee has a duty to notify the employee in writing of—

(a) the employee's right to make a request; and

(b) the date on which he intends the employee to retire,

not more than one year and not less than six months before that date.

(2) The duty to notify applies regardless of—

(a) whether there is any term in the employee's contract of employment indicating when his retirement is expected to take place,

(b) any other notification of, or information about, the employee's date of retirement given to him by the employer at any time, and

(c) any other information about the employee's right to make a request given to him by the employer at any time.

3.—(1) This paragraph applies if the employer has notified the employee in accordance with paragraph 2 or 4 or the employee has made a request before being notified in accordance with paragraph 4 (including where no notification in accordance with that paragraph is given), and—

(a) the employer and employee agree, in accordance with paragraph 7(3)(b) or 8(5)(b), that the dismissal is to take effect on a date later than the relevant date;

(b) the employer gives notice to the employee, in accordance with paragraph 7(7)(a)(ii) or, where the employee appeals, paragraph 8(9)(a)(ii), that the dismissal is to take effect on a date later than the relevant date; or

(c) the employer and employee agree that the dismissal is to take effect on a date earlier than the relevant date.

(2) This Schedule does not require the employer to give the employee a further notification in respect of dismissal taking effect on a date—

(a) agreed as mentioned in sub-paragraph (1)(a) or notified as mentioned in sub-paragraph (1)(b) that is later than the relevant date and falls six months or less after the relevant date; or

(b) agreed as mentioned in sub-paragraph (1)(c) that is earlier than the relevant date.

(3) If—

(a) a date later than the relevant date is agreed as mentioned in sub-paragraph (1)(a) or notified as mentioned in sub-paragraph (1)(b) and falls six months or less after the relevant date, or

(b) a date earlier than the relevant date is agreed as mentioned in sub-paragraph (1)(c),

the earlier or later date shall supersede the relevant date as the intended date of retirement.

(4) In this paragraph, 'the relevant date' means the date that is defined as the intended date of retirement in paragraph (a), (b) or (c) of paragraph 1(2).

Continuing duty to inform employee

4. Where the employer has failed to comply with paragraph 2, he has a continuing duty to notify the employee in writing as described in paragraph 2(1) until the fourteenth day before the operative date of termination.

Statutory right to request not to retire

5.—(1) An employee may make a request to his employer not to retire on the intended date of retirement.

(2) In his request the employee must propose that his employment should continue, following the intended date of retirement—

(a)   indefinitely,

(b)   for a stated period, or

(c)   until a stated date;

and, if the request is made at a time when it is no longer possible for the employer to notify in accordance with paragraph 2 and the employer has not yet notified in accordance with paragraph 4, must identify the date on which he believes that the employer intends to retire him.

(3) A request must be in writing and state that it is made under this paragraph.

(4) An employee may only make one request under this paragraph in relation to any one intended date of retirement and may not make a request in relation to a date that supersedes a different date as the intended date of retirement by virtue of paragraph 3(3) or 10(3)(b).

(5) A request is only a request made under this paragraph if it is made—

(a)   in a case where the employer has complied with paragraph 2, more than three months but not more than six months before the intended date of retirement, or

(b)   in a case where the employer has not complied with paragraph 2, before, but not more than six months before, the intended date of retirement.

An employer's duty to consider a request

6. An employer to whom a request is made is under a duty to consider the request in accordance with paragraphs 7 to 9.

Meeting to consider request

7.—(1) An employer having a duty under paragraph 6 to consider a request shall hold a meeting to discuss the request with the employee within a reasonable period after receiving it.

(2) The employer and employee must take all reasonable steps to attend the meeting.

(3) The duty to hold a meeting does not apply if, before the end of the period that is reasonable—

(a)   the employer and employee agree that the employee's employment will continue indefinitely and the employer gives notice to the employee to that effect; or

(b)   the employer and employee agree that the employee's employment will continue for an agreed period and the employer gives notice to the employee of the length of that period or of the date on which it will end.

(4) The duty to hold a meeting does not apply if—

(a)   it is not practicable to hold a meeting within the period that is reasonable, and

(b)   the employer complies with sub-paragraph (5).

(5) Where sub-paragraph (4)(a) applies, the employer may consider the request without holding a meeting provided he considers any representations made by the employee.

(6) The employer shall give the employee notice of his decision on the request as soon as is reasonably practicable after the date of the meeting or, if sub-paragraphs (4) and (5) apply, his consideration of the request.

(7) A notice given under sub-paragraph (6) shall—

    (a)   where the decision is to accept the request, state that it is accepted and—

        (i)   where the decision is that the employee's employment will continue indefinitely, state that fact, or

        (ii)   where the decision is that the employee's employment will continue for a further period, state that fact and specify the length of the period or the date on which it will end,

    (b)   where the decision is to refuse the request, confirm that the employer wishes to retire the employee and the date on which the dismissal is to take effect,

and, in the case of a notice falling within paragraph (b), and of a notice referred to in paragraph (a) that specifies a period shorter than the period proposed by the employee in the request, shall inform the employee of his right to appeal.

(8) All notices given under this paragraph shall be in writing and be dated.

Appeals

8.—(1) An employee is entitled to appeal against—

    (a)   a decision of his employer to refuse the request, or

    (b)   a decision of his employer to accept the request where the notice given under paragraph 7(6) states as mentioned in paragraph 7(7)(a)(ii) and specifies a period shorter than the period proposed by the employee in the request,

by giving notice in accordance with sub-paragraph (2) as soon as is reasonably practicable after the date of the notice given under paragraph 7(6).

(2) A notice of appeal under sub-paragraph (1) shall set out the grounds of appeal.

(3) The employer shall hold a meeting with the employee to discuss an appeal within a reasonable period after the date of the notice of appeal.

(4) The employer and employee must take all reasonable steps to attend the meeting.

(5) The duty to hold a meeting does not apply if, before the end of the period that is reasonable—

    (a)   the employer and employee agree that the employee's employment will continue indefinitely and the employer gives notice to the employee to that effect; or

    (b)   the employer and employee agree that the employee's employment will continue for an agreed period and the employer gives notice to the employee of the length of that period or of the date on which it will end.

(6) The duty to hold a meeting does not apply if—

    (a) it is not practicable to hold a meeting within the period that is reasonable, and

    (b) the employer complies with sub-paragraph (7).

(7) Where sub-paragraph (6)(a) applies, the employer may consider the appeal without holding a meeting provided he considers any representations made by the employee.

(8) The employer shall give the employee notice of his decision on the appeal as soon as is reasonably practicable after the date of the meeting or, if sub-paragraphs (6) and (7) apply, his consideration of the appeal.

(9) A notice under sub-paragraph (8) shall—

    (a) where the decision is to accept the appeal, state that it is accepted and—

        (i) where the decision is that the employee's employment will continue indefinitely, state that fact, or

        (ii) where the decision is that the employee's employment will continue for a further period, state that fact and specify the length of the period or the date on which it will end,

    (b) where the decision is to refuse the appeal, confirm that the employer wishes to retire the employee and the date on which the dismissal is to take effect.

(10) All notices given under this paragraph shall be in writing and be dated.

Right to be accompanied

9.—(1) This paragraph applies where—

    (a) a meeting is held under paragraph 7 or 8, and

    (b) the employee reasonably requests to be accompanied at the meeting.

(2) Where this paragraph applies the employer must permit the employee to be accompanied at the meeting by one companion who—

    (a) is chosen by the employee;

    (b) is a worker employed by the same employer as the employee;

    (c) is to be permitted to address the meeting (but not to answer questions on behalf of the employee); and

    (d) is to be permitted to confer with the employee during the meeting.

(3) If—

    (a) an employee has a right under this paragraph to be accompanied at a meeting,

    (b) his chosen companion will not be available at the time proposed for the meeting by the employer, and

    (c) the employee proposes an alternative time which satisfies sub-paragraph (4),

the employer must postpone the meeting to the time proposed by the employee.

(4) An alternative time must—

    (a) be convenient for employer, employee and companion, and

    (b) fall before the end of the period of seven days beginning with the first day after the day proposed by the employer.

(5) An employer shall permit a worker to take time off during working hours for the purpose of accompanying an employee in accordance with a request under sub-paragraph (1)(b).

(6) Sections 168(3) and (4), 169 and 171 to 173 of the Trade Union and Labour Relations (Consolidation) Act 1992(**a**) (time off for carrying out trade union duties) shall apply in relation to sub-paragraph (5) above as they apply in relation to section 168(1) of that Act.

Dismissal before request considered

10.—(1) This paragraph applies where—

    (a) by virtue of paragraph 6 an employer is under a duty to consider a request;

    (b) the employer dismisses the employee;

    (c) that dismissal is the contemplated dismissal to which the request relates; and

    (d) the operative date of termination would, but for sub-paragraph (3), fall on or before the day on which the employer gives notice in accordance with paragraph 7(6).

(2) Subject to paragraph (4), the contract of employment shall continue in force for all purposes, including the purpose of determining for any purpose the period for which the employee has been continuously employed, until the day following that on which the notice under paragraph 7(6) is given.

(3) The day following the day on which that notice is given shall supersede—

    (a) the date mentioned in sub-paragraph (1)(d) as the operative date of termination; and

    (b) the date defined as the intended date of retirement in paragraph (a), (b) or (c) of paragraph 1(2) as the intended date of retirement.

(4) Any continuation of the contract of employment under sub-paragraph (2) shall be disregarded when determining the operative date of termination for the purposes of sections 98ZA to 98ZH of the 1996 Act.

Complaint to employment tribunal: failure to comply with paragraph 2

11.—(1) An employee may present a complaint to an employment tribunal that his employer has failed to comply with the duty to notify him in paragraph 2.

(2) A tribunal shall not consider a complaint under this paragraph unless the complaint is presented—

(**a**) 1992 c 52; sections 171 and 173 have been amended by section 1(2)(a) of the Employment Rights (Dispute Resolution) Act 1998 (c 8). There are other amendments to these provisions which are not relevant for the purposes of these Regulations.

   (a) before the end of the period of three months beginning with—

      (i) the last day permitted to the employer by paragraph 2 for complying with the duty to notify, or

      (ii) if the employee did not then know the date that would be the intended date of retirement, the first day on which he knew or should have known that date; or

   (b) within such further period as the tribunal considers reasonable in a case where it is satisfied that it was not reasonably practicable for the complaint to be presented before the end of that period of three months.

(3) Where a tribunal finds that a complaint under this paragraph is well-founded it shall order the employer to pay compensation to the employee of such amount, not exceeding 8 weeks' pay, as the tribunal considers just and equitable in all the circumstances.

(4) Chapter 2 of Part 14 of the 1996 Act (calculation of a week's pay) shall apply for the purposes of sub-paragraph (3); and in applying that Chapter the calculation date shall be taken to be the date on which the complaint was presented or, if earlier, the operative date of termination.

(5) The limit in section 227(1) of the 1996 Act(**a**) (maximum amount of a week's pay) shall apply for the purposes of sub-paragraph (3).

Complaint to employment tribunal: denial of right to be accompanied

12.—(1) An employee may present a complaint to an employment tribunal that his employer has failed, or threatened to fail, to comply with paragraph 9(2) or (3).

(2) A tribunal shall not consider a complaint under this paragraph in relation to a failure or threat unless the complaint is presented—

   (a) before the end of the period of three months beginning with the date of the failure or threat; or

   (b) within such further period as the tribunal considers reasonable in a case where it is satisfied that it was not reasonably practicable for the complaint to be presented before the end of that period of three months.

(3) Where a tribunal finds that a complaint under this paragraph is well-founded it shall order the employer to pay compensation to the worker of an amount not exceeding two weeks' pay.

(4) Chapter 2 of Part 14 of the 1996 Act (calculation of a week's pay) shall apply for the purposes of sub-paragraph (3); and in applying that Chapter the calculation date shall be taken to be the date on which the relevant meeting took place (or was to have taken place).

(5) The limit in section 227(1) of the 1996 Act (maximum amount of a week's pay) shall apply for the purposes of sub-paragraph (3).

(**a**) 1996 c 18; the amount laid down in section 227 may be increased or decreased by Order made by the Secretary of State under section 34 of the Employment Relations Act 1999. The amount laid down in section 227 is currently £290: see SI 2005/3352.

Detriment and dismissal

13.—(1) An employee has the right not to be subjected to any detriment by any act by his employer done on the ground that he exercised or sought to exercise his right to be accompanied in accordance with paragraph 9.

(2) A worker has the right not to be subjected to any detriment by any act, or any deliberate failure to act, by his employer done on the ground that he accompanied or sought to accompany an employee pursuant to a request under paragraph 9.

(3) Section 48 of the 1996 Act shall apply in relation to contraventions of sub-paragraph (1) or (2) above as it applies in relation to contraventions of certain sections of that Act.

(4) Sub-paragraph (2) does not apply where the worker is an employee and the detriment in question amounts to dismissal (within the meaning of Part 10 of the 1996 Act).

(5) An employee who is dismissed shall be regarded for the purposes of Part 10 of the 1996 Act as unfairly dismissed if the reason (or, if more than one, the principal reason) for the dismissal is that he—

    (a)   exercised or sought to exercise his right to be accompanied in accordance with paragraph 9, or

    (b)   accompanied or sought to accompany an employee pursuant to a request under that paragraph.

(6) Sections 128 to 132 of the 1996 Act (interim relief) shall apply in relation to dismissal for the reason specified in sub-paragraph (5)(a) or (b) above as they apply in relation to dismissal for a reason specified in section 128(1)(b) of that Act.

SCHEDULE 7

Regulation 48

Duty to consider working beyond retirement – transitional provisions

1. In paragraphs 2 to 6—

    (a)   'the expiry date' means the date on which notice of dismissal given by an employer expires; and

    (b)   words and expressions shall have the same meanings as they do in Schedule 6.

2.—(1) This paragraph applies in a case where—

    (a)   an employer has given notice of dismissal to the employee before the commencement date of—

        (i)   at least the period required by the contract of employment; or

        (ii) where the period required by the contract exceeds four weeks, at least four weeks;

    (b)   the expiry date falls before 1st April 2007; and

(c) the employer has made the employee aware, before the commencement date, that the employer considers that the employee is being retired on the expiry date.

(2) Where this paragraph applies and the employer on or as soon as is practicable after the commencement date notifies the employee in writing of the employee's right to make a request under paragraph 5 of Schedule 6—

(a) the employer shall be treated as complying with the duty in paragraph 2 of Schedule 6;

(b) a request shall be treated as being a request made under paragraph 5 of Schedule 6 provided it—

(i) is made after the employer notified the employee of his right to make a request;

(ii) satisfies the requirements of sub-paragraphs (2) and (3) of paragraph 5 of Schedule 6; and

(iii) is made—

(aa) where practicable, at least four weeks before the expiry date; or

(bb) where that is not practicable, as soon as reasonably practicable (whether before or after the expiry date) after the employer notified the employee of his right to make a request, but not more than four weeks after the expiry date.

(3) Where this paragraph applies and the employer does not, on or as soon as is practicable after the commencement date, notify the employee in writing of the employee's right to make a request under paragraph 5 of Schedule 6—

(a) the duty to notify in accordance with paragraph 2 of Schedule 6 does not apply;

(b) the duty to notify in accordance with paragraph 4 of Schedule 6 applies as if—

(i) the employer had failed to notify in accordance with paragraph 2 of that Schedule; and

(ii) the duty was one to notify at any time before the expiry date;

(c) a request shall be treated as being a request made under paragraph 5 of Schedule 6 if it satisfies the requirements of sub-paragraphs (2) and (3) of that paragraph and is made—

(i) before any notification given in accordance with paragraph 4 of Schedule 6; or

(ii) after such notification and—

(aa) where practicable, at least four weeks before the expiry date; or

(bb) where that is not practicable, as soon as reasonably practicable (whether before or after the expiry date) after the employer notified the employee of his right to make a request, but not more than four weeks after the expiry date.

3.—(1) This paragraph applies in a case where the employer has given notice of dismissal to the employee before the commencement date and—

(a)   the expiry date falls before 1st April 2007, but

(b)   the period of notice given is shorter than the minimum period of notice required by paragraph 2(1)(a) or the employer has not complied with paragraph 2(1)(c).

(2) Where this paragraph applies—

(a)   the duty to notify in accordance with paragraph 2 of Schedule 6 does not apply;

(b)   the duty to notify in accordance with paragraph 4 of Schedule 6 applies as if—

(i)   the employer had failed to notify in accordance with paragraph 2 of that Schedule; and

(ii)   the duty was one to notify at any time before the expiry date;

(c)   a request shall be treated as being a request made under paragraph 5 of Schedule 6 if it satisfies the requirements of sub-paragraphs (2) and (3) of that paragraph and is made—

(i)   before any notification given in accordance with paragraph 4 of Schedule 6; or

(ii)   after such notification and—

(aa)   where practicable, at least four weeks before the expiry date; or

(bb)   where that is not practicable, as soon as reasonably practicable (whether before or after the expiry date) after the employer notified the employee of his right to make a request, but not more than four weeks after the expiry date.

4.—(1) This paragraph applies in a case where—

(a)   notice of dismissal is given on or after the commencement date of at least—

(i)   the period required by the contract of employment; or

(ii)   if longer, the period required by section 86 of the 1996 Act; and

(b)   the expiry date falls before 1st April 2007.

(2) Where this paragraph applies and the employer notifies the employee in writing of the employee's right to make a request under paragraph 5 of Schedule 6 before, or on the same day as, the day on which notice of dismissal is given—

(a)   the employer shall be treated as complying with the duty in paragraph 2 of Schedule 6;

(b)   a request shall be treated as being a request made under paragraph 5 of Schedule 6 provided it—

(i)   is made after the employer notified the employee of his right to make a request;

(ii)   satisfies the requirements of sub-paragraphs (2) and (3) of paragraph 5 of Schedule 6; and

(iii) is made—

    (aa)   where practicable, at least four weeks before the expiry date; or

    (bb)   where that is not practicable, as soon as reasonably practicable (whether before or after the expiry date) after the employer notified the employee of his right to make a request, but not more than four weeks after the expiry date.

(3) Where this paragraph applies but the employer does not notify the employee in writing of the employee's right to make a request under paragraph 5 of Schedule 6 before, or on the same day as, the day on which notice of dismissal is given—

(a)   the duty to notify in accordance with paragraph 2 of Schedule 6 does not apply;

(b)   the duty to notify in accordance with paragraph 4 of Schedule 6 applies as if—

    (i)   the employer had failed to notify in accordance with paragraph 2 of that Schedule; and

    (ii)   the duty was one to notify at any time before the expiry date;

(c)   a request shall be treated as being a request made under paragraph 5 of Schedule 6 if it satisfies the requirements of sub-paragraphs (2) and (3) of that paragraph and is made—

    (i)   before any notification given in accordance with paragraph 4 of Schedule 6; or

    (ii)   after such notification and—

        (aa)   where practicable, at least four weeks before the expiry date; or

        (bb)   where that is not practicable, as soon as reasonably practicable (whether before or after the expiry date) after the employer notified the employee of his right to make a request, but not more than four weeks after the expiry date.

5.—(1) This paragraph applies in a case where—

(a)   notice of dismissal is given on or after the commencement date and is for a period shorter than—

    (i)   the period required by the contract of employment; or

    (ii)   if longer, the period required by section 86 of the 1996 Act; and

(b)   the period of notice expires on a date falling before 1st April 2007.

(2) Where this paragraph applies—

(a)   the duty to notify in accordance with paragraph 2 of Schedule 6 does not apply;

(b)   the duty to notify in accordance with paragraph 4 of Schedule 6 applies as if—

    (i)   the employer had failed to notify in accordance with paragraph 2 of that Schedule; and

    (ii)   the duty was one to notify at any time before the expiry date;

(c) a request shall be treated as being a request made under paragraph 5 of Schedule 6 if it satisfies the requirements of sub-paragraphs (2) and (3) of that paragraph and is made—

  (i) before any notification given in accordance with paragraph 4 of Schedule 6; or

  (ii) after such notification and—

    (aa) where practicable, at least four weeks before the expiry date; or

    (bb) where that is not practicable, as soon as reasonably practicable (whether before or after the expiry date) after the employer notified the employee of his right to make a request, but not more than four weeks after the expiry date.

6. In every case to which paragraph 2, 3, 4 or 5 applies—

  (a) paragraph 10 of Schedule 6 does not apply; and

  (b) the employer is under a duty to consider any request which complies with the requirements of paragraph 2(2)(b), 2(3)(c), 3(2)(c), 4(2)(b), 4(3)(c) or 5(2)(c) in accordance with paragraphs 7 to 9 of Schedule 6.

SCHEDULE 8

Regulation 49(1)

Amendments to legislation and related transitional provisions

Part 1

Primary legislation

The Mines and Quarries Act 1954

1. The Mines and Quarries Act 1954(**a**) is amended as follows.

2.—(1) In section 42(1) (charge of winding and rope haulage apparatus when persons are carried) omit the words 'who has attained the age of twenty-two years'.

(2) In section 43(2) (charge of winding and rope haulage apparatus when persons are not carried) omit the words 'who has attained the age of eighteen years'.

(3) In section 44 (charge of conveyors at working faces) omit the words 'who has attained the age of eighteen years'.

(**a**) 1954 c 70; relevant amendments to sections 42, 43 and 44 are made by the Employment Act 1989 (c 38), sections 9 and 29(4) and by Schedule 7.

The Parliamentary Commissioner Act 1967

3. The Parliamentary Commissioner Act 1967**(a)** is amended as follows—

4.—(1) Section 1 (appointment and tenure of office) is amended in accordance with this paragraph.

(2) In subsection (2) omit the words from ', and any person' to 'during good behaviour'.

(3) After subsection (2) insert—

"(2A) A person appointed to be the Commissioner shall hold office until the end of the period for which he is appointed.

(2B) That period must be not more than seven years.

(2C) Subsection (2A) is subject to subsections (3) and (3A).".

(4) For subsection (3) substitute—

"(3) A person appointed to be the Commissioner may be—

(a) relieved of office by Her Majesty at his own request, or

(b) removed from office by Her Majesty, on the ground of misbehaviour, in consequence of Addresses from both Houses of Parliament.".

(5) After subsection (3A) insert—

"(3B) A person appointed to be the Commissioner is not eligible for re-appointment.".

5.—(2) Section 3A (appointment of acting Commissioner) is amended in accordance with this paragraph.

(2) After subsection (1) insert—

"(1A) A person appointed to act as the Commissioner ('an acting Commissioner') may have held office as the Commissioner.

(1B) A person appointed as an acting Commissioner is eligible for appointment as the Commissioner unless he has already held office as the Commissioner.".

(3) In subsection (2) for the words 'under this section' substitute 'as an acting Commissioner'.

(4) For subsection (3) substitute—

"(3) A person appointed as an acting Commissioner shall, while he holds office, be treated for all purposes, except for the purposes of section 1 and 2, and this section of this Act, as the Commissioner.".

6. The amendments made to the Parliamentary Commissioner Act 1967 apply in relation to appointments made on or after the commencement date.

(a) 1967 c 13; section 1(3A) was inserted by the Parliamentary and Health Services Commissioners Act 1987 (c 13), section 2(1).

The Pilotage Act 1987

7.—(1) The Pilotage Act 1987(**a**) is amended in accordance with this paragraph.

(2) In section 3(2) (authorisation of pilots) omit the word 'age,'.

The Social Security Contributions and Benefits Act 1992

8. The Social Security Contributions and Benefits Act 1992(**b**) is amended as follows.

9.—(1) Section 163(1) (interpretation of Part 11 and supplementary provisions) is amended in accordance with this paragraph.

(2) In the definition of 'employee' omit paragraph (b) and the word 'and' preceding it.

(3) For the definition of 'employer' substitute—

"'employer', in relation to an employee and a contract of service of his, means a person who—

    (a) under section 6 above is liable to pay secondary Class 1 contributions in relation to any earnings of the employee under the contract, or

    (b) would be liable to pay such contributions but for—

        (i) the condition in section 6(1)(b), or

        (ii) the employee being under the age of 16:".

10.—(1) Section 171(1)(**c**) (interpretation of Part 12 and supplementary provisions) is amended in accordance with this paragraph.

(2) In the definition of 'employee' omit paragraph (b) and the word 'and' preceding it.

(3) For the definition of 'employer' substitute—

"'employer', in relation to a woman who is an employee, means a person who—

    (a) under section 6 above is liable to pay secondary Class 1 contributions in relation to any of her earnings; or

    (b) would be liable to pay such contributions but for—

        (i) the condition in section 6(1)(b), or

        (ii) the employee being under the age of 16:".

(4) This paragraph applies in relation to any case where the expected week of confinement begins on or after 14th January 2007.

(**a**) 1987 c 21.

(**b**) 1992 c 4; the definition of 'employee' has been amended but in a way not relevant for the purposes of these Regulations. The definition of 'employer' has been amended by the Social Security Act 1998, (c 14), section 86(1), and Schedule 7, paragraph 74.

(**c**) The definition of 'employee' has been amended but in a way not relevant for the purposes of these Regulations. The definition of 'employer' has been amended by the Social Security Act 1998, section 86(1), and Schedule 7, paragraph 75.

11.—(1) Section 171ZJ(**a**) (Part 12ZA: supplementary) is amended in accordance with this paragraph.

(2) In subsection (1) for the definition of 'employer' substitute—

"'employer', in relation to a person who is an employee, means a person who—

(a) under section 6 above is, liable to pay secondary Class 1 contributions in relation to any of the earnings of the person who is an employee; or

(b) would be liable to pay such contributions but for—

(i) the condition in section 6(1)(b), or

(ii) the employee being under the age of 16;".

(3) In subsection (2) omit paragraph (b) and the word 'and' preceding it.

(4) This paragraph applies in relation to an entitlement to—

(a) statutory paternity pay (birth) in respect of children whose expected week of birth begins on or after 14th January 2007;

(b) statutory paternity pay (adoption) in respect of children—

(i) matched with a person who is notified of having been matched on or after the commencement date; or

(ii) placed for adoption on or after the commencement date.

12.—(1) Section 171ZS(**b**) (Part 12ZB: supplementary) is amended in accordance with this paragraph.

(2) In subsection (1) for the definition of 'employer' substitute—

"'employer', in relation to a person who is an employee, means a person who—

(a) under section 6 above is liable to pay secondary Class 1 contributions in relation to any of the earnings of the person who is an employee; or

(b) would be liable to pay such contributions but for—

(ii) the condition in section 6(1)(b), or

(ii) the employee being under the age of 16;".

(3) In subsection (2) omit paragraph (b) and the word 'and' preceding it.

(4) This paragraph applies in relation to an entitlement to statutory adoption pay in respect of children—

(a) matched with a person who is notified of having been matched on or after the commencement date; or

(b) placed for adoption on or after that commencement.

13.—(1) In Schedule 11 omit paragraph 2(a) (period of entitlement not to arise if at the relevant date the employee is over 65).

(**a**) Section 171ZJ was inserted by the Employment Act 2002 (c 22), section 2.
(**b**) Section 171ZS was inserted by the Employment Act 2002, section 4.

(2) Sub-paragraph (1) applies in relation to a period of incapacity for work which—

(a)   begins on or after the commencement date, or

(b)   begins before and continues on or after the commencement date.

(3) But in a case falling within sub-paragraph (2)(b), sub-paragraph (1) does not affect the application of paragraph 1 of Schedule 11 to the 1992 Act in relation to the part of the period of incapacity for work that falls before the commencement date.

The Health Service Commissioners Act 1993

14. The Health Service Commissioners Act 1993(**a**) is amended as follows.

15.—(1) Schedule 1 (the English Commissioner)(**b**) is amended in accordance with this paragraph.

(2) For paragraph 1 (appointment of Commissioners) substitute the following new paragraphs—

> '**1.** Her Majesty may by Letters Patent appoint a person to be the Commissioner.
>
> **1A.** Subject to paragraphs 1C and 1D a person appointed to be the Commissioner shall hold office until the end of the period for which he is appointed.
>
> **1B.** That period must be not more than seven years.
>
> **1C.** A person appointed to be the Commissioner may be relieved of office by Her Majesty at his own request.
>
> **1D.** A person appointed to be the Commissioner may be removed from office by Her Majesty, on the ground of misbehaviour, in consequence of Addresses from both Houses of Parliament.
>
> **1E.** A person appointed to be the Commissioner is not eligible for re-appointment.'.

(3) In paragraph 2 (appointment of acting Commissioners)—

(a)   after sub-paragraph (1) insert—

> '(1A) A person appointed to act as the Commissioner ("an acting Commissioner") may have held office as the Commissioner.
>
> (1B) A person appointed as an acting Commissioner is eligible for appointment as the Commissioner unless he has already held office as the Commissioner.';

(b)   in sub-paragraph (2) for the words 'under this paragraph' substitute 'as acting Commissioner,'; and

---

(**a**)   1993 c 46.
(**b**)   The schedule heading was amended by the Government of Wales Act 1998 (c 38), section 112, and Schedule 10, paragraph 16(2).

(c)   for sub-paragraph (3), substitute—

'(3) A person appointed as an acting Commissioner shall, while he holds office, be treated for all purposes, except for the purposes of paragraphs 1, 4 to 10 and this paragraph, as the Commissioner.'.

16. The amendments made to the Health Service Commissioners Act 1993 apply in relation to appointments made on or after the commencement date.

The Statutory Sick Pay Act 1994

17.—(1) The Statutory Sick Pay Act 1994(**a**) is amended in accordance with this paragraph.

(2) In section 1(2) omit the words after paragraph (b).

The Employment Tribunals Act 1996

18. The Employment Tribunals Act 1996(**b**) is amended as follows.

19.—(1) Section 18(1)(**c**) (conciliation) is amended in accordance with this paragraph.

(2) At the end of paragraph (p), omit 'or'.

(3) After paragraph (q), insert

'or

　　　　(r)   under regulation 36 of the Employment Equality (Age) Regulations 2006.'.

20.—(1) Section 21(1)(**d**) (jurisdiction of Appeal Tribunal) is amended in accordance with this paragraph.

(2) At the end of paragraph (q), omit 'or'.

(3) After paragraph (r) insert—

'or

　　　　(s)   the Employment Equality (Age) Regulations 2006.'.

The Employment Rights Act 1996

21. The 1996 Act is amended as follows.

22.—(1) Section 98 (fairness of dismissal: general) is amended as follows.

(2) In subsection (2), after paragraph (b) insert—

　　　　'(ba)   is retirement of the employee,'.

(**a**) 1994 c 2.
(**b**) 1996 c 17.
(**c**) Section 18(1)(p) was amended by SI 2004/3426, regulation 34(c). Section 18(1)(q) was inserted by SI 2006/349, Schedule 1, paragraph 9.
(**d**) Section 21(1)(q) was amended by SI2004/3426, regulation 37(c). Section 21(r) was inserted by SI 2006/349, Schedule 1, paragraph 10.

(3) After subsection (2) insert—

'(2A) Subsections (1) and (2) are subject to sections 98ZA to 98ZF.'.

(4) After subsection (3) insert—

'(3A) In any case where the employer has fulfilled the requirements of subsection (1) by showing that the reason (or the principal reason) for the dismissal is retirement of the employee, the question whether the dismissal is fair or unfair shall be determined in accordance with section 98ZG. '.

(5) In subsection (4) for 'Where' substitute 'In any other case where'.

23. After section 98 insert—

'Retirement

No normal retirement age: dismissal before 65

98ZA.—(1) This section applies to the dismissal of an employee if—

    (a) the employee has no normal retirement age, and

    (b) the operative date of termination falls before the date when the employee reaches the age of 65.

(2) Retirement of the employee shall not be taken to be the reason (or a reason) for the dismissal.

No normal retirement age: dismissal at or after 65

98ZB.—(1) This section applies to the dismissal of an employee if—

    (a) the employee has no normal retirement age, and

    (b) the operative date of termination falls on or after the date when the employee reaches the age of 65.

(2) In a case where—

    (a) the employer has notified the employee in accordance with paragraph 2 of Schedule 6 to the 2006 Regulations, and

    (b) the contract of employment terminates on the intended date of retirement,

retirement of the employee shall be taken to be the only reason for the dismissal by the employer and any other reason shall be disregarded.

(3) In a case where—

    (a) the employer has notified the employee in accordance with paragraph 2 of Schedule 6 to the 2006 Regulations, but

    (b) the contract of employment terminates before the intended date of retirement,

retirement of the employee shall not be taken to be the reason (or a reason) for dismissal.

(4) In a case where—

(a) the employer has not notified the employee in accordance with paragraph 2 of Schedule 6 to the 2006 Regulations, and

(b) there is an intended date of retirement in relation to the dismissal, but

(c) the contract of employment terminates before the intended date of retirement,

retirement of the employee shall not be taken to be the reason (or a reason) for dismissal.

(5) In all other cases where the employer has not notified the employee in accordance with paragraph 2 of Schedule 6 to the 2006 Regulations, particular regard shall be had to the matters in section 98ZF when determining the reason (or principal reason) for dismissal.

Normal retirement age: dismissal before retirement age

98ZC.—(1) This section applies to the dismissal of an employee if—

(a) the employee has a normal retirement age, and

(b) the operative date of termination falls before the date when the employee reaches the normal retirement age.

(2) Retirement of the employee shall not be taken to be the reason (or a reason) for the dismissal.

Normal retirement age 65 or higher: dismissal at or after retirement age

98ZD.—(1) This section applies to the dismissal of an employee if—

(a) the employee has a normal retirement age,

(b) the normal retirement age is 65 or higher, and

(c) the operative date of termination falls on or after the date when the employee reaches the normal retirement age.

(2) In a case where—

(a) the employer has notified the employee in accordance with paragraph 2 of Schedule 6 to the 2006 Regulations, and

(b) the contract of employment terminates on the intended date of retirement,

retirement of the employee shall be taken to be the only reason for the dismissal by the employer and any other reason shall be disregarded.

(3) In a case where—

(a) the employer has notified the employee in accordance with paragraph 2 of Schedule 6 to the 2006 Regulations, but

(b) the contract of employment terminates before the intended date of retirement,

retirement of the employee shall not be taken to be the reason (or a reason) for dismissal.

(4) In a case where—

(a) the employer has not notified the employee in accordance with paragraph 2 of Schedule 6 to the 2006 Regulations, and

(b) there is an intended date of retirement in relation to the dismissal, but

(c) the contract of employment terminates before the intended date of retirement,

retirement of the employee shall not be taken to be the reason (or a reason) for dismissal.

(5) In all other cases where the employer has not notified the employee in accordance with paragraph 2 of Schedule 6 to the 2006 Regulations, particular regard shall be had to the matters in section 98ZF when determining the reason (or principal reason) for dismissal.

Normal retirement age below 65: dismissal at or after retirement age

98ZE.—(1) This section applies to the dismissal of an employee if—

(a) the employee has a normal retirement age,

(b) the normal retirement age is below 65, and

(c) the operative date of termination falls on or after the date when the employee reaches the normal retirement age.

(2) If it is unlawful discrimination under the 2006 Regulations for the employee to have that normal retirement age, retirement of the employee shall not be taken to be the reason (or a reason) for dismissal.

(3) Subsections (4) to (7) apply if it is not unlawful discrimination under the 2006 Regulations for the employee to have that normal retirement age.

(4) In a case where—

(a) the employer has notified the employee in accordance with paragraph 2 of Schedule 6 to the 2006 Regulations, and

(b) the contract of employment terminates on the intended date of retirement,

retirement of the employee shall be taken to be the only reason for dismissal by the employer and any other reason shall be disregarded.

(5) In a case where—

(a) the employer has notified the employee in accordance with paragraph 2 of Schedule 6 to the 2006 Regulations, but

(b) the contract of employment terminates before the intended date of retirement,

retirement of the employee shall not be taken to be the reason (or a reason) for dismissal.

(6) In a case where—

(a) the employer has not notified the employee in accordance with paragraph 2 of Schedule 6 to the 2006 Regulations, and

(b) there is an intended date of retirement in relation to the dismissal, but

(c) the contract of employment terminates before the intended date of retirement,

retirement of the employee shall not be taken to be the reason (or a reason) for dismissal.

(7) In all other cases where the employer has not notified the employee in accordance with paragraph 2 of Schedule 6 to the 2006 Regulations, particular regard shall be had to the matters in section 98ZF when determining the reason (or principal reason) for dismissal

Reason for dismissal: particular matters

98ZF.—(1) These are the matters to which particular regard is to be had in accordance with section 98ZB(5), 98ZD(5) or 98ZE(7)—

(a) whether or not the employer has notified the employee in accordance with paragraph 4 of Schedule 6 to the 2006 Regulations;

(b) if the employer has notified the employee in accordance with that paragraph, how long before the notified retirement date the notification was given;

(c) whether or not the employer has followed, or sought to follow, the procedures in paragraph 7 of Schedule 6 to the 2006 Regulations.

(2) In subsection (1)(b) "notified retirement date" means the date notified to the employee in accordance with paragraph 4 of Schedule 6 to the 2006 Regulations as the date on which the employer intends to retire the employee.

Retirement dismissals: fairness

98ZG.—(1) This section applies if the reason (or principal reason) for a dismissal is retirement of the employee.

(2) The employee shall be regarded as unfairly dismissed if, and only if, there has been a failure on the part of the employer to comply with an obligation imposed on him by any of the following provisions of Schedule 6 to the 2006 Regulations—

(a) paragraph 4 (notification of retirement, if not already given under paragraph 2),

(b) paragraphs 6 and 7 (duty to consider employee's request not to be retired),

(c) paragraph 8 (duty to consider appeal against decision to refuse request not to be retired).

Interpretation

98ZH. In sections 98ZA to 98ZG—

"2006 Regulations" means the Employment Equality (Age) Regulations 2006;

"intended date of retirement" means the date which, by virtue of paragraph 1(2) of Schedule 6 to the 2006 Regulations, is the intended date of retirement in relation to a particular dismissal;

"normal retirement age", in relation to an employee, means the age at which employees in the employer's undertaking who hold, or have held, the same kind of position as the employee are normally required to retire;

"operative date of termination" means—

(a) where the employer terminates the employee's contract of employment by notice, the date on which the notice expires, or

(b) where the employer terminates the contract of employment without notice, the date on which the termination takes effect.

Other dismissals".

24. In section 108(**a**) (qualifying period of employment) in subsection (3) (cases where no qualifying period of employment is required)—

(a) at the end of paragraph (l) omit 'or'; and

(b) after paragraph (m) insert—

'or

(n) paragraph (a) or (b) of paragraph 13(5) of Schedule 6 to the Employment Equality (Age) Regulations 2006 applies.'.

25. Omit section 109(**b**) (upper age limit on unfair dismissal right).

26.—(1) Section 112(**c**) (remedies for unfair dismissal: orders and compensation) is amended as follows.

(2) In subsection (5)(a) after 'section' insert '98ZG or'.

27.—(1) Section 119 (basic award) is amended as follows.

(2) Omit subsections (4) and (5).

28.—(1) Section 120(**d**) (basic award: minimum in certain cases) is amended as follows.

(2) In subsection (1A) after 'section' insert '98ZG or'.

29. In section 126(1)(**e**) (acts which are both unfair dismissal and discrimination), for paragraph (b) substitute—

'(b) any one or more of the following—

(i) the Sex Discrimination Act 1975;

(**a**) Section 108(1) was amended by SI 2004/3426, regulation 31(2)(b). Section 108(m) was inserted by SI 2006/1349, Schedule 1, paragraph 6.

(**b**) Section 109 has been amended but the amendments are not relevant for the purposes of these Regulations.

(**c**) Subsection (5) was inserted by the Employment Act 2002 (c 22), section 34(3).

(**d**) Subsection (1A) inserted by the Employment Act 2002, sections 34(1) and (6).

(**e**) Section 126(1)(b) was substituted by the Employment Rights (Dispute Resolution) Act 1998 (c 8), section 14(3), and has been amended since, but the amendments are not relevant for the purposes of these Regulations.

    (ii) the Race Relations Act 1976;

    (iii) the Disability Discrimination Act 1995;

    (iv) the Employment Equality (Sexual Orientation) Regulations 2003;

    (v) the Employment Equality (Religion or Belief) Regulations 2003;

    (vi) the Employment Equality (Age) Regulations 2006.'.

30. Section 156 (upper age limit) is repealed.

31. Section 158 (pension rights) is repealed.

32.—(1) Section 162 (amount of a redundancy payment) is amended in accordance with this paragraph.

(2) Subsections (4), (5) and (8) are repealed.

(3) In subsection (6), for the words 'Subsections (1) to (5)'substitute 'Subsections (1) to (3)'.

33. In relation to any case where the date that is the relevant date by virtue of section 153 of the 1996 Act falls before the commencement date, paragraphs 30 to 32 do not apply.

34.—(1) Section 209 (powers to amend Act) is amended as follows.

(2) In subsection (5)(**a**) omit '109(1),'.

35.—(1) Section 211 (period of continuous employment) is amended in accordance with this paragraph.

(2) In paragraph (a) of subsection (1) for the words 'subsections (2) and' substitute 'subsection'.

(3) Subsection (2) is repealed.

The Employment Act 2002

36.—(1) The Employment Act 2002 is amended in accordance with this paragraph.

(2) At the end of each of the following Schedules—

    (a) Schedule 3 (tribunal jurisdictions to which section 31 applies for adjustment of awards for non-completion of statutory procedure);

    (b) Schedule 4 (tribunal jurisdictions to which section 32 applies for complaints where the employee must first submit a statement of grievance to employer); and

    (c) Schedule 5 (tribunal jurisdictions to which section 38 applies in relation to proceedings where the employer has failed to give a statement of employment particulars),

---

(**a**) Section 209(5) was amended by the Employment Relations Act 1999 (c 26), Section 44 and Schedule 9.

insert—

>   'Regulation 36 of the Employment Equality (Age) Regulations 2006 (discrimination in the employment field)'.

The Equality Act 2006

37. The Equality Act 2006(**a**) is amended as follows.

38.—(1) Section 14(1) (codes of practice) is amended in accordance with this paragraph.

(2) At the end of paragraph (g) omit 'and'.

(3) After paragraph (h) insert—

>   'and

>>   (i) Parts 2 and 3 of the Employment Equality (Age) Regulations 2006.'.

39.—(1) Section 27(1) (conciliation) is amended in accordance with this paragraph.

(2) At the end of paragraph (f) omit 'or'.

(3) After paragraph (g) insert—

>   'or

>>   (h) regulation 39 of the Employment Equality (Age) Regulations 2006 (Jurisdiction of County and Sheriff Courts).'.

40.—(1) Section 33(1) (equality and human rights enactments) is amended in accordance with this paragraph.

(2) At the end of paragraph (g) omit 'and'.

(3) After paragraph (h) insert—

>   'and

>>   (i) the Employment Equality (Age) Regulations 2006.'.

Part 2

Other legislation

41.—(1) The Coal and Other Mines (Locomotives) Regulations 1956(**b**), Schedule 1 to the Coal and Other Mines (Locomotives) Order 1956 is amended in accordance with this paragraph.

(2) In regulation 17(1) (drivers of locomotives) omit the words 'and no appointed driver shall operate a locomotive hauling persons in vehicles unless he has attained the age of—

>   (a)   in the case of a mine of shale, eighteen years;

(**a**) 2006 c 3.
(**b**) SI 1956/1771.

(b)   in the case of any other mine, twenty-one years'.

42.—(1) The Stratified Ironstone, Shale and Fireclay Mines (Explosives) Regulations 1956(**a**) are amended in accordance with this paragraph.

(2) In regulation 3 (qualification of shot firers) omit the words 'he has attained the age of twenty-one years; and'.

43.—(1) The Miscellaneous Mines (Explosives) Regulations 1959(**b**) are amended in accordance with this paragraph.

(2) Omit regulation 6(2).

(3) In regulation 8(2) (control of issue of detonators) omit the words 'has attained the age of eighteen years and'.

44.—(1) The Lynemouth Mine (Diesel Vehicles and Storage Battery Vehicles) Special Regulations 1961(**c**) are amended in accordance with this paragraph.

(2) In regulation 15 after the words 'Regulations 17' insert 'as amended by the Employment Equality (Age) Regulations 2006'.

45.—(1) The South Crofty Mine (Locomotive) Special Regulations 1965(**d**) are amended in accordance with this paragraph.

(2) In regulation 11(2) omit the words 'has attained the age of twenty-one years and'.

46.—(1) The Glebe Mine (Locomotives and Diesel Vehicles) Special Regulations 1967(**e**) are amended in accordance with this paragraph.

(2) In regulation 15(2) omit the words 'has attained the age of eighteen years and'.

47.—(1) The Winsford Rock Salt Mine (Diesel Vehicles and Storage Battery Vehicles) Special Regulations 1971(**f**) are amended in accordance with this paragraph.

(2) In regulation 14(2) omit the words 'is under the age of twenty-one years and'.

48.—(1) The Thoresby Mine (Cable Reel Load-Haul-Dump Vehicles) Special Regulations 1978(**g**) are amended in accordance with this paragraph.

(2) In regulation 17 after the words 'Regulations 17' insert 'as amended by the Employment Equality (Age) Regulations 2006'.

49. The Statutory Sick Pay (General) Regulations 1982(**h**) are amended as follows.

50.—(1) Regulation 16 (meaning of 'employee') is amended in accordance with this paragraph.

(**a**) SI 1956/1943.
(**b**) SI 1959/2258.
(**c**) SI1961/2445.
(**d**) SI 1965/759.
(**e**) SI 1967/1335.
(**f**) SI 1971/50.
(**g**) SI 1978/119.
(**h**) SI 1982/894; regulation 17(2) was amended by SI 1999/567, regulation 13.

(2) In paragraph (1)—

    (a)   at the beginning insert the words 'Subject to paragraph (1ZA),', and

    (b)   omit the words 'over the age of 16'.

(3) After paragraph (1) insert—

> '(1ZA) Any person under the age of 16 who would have been treated as an employed earner or, as the case may be, would have been treated otherwise than as an employed earner by virtue of the Social Security (Categorisation of Earners) Regulations 1978 had he been aged 16 or over, shall be treated as if he is aged 16 or over for the purposes of paragraph (1).'.

51.—(1) Regulation 17(2) (meaning of 'earnings') is amended in accordance with this paragraph.

(2) At the end of sub-paragraph (a) insert '(or would have been so excluded had he not been under the age of 16)'.

(3) At the end of sub-paragraph (b) insert '(or where such a payment or amount would have been so excluded and in consequence he would not have been entitled to statutory sick pay had he not been under the age of 16)'.

52. The Statutory Maternity Pay (General) Regulations 1986(**a**) are amended as follows.

53.—(1) Regulation 17 (meaning of 'employee') is amended in accordance with this paragraph.

(2) In paragraph (1)—

    (a)   at the beginning insert the words 'Subject to paragraph (1A),', and

    (b)   omit the words 'over the age of 16'.

(3) After paragraph (1) insert—

> '(1A) Any woman under the age of 16 who would have been treated as an employed earner or, as the case may be, would have been treated otherwise than as an employed earner by virtue of the Social Security (Categorisation of Earners) Regulations 1978 had she been aged 16 or over, shall be treated as if she is aged 16 or over for the purposes of paragraph (1).'.

54.—(1) Regulation 20(2)(**b**) (Meaning of 'earnings') is amended in accordance with this paragraph.

(2) At the end of sub-paragraph (a) insert '(or would have been so excluded had she not been under the age of 16)'.

(3) At the end of sub-paragraph (b) insert '(or where such a payment or amount would have been so excluded and in consequence she would not have been entitled to statutory maternity pay had she not been under the age of 16)'.

(4) This paragraph applies in relation to any case where the expected week of confinement begins on or after 14th January 2007.

(**a**) SI 1986/1960.
(**b**) Regulation 20(2) was amended by SI 1999/567, regulation 12.

55.—(1) The Coal and Other Safety-Lamp Mines (Explosives) Regulations 1993(**a**) are amended in accordance with this paragraph.

(2) In regulation 4(4) (appointment of shotfirers and trainee shotfirers) omit the words 'he is at least 21 years of age and'.

56.—(1) The Employment Tribunals (Interest on Awards In Discrimination Cases) Regulations 1996(**b**) are amended in accordance with this paragraph.

(2) In sub-paragraph (b) of the definition of 'an award under the relevant legislation' in regulation 1(2) (interpretation)—

    (a) after 'regulation 30(1)(b) of the Employment Equality (Sexual Orientation) Regulations 2003' omit 'or'; and

    (b) after 'regulation 30(1)(b) of the Employment Equality (Religion or Belief) Regulations 2003' insert—

        'or regulation 38(1)(b) of the Employment Equality (Age) Regulations 2006'.

57.—(1) The Employment Protection (Continuity of Employment) Regulations 1996(**c**) are amended in accordance with this paragraph.

(2) In regulation 2 (application)—

    (a) omit the word 'or' at the end of paragraph (e); and

    (b) after paragraph (f) insert—

    ', or

        (g) a decision taken arising out of the use of the statutory duty to consider procedure contained in Schedule 6 to the Employment Equality (Age) Regulations 2006.'.

58.—(1) The National Minimum Wage Regulations 1999(**d**) are amended in accordance with this paragraph.

(2) Omit regulation 12(2)(a).

(3) Omit paragraphs (2) to (6) of regulation 13.

(4) In regulation 13(7) for the words 'Paragraphs (1) and (2) do' substitute 'Paragraph (1) does'.

(5) In relation to any case where, before the commencement date, a worker within the meaning of regulation 12(2) has attained the age of 26, sub-paragraph (2) does not apply.

59. The Statutory Paternity Pay and Statutory Adoption Pay (General) Regulations 2002(**e**) are amended as follows.

(**a**) SI 1993/208.
(**b**) SI 1996/2803; regulation 1(2) was amended by SI 2003/1661, regulation 1(1), and SI 2003/1660, regulation 1(1).
(**c**) SI 1996/3147; regulation 2(c) was inserted by SI 2001/1188, regulation 1(1), and regulation 2(f) was amended by SI 2004/752, regulation 17(e).
(**d**) SI 1999/584; regulation 13 has been amended, but the amendments are not relevant for the purposes of these Regulations.
(**e**) SI 2002/2822.

60.—(1) Regulation 32 (Treatment of persons as employees) is amended in accordance with this paragraph.

(2) In paragraph (1)–

    (a)   at the beginning insert the words 'Subject to paragraph (1A),', and

    (b)   omit the words 'over the age of 16'.

(3) After paragraph (1) insert—

    '(1A) Any person under the age of 16 who would have been treated as an employed earner or, as the case may be, would have been treated otherwise than as an employed earner by virtue of the Social Security (Categorisation of Earners) Regulations 1978 had he been aged 16 or over, shall be treated as if he is aged 16 or over for the purposes of paragraph (1).'.

61.—(1) Regulation 39(2) (Meaning of 'earnings') is amended in accordance with this paragraph.

(2) At the end of sub-paragraph (a) insert '(or would have been so excluded had he not been under the age of 16)'.

(3) At the end of sub-paragraph (b) insert '(or where such a payment or amount would have been so excluded and in consequence he would not have been entitled to statutory paternity pay or, as the case may be, statutory adoption pay had he not been under the age of 16)'.

62.—(1) Schedule 1A (occupational pension schemes) to the Employment Equality (Religion or Belief) Regulations 2003(**a**) is amended in accordance with this paragraph.

(2) In paragraph 1(1)—

    (a)   in the definition of 'active member', 'deferred member', 'managers', 'pensioner member' and 'trustees or managers', omit the words 'as at the date of the coming into force of these Regulations', and

    (b)   in the definition of 'occupational pension scheme' omit the words 'as at the date of the coming into force of these Regulations'.

(3) In paragraph 1(2) omit the words 'as at the date of the coming into force of these Regulations'.

63.—(1) Schedule 1A (occupational pension schemes) to the Employment Equality (Sexual Orientation) Regulations 2003(**b**) is amended in accordance with this paragraph.

(2) In paragraph 1(1)—

    (a)   in the definition of 'active member', 'deferred member', 'managers', 'pensioner member' and 'trustees or managers', omit the words 'as at the date of the coming into force of these Regulations', and

    (b)   in the definition of 'occupational pension scheme' omit the words 'as at the date of the coming into force of these Regulations'.

(**a**) SI 2003/1660; Schedule 1A was inserted by SI 2003/2828, regulation 3.
(**b**) SI 2003/1661; Schedule 1A was inserted by SI 2003/2827, regulation 3.

(3) In paragraph 1(2) omit the words 'as at the date of the coming into force of these Regulations'.

64.—b) The Employment Act 2002 (Dispute Resolution) Regulations 2004(**a**) are amended in accordance with this paragraph.

(2) In regulation 4(1) (dismissals to which the dismissal and disciplinary procedures do not apply)—

    (a)   omit the word 'or' at the end of sub-paragraph (f); and

    (b)   after sub-paragraph (g) insert —

      ', or

          (h)   the reason (or, if more than one, the principal reason) for the dismissal is retirement of the employee (to be determined in accordance with section 98ZA to 98ZF of the 1996 Act(**b**))'.

SCHEDULE 9

Regulation 49(2)

Repeals and revocations

(1) Repeals	
Short title and chapter	Extent of repeal
Marriage (Scotland) Act 1977 (c 15)	In section 9(1) the proviso, In section 12 the proviso, and In section 17 the proviso
Education (Scotland) Act 1980 (.44)	Section 89
Solicitors (Scotland) Act 1980 (c 46)	Section 6(1)(a)
Weights and Measures Act 1985 (c 72)	Section 73(3)
Electricity Act 1989 (c 29)	In Schedule 10, paragraph 9(3)
Judicial Pensions and Retirement Act 1993(c 8)	In Schedule 6, paragraph 66
Scottish Public Services Ombudsman Act 2002 (asp 11)	In Schedule 1, paragraph 4(1)(c) In Schedule 1, in paragraph 4(3), the words in brackets
Freedom of Information (Scotland) Act 2002 (asp 13)	Section 42(4)(b) In Section 42(5), the words in brackets

(2) Revocations	
Title and reference	Extent of revocation
Coal and Other Mines (Sidings) Regulations 1956, Schedule to the Coal and Other Mines (Sidings) Order 1956	Regulation 21 In Regulation 22, the definition of locomotive

---

(**a**) SI 2004/752.
(**b**) Sections 98ZA to 98ZF are inserted by regulation 49 of, and paragraph 23 of Schedule 8 to, these Regulations.

(2) Revocations	
Title and reference	Extent of revocation
(SI 1956/1773)	
The Management and Administration of Safety and Health in Mines Regulations 1993 (SI 1993/1897)	Regulation 17(2)

EXPLANATORY NOTE

(This note is not part of the Regulations)

These Regulations, which are made under section 2(2) of the European Communities Act 1972 (c .68), implement (in Great Britain) Council Directive 2000/78/EC of 27 November 2000 establishing a general framework for equal treatment in employment (OJ L 303, 2.12.2000, p 16) so far as it relates to discrimination on grounds of age. The Regulations make it unlawful to discriminate on grounds of age in employment and vocational training. They prohibit direct discrimination, indirect discrimination, victimisation, instructions to discriminate and harassment.

Direct discrimination, defined in regulation 3(1)(a), arises where a person is treated less favourably than another on grounds of his age or apparent age. Indirect discrimination, defined in regulation 3(1)(b), arises where a provision, criterion or practice, which is applied generally, puts persons of a particular age or age group at a disadvantage. Discrimination will occur where the difference in treatment or disadvantage cannot be shown to be a proportionate means of achieving a legitimate aim. Victimisation, defined in regulation 4, occurs where a person receives less favourable treatment than others by reason of the fact that he has brought (or given evidence in) proceedings, made an allegation or otherwise done anything under or by virtue of the Regulations. Instructions to discriminate are dealt with in regulation 5. It is a form of discrimination to treat a person less favourably than another because he has failed to carry out an instruction to discriminate or because he has complained about receiving such an instruction. Harassment, defined in regulation 6, occurs where a person is subjected to unwanted conduct on grounds of age with the purpose or effect of violating his dignity, or creating an intimidating, hostile, degrading, humiliating or offensive environment for him.

Regulations 7 to 24 prohibit discrimination, victimisation and harassment in the fields of employment and vocational training. In particular, they protect employees (regulation 7), contract workers (regulation 9), office-holders (including police and those seconded to the Serious Organised Crime Agency (regulations 12, 13 and 14)), and partners in firms (regulation 17). They not only prohibit discrimination etc by employers, but also by trustees and managers of occupational pension schemes (regulation 11), trade organisations (regulation 18), qualifications bodies (regulation 19), providers of vocational training (regulation 20), employment agencies (regulation 21) and institutions of further and higher education (regulation 23). By virtue of regulation 24, discrimination, victimisation or harassment occurring after the relevant relationship has ended is unlawful if it arises out of, and is closely connected to, the relationship. The Regulations also apply to Crown servants and Parliamentary staff (regulations 44, 45 and 46). Regulation 43 and Schedule 5 address the validity of discriminatory terms in contracts and collective agreements.

Not all differences of treatment on grounds of age are unlawful. There are exceptions: in regulation 27 in relation to acts done in order to comply with a statutory provision; in regulation 28 in relation to acts related to national security; in regulation 29 for positive action; in regulation 30 in relation to retirement; in regulation 31 in relation to the national minimum wage; in regulation 32 in relation to the provision of certain employment benefits based on length of service; in regulation 33 in relation to the provision of enhanced redundancy payments; and in regulation 34 in relation to the provision of life assurance cover to workers who have had to retire early on grounds of ill-health. Regulation 8 provides an exception where possessing a characteristic related to age is a genuine and determining occupational requirement for a post if it is proportionate to apply the requirement in the particular case. Schedule 2 provides exceptions for various rules, practices actions and decisions relating to occupational pension schemes.

Regulations 35 to 42 deal with enforcement and provide remedies for individuals, including compensation, by way of proceedings in employment tribunals and in the county or sheriff courts. There are special provisions about the burden of proof in those cases in regulations 37 and 40, which transfer the burden to a respondent to a case once a complainant has established facts from which a court or tribunal could conclude, in the absence of an adequate explanation, that an act of discrimination or harassment has been committed by the respondent. Regulation 41 and Schedules 3 and 4 also include a questionnaire procedure to assist complainants in obtaining information from respondents.

Schedule 6 establishes a new duty on employers to consider requests by employees to continue working beyond retirement. Schedule 7 contains transitional provisions in relation to that new duty.

Schedule 8 amends legislation containing age-discriminatory provisions that cannot be shown to be a proportionate means of achieving a legitimate aim. It also includes amendments to the Employment Rights Act 1996 (c 18), which introduce a new potentially fair ground for dismissal of employees – dismissal on the grounds of retirement (where the duty to consider procedure in Schedule 6 has been followed).

Schedule 9 contains repeals and revocations.

A full Regulatory Impact Assessment report of the effect that these Regulations will have on the costs to business and a Transposition Note are freely available to the public from the Selected Employment Rights Branch, Bay 391, Department of Trade and Industry, 1 Victoria Street, London SW1H 0ET. Copies have also been placed in the libraries of both Houses of Parliament.

Appendix 2

ACAS: A GUIDE FOR EMPLOYERS[1]

CONTENTS

---

[1]   ACAS A Guide for Employers: Age and the Workplace: Putting the Employment Equality (Age) Regulations 2006 into practice.

INTRODUCTION

From 1 October 2006 the Employment Equality (Age) Regulations make it unlawful to discriminate against workers, employees, job seekers and trainees because of their age. This booklet describes the regulations and gives you guidance on how to implement them.

Terms in this guide – workers and employees

Workers are covered in the regulations and in this guidance. Workers often undertake roles similar to employees but do not have contracts of employment like employees, these include office holders, police, barristers and partners in a business.

Our Guidance uses the term 'employee' throughout to cover all workers except under length of service issues, retirement, and right to request which are for a narrower range of employees.

Fairness at work and good job performance go hand in hand. Tackling discrimination helps to attract, motivate and retain staff and enhances your reputation as an employer. Eliminating discrimination helps everyone to have an equal opportunity to work and to develop their skills.

Employees who are subjected to discrimination, harassment or victimisation may:

- be unhappy, less productive and less motivated
- resign
- make a complaint to an employment tribunal.

In addition employers may find:

- their reputation as a business and as an employer may be damaged
- the cost of recruitment and training will increase because of higher employee turnover
- they may be liable to pay compensation following a claim to an employment tribunal – there is no upper limit to the amount of this compensation.

There is already legislation to protect people against discrimination on the grounds of sex, race, disability, gender reassignment, sexual orientation and religion or belief.

The new regulations should pose few difficulties in organisations where people are treated fairly and with consideration.

This guidance aims to:

- help employers and vocational training providers fulfil their obligations under the Employment Equality (Age) Regulations 2006

- make employees, job seekers and trainees aware of how they will be affected by the regulations.

WHAT THE REGULATIONS SAY – IN SUMMARY

These regulations apply to all employers, private and public sector vocational training providers, trade unions, professional organisations, employer organisations and trustees and managers of occupational pension schemes. In this context an employer is anyone who has employees or who enters into a contract with a person for them to do work. The regulations cover recruitment, terms and conditions, promotions, transfers, dismissals and training. They do not cover the provision of goods and services.

The regulations make it unlawful on the grounds of age to:

- discriminate directly against anyone – that is, to treat them less favourably than others because of their age – unless objectively justified

- discriminate indirectly against anyone – that is, to apply a criterion, provision or practice which disadvantages people of a particular age unless it can be objectively justified

- subject someone to harassment. Harassment is unwanted conduct that violates a person's dignity or creates an intimidating, hostile, degrading, humiliating or offensive environment for them having regard to all the circumstances including the perception of the victim

- victimise someone because they have made or intend to make a complaint or allegation or have given or intend to give evidence in relation to a complaint of discrimination on grounds of age

- discriminate against someone, in certain circumstances, after the working relationship has ended.

Employers could be responsible for the acts of employees who discriminate on grounds of age. This makes it important to train staff about the regulations.

Upper age limits on unfair dismissal and redundancy will be removed.

There will be a national default retirement age of 65, making compulsory retirement below 65 unlawful unless objectively justified.

Employees will have the right to request to work beyond 65 or any other retirement age set by the company. The employer has a duty to consider such requests.

There are limited circumstances when discrimination may be lawful (see section on genuine occupational requirements, objective justifications, exceptions and exemptions).

This guide does not use the precise legal terms contained within the regulations – reference needs to be made to the regulations.

GUIDANCE FOR EMPLOYERS

What do the regulations mean? A brief explanation of the regulations

Direct discrimination

Direct discrimination is less favourable treatment because of someone's age.

For example it will be unlawful on the grounds of age to:

- decide not to employ someone
- dismiss them
- refuse to provide them with training
- deny them promotion
- give them adverse terms and conditions
- retire an employee before the employer's usual retirement age (if there is one) or retire an employee before the default retirement age of 65 without an objective justification (see page [220]).

    Example: Whilst being interviewed, a job applicant says that she took her professional qualification 30 years ago. Although she has all the skills and competences required of the job holder, the organisation decides not to offer her the job because of her age. This is direct discrimination.

    Note: A job applicant can make a claim to an employment tribunal, it is not necessary for them to have been employed by the organisation to make a claim of discrimination.

Indirect discrimination

Indirect discrimination means selection criteria, policies, benefits, employment rules or any other practices which, although they are applied to all employees, have the effect of disadvantaging people of a particular age unless the practice can be justified. Indirect discrimination is unlawful whether it is intentional or not.

Lawful discrimination

There are limited circumstances when it is lawful to treat people differently because of their age.

It is not unlawful to discriminate on the grounds of age if:

- there is an objective justification for treating people differently – for example, it might be necessary to fix a maximum age for the recruitment or promotion of employees (this maximum age might reflect the training requirements of the post or the need for a reasonable period of employment before retirement)

- where a person is older than, or within six months of, the employer's normal retirement age, or 65 if the employer doesn't have one, there is a specific exemption allowing employers to refuse to recruit that person.

- the discrimination is covered by one of the exceptions or exemptions given in the regulations – for example pay related to the National Minimum Wage

- there is a genuine occupational requirement (GOR) that a person must be of a certain age – for example, if you are producing a play which has parts for older or younger characters.

For more details see the section on genuine occupational requirements, objective justifications, exceptions and exemptions on page [218].

Harassment

Harassment includes behaviour that is offensive, frightening or in any way distressing. It may be intentional bullying which is obvious or violent, but it can also be unintentional, subtle and insidious. It may involve nicknames, teasing, name calling or other behaviour which is not with malicious intent but which is upsetting. It may be about the individual's age or it may be about the age of those with whom the individual associates. It may not be targeted at an individual(s) but consist of a general culture which, for instance, appears to tolerate the telling of ageist jokes.

You may be held responsible for the actions of your employees – as well as the employees being individually responsible. If harassment takes place in the workplace or at a time and place associated with the workplace, for example a work-related social gathering, you may be liable. You may be ordered to pay compensation unless it can be shown that you took reasonable steps to prevent harassment. Individuals who harass may also be ordered to pay compensation.

It is good practice to protect your workers from harassment by third parties, such as service users and customers.

When you are investigating claims of harassment, consider all the circumstances before reaching a conclusion. Harassment is often subjective so think carefully about the complainant's perception of what has happened to them. Ask yourself if what has taken place could 'be reasonably considered to have caused offence?'

> **Example:** A young employee is continually told he is 'wet behind the ears' and 'straight out of the pram' which he finds humiliating and distressing. This is harassment.

> **Example:** An employee has a father working in the same workplace. People in the workplace often tell jokes about 'old fogies' and tease the employee about teaching 'old dogs new tricks'. This may be harassment on the grounds of age, even though it is not the victim's own age that is the subject of the teasing.

Victimisation

Victimisation is when an individual is treated detrimentally because they have made a complaint or intend to make a complaint about discrimination or harassment or have given evidence or intend to give evidence relating to a complaint about discrimination or harassment.

They may become labelled 'troublemaker', denied promotion or training, or be 'sent to Coventry' by their colleagues. If this happens or if you fail to take reasonable steps to prevent it from happening, you may be ordered to pay compensation. Individuals who victimise may also be ordered to pay compensation.

> **Example:** An employee claims discrimination against their employer on the grounds of age. A work colleague gives evidence on their behalf at the employment tribunal. When the work colleague applies for promotion her application is rejected even though she is able to show she has all the necessary skills and experience. Her manager maintains she is a 'troublemaker' because she had given evidence at the tribunal and should not be promoted. This is victimisation.

Discrimination, harassment or victimisation following the end of a working relationship covers issues such as references either written or verbal.

> **Example:** A manager is approached by someone from another organisation. He says that Ms 'A' has applied for a job and asks for a reference. The manager

says that he cannot recommend her as she was not accepted by other staff because she was 'too young and inexperienced'. This is direct discrimination because of age.

An equality policy and action plan

You can start to address fairness at work by writing an equality policy or updating an existing one – with an action plan to back it up. You may already have equal opportunity or diversity policies which cover age but, if not, age should now be included. It is good practice in drawing up a policy to consult with your workforce or their representatives.

To make sure age discrimination is eliminated in your workforce draw up an action plan to review your policies for:

- recruitment, selection and promotion
- training
- pay, benefits and other conditions
- bullying and harassment
- retirement.

Also consider the make up of your workforce and whether positive action is required to tackle any age imbalance (guidance on positive action can be found on page [219]).

Ensure that all employees know about your equality policy and what is expected of them; a communications strategy should be a key part of your action plan.

Employees are often attracted to an organisation if it has a robust equality policy. Although not a legal necessity, such a policy makes applicants feel confident and discourages those who do not embrace equality of opportunity.

Acas can help you to draw up and implement an equality policy and to train you and your employees to use it. For further information see the Acas booklet *Tackling discrimination and promoting equality – good practice guidance for employers*.

Recruitment

See comment about specific recruitment exemption – on page [205].

Base your decisions about recruitment on the skills required to do the job. Provide training to help those making judgements to be objective and avoid stereotyping people because of their age.

Application form

Remove age/date of birth from the main application form and include it in a diversity monitoring form to be retained by HR/Personnel. In addition review your application form to ensure that you are not asking for unnecessary information about periods and dates. Asking for age-related information on an application form could allow discrimination to take place.

Monitor your decisions for any evidence of age bias, particularly after shortlisting (see page [209]).

Job description and person specification

A job description outlines the duties required of a particular post holder. A person specification gives the skills, knowledge and experience required to carry out these duties.

Avoid references, however oblique, to age in both the job description and the person specification. For example, avoid asking for 'so many years' experience. This may rule out younger people who have the skills required but have not had the opportunity to demonstrate them over an extended period. A jobseeker could challenge any time requirement and you may have to justify it in objective terms.

> **Example:** Scrape and Co, a local driving school have been advertising for instructors who must be qualified and have a minimum of 10 years driving experience. Effectively this would prevent people under 28 applying for this job and could therefore be discriminatory. Scrape would need to justify this 10 year experience criterion if challenged by a jobseeker under 28 especially as only four years experience is formally required to qualify as a driving instructor.

Educational and vocational qualifications have changed and developed over the years. Make sure that the qualifications you specify are not disadvantaging people at different ages.

Ask yourself:

- are the qualifications really necessary?
- are they still current?
- are there other ways of specifying the skill level you require?

If you are going to be specific about qualifications be sure you can justify their need in objective terms and make it clear you will consider equivalent or similar level alternative qualifications.

Advertising

It makes sound business sense to attract a wide field of applicants – if you rely on the friends or family of current staff you will miss the opportunity to tap into the diverse skills of your local community.

Advertise in a way that will be accessible to a large audience. For instance, avoid using a publication or employment agency that is focused on a niche market. This may limit the diversity of applicants and may constitute indirect discrimination.

Example: An advertisement placed only in a magazine aimed at young people may indirectly discriminate against older people because they are less likely to subscribe to the magazine and therefore less likely to find out about the vacancy and apply.

Write your job advert using the information in the job description and person specification. Avoid using language that might imply that you would prefer someone of a certain age, such as 'mature', 'young' or 'energetic'.

Example: Try to avoid stereotyping. For example, which vacancy is asking for an older person and which a younger person?

1   'We require an enthusiastic person, flexible enough to fit in with our fast moving market place, not afraid of challenging the status quo and in touch with latest thinking'
2   'Our ideal candidate will need to manage competing demands. He or she should be reflective, and have boardroom presence and gravitas'.

Be clear about what skills you actually need for the post – and what skills are merely desirable or reflect the personal preferences of the selector. Recruit and/or promote for these essential skills and aptitudes – you can always decide not to recruit or promote someone if the applicant does not have these necessary skills or abilities.

As well as considering the language you use in adverts think also about the hidden messages that may be present in any promotional literature that you have, particularly the pictures.

Graduates

If you ask for graduates, remember that the term can be interpreted as code for someone in their early twenties. Graduates can be almost any age. Make it clear that you are interested in the qualification and not the age of the applicant.

A local engineering company is looking for a new Personnel Officer and asks for applicants to be graduates and hold the IPD qualification. As many more people attend university today than say 25 years ago, there is a lower chance that older Personnel Officers will be university graduates even though holding the IPD qualification and having considerable practical experience. This graduate requirement might thus be indirect age discrimination if the employer is unable to justify it. Remember also that the IPD qualification was formerly the IPM qualification.

If you limit your recruitment to university 'milk rounds' only, you may find that this is indirect age discrimination as this practice would severely restrict the chances of someone over say, 25 applying for your vacancies. If challenged you would need to objectively justify this practice (see section on genuine occupational requirements, objective justifications, exceptions and exemptions).

Consider enhancing any 'milk round' programme with a broader recruitment strategy, using other avenues to capture a wider pool of applicants of differing ages.

Shortlisting

If you have removed age-related material from your application form then you will generally not know a person's age although applicants may make reference to their age on the form so this is not always the case.

Whether or not you know someone's age, it is important that those doing the shortlisting, ideally more than one person, base their decisions on skills and ability alone. They should be trained, reminded of their responsibility not to discriminate on age grounds and use the requirements of the person specification to judge applicants.

Before moving on to the next stage of the recruitment process, check that no bias, deliberate or unintentional, has influenced decisions. In all organisations this check should be carried out by someone who has not been involved in the shortlisting. In all instances, you should record your decisions and retain these records, ideally for 12 months.

Interviewing

Interviews should preferably not be carried out by one person on their own. When interviewing, try to avoid:

- Asking questions related to age, for example, 'how would you feel about managing older/younger people?'

- Throwaway comments such as 'you're a bit young for a post of this responsibility' or 'don't you think someone like you should be looking for something with more responsibility'.

Focus on the applicant's competence and where more than one demonstrates the required competence the one who is more competent or offers the best skill mix should be appointed.

Check decisions for any bias and make sure interviewers have received training in the skills required and equal opportunities/ diversity.

Again, in all instances, record your decisions and retain these records, ideally for 12 months from the date of the interviews.

Working with employment agencies

If you use a recruitment agency you need to be sure the agency acts appropriately and in accordance with your company's equality and diversity policies.

If you tell an employment agency to discriminate on age grounds because you consider you have objective justification for doing so, then the regulations enable the agency to rely on this justification if challenged. In such circumstances the agency should obtain this justification in writing from the employer and if at all unhappy to raise that with the employer.

Vocational training

As well as training provided by employers for their own employees, the regulations also cover organisations providing vocational education and training to the wider community. For the purpose of anti-discrimination law, all forms of vocational training including general educational provision at further, higher and other adult education institutions will be covered.

This means that vocational training providers will not be able to set age limits or age related criteria:

- for entry to training; or
- in the terms under which they provide training, for example when offering help with costs to encourage participation among under represented groups of people.

As an employer, training provider, college or university you will need to consider the following questions:

- do you set a minimum or maximum age for entry generally or in relation to admission or access to particular courses? If so, what are the justifications for these?
- even if you do not have formal minimum or maximum ages, is age taken into account when you consider applications for admission or access, eg do you offer preferential fee discount arrangements based on age?

In either case, you need to consider:

- can you objectively justify any age-related criterion, eg what evidence have you in support of restricting such financial help to a particular age group?

- what legitimate aim does any age-related criterion help you achieve, eg have you clear evidence that demonstrates particular age groups would be excluded from your learning provision if they had to pay full fees?

- are your age-related criteria a proportionate means of achieving that aim?

- is there another way of achieving that aim without resorting to discrimination?

The EU Employment Directive allows for the setting of age requirements relating to institutions of further and higher education and in respect of access to vocational training if they can be objectively justified, for example on the grounds of vocational integration.

Retaining good staff

Many factors motivate employees and make them want to stay with an organisation. People are more likely to feel positive about an organisation if they are treated fairly and with consideration regardless of their age.

Promotion and training

Opportunities for promotion and training should be made known to all employees and be available to everyone on a fair and equal basis.

Where employees apply for internal transfers take care with informal and verbal references between departmental heads, supervisors, etc. These references are covered by the regulations and should be fair and non-discriminatory.

Job-related training or development opportunities should be available to all employees regardless of age – monitor the training to make sure no particular age group is missing out.

Review the style and location of training to ensure:

- there are no barriers to any particular age group participating

- it is suitable for people of all ages

- everyone is encouraged to participate.

For example, if you are using computer-based training, do not assume everyone will be fully competent using a PC.

Age discrimination awareness

However large or small an organisation, it is good practice for them to have an Equality Policy and to train all employees and update them on a regular basis. This will help to reduce the likelihood of discrimination, harassment and victimisation taking place and may help to limit liability if a complaint is made.

All employees should understand:

- what the terms 'discrimination' and 'harassment' mean
- why discrimination and harassment are hurtful, unlawful and totally unacceptable.

Tell all employees about your company policy on age discrimination and train those who make decisions that affect others. Training should apply not only to those who recruit and select but also to those involved in day-to-day decisions about work allocation, performance appraisal, etc. Supervisors and managers also need training in recognising and dealing with bullying and harassment.

Performance appraisal

Check any performance appraisal system you have to ensure that it is working fairly and without bias. Many people have preconceptions about age and these can influence the judgements we make about people. If these preconceptions appear in performance appraisals through use of inappropriate comments – such as 'does well despite their age' or 'shows remarkable maturity for their age' – they will undermine the whole basis of a fair appraisal system. Such comments could also lead to further discrimination when decisions about promotion or work allocation are being made.

A fair and transparent appraisal system will become increasingly important when the changes to the retirement age are introduced. However, young people in the early stages of their career also need to be assessed on their actual performance unclouded by any preconceptions about their age.

> **Example:** Two candidates have done equally well for the post on offer, so the selectors decide to review previous assessments to try and draw a fair distinction between them. On one they read: 'Despite his many years with the company John remains capable and enthusiastic' and 'John does very well at work considering his age'.

> There are no such comments on Mark's assessments.

Which candidate now has a question mark against them?

Treat all employees the same when setting objectives or measuring performance. Ignoring shortfalls in performance because an employee is nearing retirement may be discriminatory – particularly if the same shortfalls are addressed in younger employees.

Redundancy selection

Check that your selection processes for redundancy are free of age discrimination. This means that practices such as last in first out (LIFO), and using length of service in any selection criteria are likely to be age discriminatory.

Policies and procedures

Review policies and procedures for age bias, including those covering:

- sick absence
- leave and holidays
- discipline and grievances
- staff transfers
- flexible working
- use of computers
- individual space requirements (ergonomic policies).

Annex 3 shows you how to use an age impact assessment to carry out these kinds of reviews.

Bullying and harassment

Every individual member of staff has the right to be treated fairly and with dignity and respect. Harassment occurs when someone engages in unwanted conduct which has the purpose or effect of violating someone else's dignity or creating an intimidating, hostile, degrading, humiliating or offensive environment.

It is not the intention of the perpetrator which defines whether a particular type of conduct is harassment but the effect it has on the recipient.

Bullying is just as unacceptable as any other form of harassment.

People can become targets of harassment because of their age. Harassment could take the form of:

- inappropriate comments – for example, by suggesting someone is too old ('over the hill') or too young ('wet behind the ears')
- offensive jokes
- exclusion from informal groups such as social events.

  Example: George is in his 60s and works in an office with a team of younger colleagues in their 20s and 30s. The team, including the manager, often go out socialising. They do not ask George because they feel that he wouldn't like the venues they choose for such events. However, George finds out that many workplace issues and problems are discussed and resolved during these informal meetings. George feels undervalued and disengaged by this unintended action. This is a form of harassment, even though unintended, as George is being excluded from the team. To prevent this, the manager ought to consider office-based meetings to consult more fully with all staff in decision-making to prevent George feeling excluded because of his age.

Dealing with harassment

Make sure your anti-harassment policy covers age. You may have a stand alone policy or one that is part of a wider equal opportunities policy (for more detailed information see the Acas booklet *Tackling discrimination and promoting equality*).

If managers see unacceptable behaviour whether or not a complaint is made they need to treat the matter seriously and take action to eliminate the behaviour in question. This may involve just pointing out to someone the effect that their behaviour has on others and getting them to stop. If this informal approach fails, or in more serious cases, or where the person being harassed prefers it will be necessary to take formal action within the normal disciplinary procedures of the company or within the guidelines laid down by a specific anti-harassment policy.

For further information see the Acas leaflet *Bullying and harassment at work: a guide for managers and employers.*

Retirement

Pension age is when an employee can draw down their pension; for many, but not all, it is also the time when they can retire if they wish.

Retirement age in this guidance is either the employer's normal retirement age (if there is one) or the default retirement age of 65.

Normal retirement age means the age at which the employer requires employees in the same kind of position as the employee to retire.

The regulations set a default retirement age of 65 (to be reviewed in 2011). This means you can retire employees or set retirement ages within your company at or above 65. Retirements or retirement ages below the default retirement age will need to satisfy the test of objective justification (see page [220]).

However, you do not have to have a fixed retirement age. Indeed, there are many business benefits to adopting a flexible approach to the employment and work patterns of older workers. Employees will have the right to request to continue working beyond their retirement date and you have a duty to give consideration to such requests.

Think about each request on an individual basis – taking into account opportunities to vary the employee's hours or the duties they perform. You are under no obligation to agree to such requests.

Fair retirement

A fair retirement is one that:

- takes effect on or after the default retirement age (or on or after the employer's normal retirement age – if there is one) and

- where the employer has given the employee written notice of the date of their intended retirement and told them about their right to request to continue working. (See below for the timing requirements of this notice).

If the employer's normal retirement age is below the age of 65, it must be objectively justified.

For the retirement to be classed as 'fair' you need to have informed the employee in writing of their intended retirement date and of their right to make a request to work beyond retirement age at least six months in advance (but no more than 12 months before the intended date). If they do make such a request, you must have followed the correct procedure for dealing with it. Annex 5 sets out a guidance flowchart for fair retirements.

Working beyond retirement date –Notification of right to request to continue working

You should notify the employee in writing of their right to request to go on working beyond their retirement date (at least six months in advance but no more than 12 months before the intended date).

When you write to the employee it is good practice to set out how you will manage the retirement process. Remind them of your obligation to give consideration to any request to work after the normal retirement age and in order not to raise the expectations of the employee, explain that you are entitled to refuse the request. You are not required to give a reason for your decision as – if you have followed the retirement procedure correctly (see Annex 5) – the reason for their dismissal will always be retirement.

However giving reasons and a more detailed explanation of your retirement policy may enable the employee to leave with dignity and respect and help you maintain good workplace relationships with other employees. This would be in line with normal good practice recommended by Acas.

If you choose to give reasons, take the time to consider what you are going to say and how you are going to say it. You must be careful not to suggest that you might be discriminating against the employee on the grounds of race, gender, disability, sexual orientation or religion or belief.

If the employee has been properly notified (as above) and wishes to continue working, they must request to do so no less than three months before the intended retirement date.

If you fail to notify the employee six months in advance of retirement, you may be liable for compensation and you have an ongoing duty (up until two weeks before the retirement dismissal) to inform the employee of both the intended date and their right to request working longer. Failure to do this will make the dismissal automatically unfair.

If you fail to inform the employee of their intended retirement date and of their right to request to continue working, the employee will still be able to make a request not to retire at any stage until dismissal. If the employee does make a request the employment must continue until the day after the employer notifies the employee of their decision on the request.

Employees should be able to retire with dignity so try and use as much tact and sensitivity as possible.

Dealing with the request

If the employee requests in writing not to be retired this request must be considered before the employee is retired. Failure to do so will make the dismissal automatically unfair. You must meet the employee to discuss their request within a reasonable period of receiving it (unless agreeing to the request or it is not practicable to hold a meeting) and inform them in writing of your decision as soon as is reasonably practicable. The employee's employment continues until you have informed them of your decision on the request.

As preparation for this meeting, it would be good practice for you to reflect on the positive reasons why you should grant an extension, in particular:

• savings to the organisation in recruitment and training costs

- retaining the valuable experience and knowledge of the employee

Try to avoid making stereotypical assumptions about the capabilities of the employee. At the meeting the employee has a right to be accompanied by a colleague. There is the same right in relation to any subsequent appeal meeting.

The individual accompanying the employee must be:

- chosen by the employee

- a worker or trade union representative employed by the same employer as the employee

- permitted to address the meeting but not answer questions on behalf of the employee; and

- permitted to confer with the employee during the meeting.

The employee may appeal against your decision as soon as is reasonably practicable after receiving notification of your decision. If the employee does appeal, the appeal meeting should be held as soon as is reasonable. The employee may appeal the decision if you refuse the request in its entirety or if you accept it but decide to continue employing the employee for a shorter period than the employee requested. The appeal meeting can be held after the retirement has taken effect.

This procedure must be repeated each time an individual nears an extended point for retirement. Annex 6 sets out a guidance framework for retirement and the duty to consider.

As long as employers follow this procedure correctly they may rely on their normal retirement age (if they have one) or the default retirement age without the dismissal being regarded as unfair or age discriminatory. Where a dismissal is for reasons of retirement, the statutory dismissals procedure does not apply.

Transitional arrangements

There are transitional arrangements produced by the Department for Trade and Industry (DTI) for employees who are retiring on or shortly after 1 October 2006. These arrangements are available at the DTI website and are summarised at Annex 12 of this guide (see page [243]).

Know your employees

You will probably have information that shows the ages of your employees. It makes sense to analyse this information (probably in age bands – see Annex 4) to get an age profile of your workforce.

This profile will help you decide whether there is a need for any remedial action.

For example, do you need to:

- plan for a retirement peak?
- take positive action to rectify any obvious imbalance in the age bands?

You can also use this profile to check that your entire workforce is getting access to training and other facilities.

Staff attitude surveys and exit interviews can also give you valuable insights into how people view their work and you as an employer, and help you to create a positive working environment.

It is important to monitor in this way if you wish to claim an objective justification or, when reviewing service related benefits, 'conclude' a business benefit (see section on genuine occupational requirements, objective justifications, exceptions and exemptions). In considering these matters you should always use evidence in your decision-making rather than merely continuing old working practices or relying on 'gut feeling' as these may be based on unfounded assumptions.

Annex 4 sets out a framework for age monitoring.

Positive action

You can take positive action to prevent or compensate for disadvantages linked to age.

This might involve:

- giving people of a particular age access to vocational training; or
- encouraging people of a particular age to take up employment opportunities.

Where it reasonably appears to the person undertaking such positive action that it will prevent or compensate for disadvantages linked to age that they have or may suffer.

For example, you might place advertisements where they are more likely to be seen by people in a disadvantaged group. Or you might limit access to a computer training course to those over 60 because they may have had less exposure to such training in the past.

Positive action on age can help you to attract people from all age groups in your local community.

Example: Green and Co, a transport company, see from their internal monitoring processes that the company has a mature age profile with disproportionately few workers under 40. Not wanting to miss out on the talents of all the local community, they include a statement in their next adverts saying 'We welcome applications from everyone irrespective of age but, as we are under-represented by people under 40, would especially welcome applications from these jobseekers. Appointment will be on merit alone'.

Objective justifications, exceptions, exemptions and genuine occupational requirements

Treating people differently because of their age will only be justifiable in the following exceptional circumstances.

Objective justification

You may treat people differently on the grounds of their age if you have an objective justification.

An objective justification allows employers to set requirements that are directly age discriminatory. Remember that different treatment on grounds of age will only be possible exceptionally for good reasons (see below).

You will need to provide real evidence to support any claim of objective justification. Assertion alone will not be sufficient and each case must be considered on its individual merits.

Both direct and indirect discrimination will be justified if it is:

- a proportionate means (of)
- achieving a legitimate aim.

WHAT IS PROPORTIONATE?

This means:

- what you are doing must actually contribute to a legitimate aim, eg if your aim is to encourage loyalty then you ought to have evidence that the provision or criterion you introduce is actually doing so
- the discriminatory effect should be significantly outweighed by the importance and benefits of the legitimate aim
- you should have no reasonable alternative to the action you are taking. If the legitimate aim can be achieved by less or nondiscriminatory means then these must take precedence.

WHAT IS A LEGITIMATE AIM?

A legitimate aim might include:

- economic factors such as business needs and efficiency
- the health, welfare and safety of the individual (including protection of young people or older workers)
- the particular training requirements of the job.

A legitimate aim must correspond with a real need of the employer – economic efficiency may be a real aim but saving money because discrimination is cheaper than non-discrimination is not legitimate. The legitimate aim cannot be related to age discrimination itself.

The test of objective justification is not an easy one and it will be necessary to provide evidence if challenged; assertions alone will not be enough.

> Jones and Company are unsure if they need an objective justification. To help make the decision they ask themselves:
>
> - STOP – Why do we want to do this?
> - Set out the reason clearly on paper
> - Do we have evidence to support us in this reason?
> - Are we certain this is real hard evidence and not just based on assumptions?
> - Is there an alternative less or non-discriminatory way of achieving the same result?
>
> The HR director seeks a second opinion from the Board and keeps all records of how the decision was made in case it is reviewed in the future.
>
> In a smaller company, you could consult your partner or colleague.

Exceptions and exemptions

There are also exceptions to or exemptions from the age regulations in the following areas:

- pay and other employment benefits based on length of service
- pay related to the National Minimum Wage
- acts under statutory authority
- enhanced redundancy
- life assurance
- retirement (see separate section on page [215])
- occupational pension systems (not covered in this guidance).

Exemptions based on length of service

In many cases employers require a certain length of service before increasing or awarding a benefit such as holiday entitlement. Without the exemptions contained in the regulations this could often amount to indirect age discrimination because some age groups are more likely to have completed the length of service than others.

Any benefit earned by five years service or less will be exempt. Employers may use pay scales that reflect growing experience or limit the provision of non-pay benefits to those who have served a qualifying period, subject to the five-year limit.

The use of length of service of more than five years for all types of employment benefits is lawful if:

- awarding or increasing the benefit is meant to reflect a higher level of experience of the employee, or to reward loyalty, or to increase or maintain the motivation of the employee;

- the employer has reasonable grounds for concluding that using length of service in this way fulfils a business need of his undertaking.

In order to meet these requirements employers would need evidence from which they can conclude there is a benefit to the organisation. This could include information the employer might have gathered through monitoring, staff attitude surveys or focus groups for example.

National Minimum wage

Nothing in the regulations will alter the provisions of the National Minimum Wage. The exemption linked to the National Minimum Wage will allow employers using exactly the same age bands, ie 16 and 17, 18 to 21 and 22 and over, to pay at or above the national minimum rates provided those in the lower age group(s) are paid less than the adult minimum wage.

This will allow an employer to pay those aged 22 and over more than those aged under 22 as long as those under 22 are paid less than the minimum adult rate; likewise an employer may pay those aged 18 to 21 more than those under 18 as long as those under 18 are paid less than the minimum adult rate. The exemption does not allow employers to pay different rates to those in the same age category. Apprentices not entitled to the National Minimum Wage may continue to be paid at a lower rate than those that are.

Acts under statutory authority

Age criteria are widely used in legislation, notably to qualify for various licences. Where this is the case the employer must follow the criteria laid down by statute and will not be contravening the age regulations by doing so.

Enhanced redundancy payments

The statutory redundancy scheme will not substantially change (except in respect of the years worked when an employee was below 18 or over 64). Both the statutory authority exemption and this regulation make it clear that, even though statutory redundancy payments are calculated using age-related criteria, such payments are lawful.

The exemption linked to statutory redundancy payments is for an employer who wants to make more generous redundancy payments than under the statutory scheme. It allows the employer to use one of the methods specified, based on the statutory redundancy scheme, to calculate the amount of redundancy payment. An employer can use a different method of their own to calculate the amount of redundancy payment, but if it is based on length of service and if an employee brings a discrimination claim under the regulations, the employer will have to objectively justify it in so far as age discrimination arises. (This is because the exception for pay and benefits based on length of service does not apply to redundancy payments.)

The exemption allows the employer to either raise or remove the maximum amount of a week's pay so that a higher amount of pay is used in the calculation, or multiply the total amount calculated by a figure of more than one, or both. Having done this, the employer may again multiply the total by a figure of more than one.

The exemption also allows an employer to make a redundancy payment to an employee who has taken voluntary redundancy, and an employee with less than two years continuous employment. In such cases, where no statutory redundancy payment is required, an employer may make a payment equivalent to the statutory minimum payment, or if they so wish an enhanced payment as above.

Life assurance cover

Some employers provide life assurance cover for their workers. If a worker retires early due to ill health, the employer may continue to provide that life assurance cover for that worker. This exemption allows an employer to stop doing so when the worker reaches the age at which he would have retired had he not fallen ill. If there was no normal retirement age at which the worker would have retired, the employer can stop providing life assurance cover when the worker reaches 65.

Genuine occupational requirement (GOR)

In very limited circumstances, it will be lawful for an employer to treat people differently if it is a genuine occupational requirement that the job holder must be of a particular age. When deciding if this applies, it is necessary to consider the nature of the work and the context in which it is carried out. Jobs may change over time and you should review whether the requirement continues to apply, particularly when recruiting.

> **Example:** An organisation advising on and promoting rights for older people **may be able** to show that it is essential that its chief executive – who will be the public face of the organisation – is of a certain age. The age of the holder of the post may be a genuine occupational requirement.

GUIDANCE FOR THE INDIVIDUAL

What do I do if I think I have suffered discrimination or harassment?

Expressing your concerns

If you think you are being harassed or discriminated against it is a good idea to make it clear to the person who is harassing you that their behaviour is unwelcome and that you want it to stop. However, you do not have to do this, particularly if you are feeling bullied or intimidated. If you do choose to address your concerns to the person, be clear and assertive but take care that you are not perceived to be bullying the individual. Some people may find it helpful to ask a friend, colleague, welfare officer or trade union representative to be with them in a support role.

If speaking to the person in question has failed to stop the problem, you should talk to your manager or your trade union representative. If it is your manager or supervisor who is harassing you, speak to someone higher up. Employers should deal with such complaints quickly, thoroughly and sympathetically.

It is usually best to try and sort things out quickly and as close to the problem as possible. If your organisation has a personnel or human resources department or an equality adviser you might find it helpful to talk to them. Discrimination can happen accidentally or through thoughtlessness. Harassment can be unintentional. Often, once a manager understands the problem, he or she will be willing to try and put things right.

Using the grievance procedure

If your manager is unable to help you, or refuses to help you, you must use your organisation's grievance procedure if you wish to proceed with your complaint. All organisations should have a grievance procedure by law. You also have a legal right to be accompanied by a trade union representative or a work colleague at any hearing into your grievance.

If you are not satisfied with the result of a grievance procedure, you have a right of appeal which should be heard, if the organisation's size allows it, by someone different from the person who conducted the original grievance hearing. You have a right to be accompanied by a trade union representative or a work colleague during the appeal hearing.

Making a claim to an employment tribunal

When you have tried all these things, or if your employer does not have a grievance procedure, or if you feel too intimidated to use the internal procedures, you may be able to bring a complaint to an employment tribunal under the age regulations. You do not have to hand in your notice to bring such a complaint. As part of your employment tribunal claim, you can require your employer to answer a set of questions about discrimination in your workplace. A questionnaire is available on the DTI website (www.dti.gov.uk) and from jobcentres and citizens advice bureaux.

You and any witnesses have a right not to be victimised for following up a grievance or complaining to an employment tribunal under these regulations provided the complaint was made in good faith.

If you have been dismissed because you objected to conduct towards you, you may be able to bring a complaint of unfair dismissal to an employment tribunal.

Complaints to an employment tribunal must normally be brought within three months of the act you are complaining about. Care should be taken to ensure that the three month point is not exceeded during any internal grievance/appeals process.

Retirement

You now have the right to request to continue working beyond your expected retirement date. If you do so your employer must give consideration to your request if you have made it in time and if they turn it down you have the right to appeal to the employer. If you do not make the request to continue working no less than three months before your expected date of retirement you may lose your opportunity to continue working.

You will not automatically be allowed to work beyond your expected retirement. Your employer does not have to agree to your request or give you a reason for turning it down.

If you want to continue working beyond your expected retirement date, but perhaps with alternative or variable working patterns take the initiative and discuss this with your employer at an early stage. Your employer does not have to agree to vary your job but early discussion could help highlight the mutual benefits of a different pattern of work or combination of duties.

Take advantage of training and development opportunities in the years approaching retirement. It will help you to make a stronger case for continuing to work.

Your employer should inform you of their intended retirement date for you and your right to request to continue working at least six months, but no more than twelve months, before the intended date. If your employer does not do this you may have the right to eight weeks pay as compensation.

If you ask to continue working, your employer should hold a meeting with you to consider your request. You have a right to be accompanied by a work colleague or trade union representative at the meeting. The trade union representative must also be a work colleague. You must be told the result of your request as soon as is reasonably practicable after the meeting. You can appeal against the decision if your request is not met. You will need to give your employer notice of the appeal as soon as is reasonably practicable after you have received his decision.

There will no longer be an upper age limit on unfair dismissal claims. The statutory redundancy payments scheme is also being adjusted to remove upper and lower age limits as is statutory sick pay and maternity pay.

FURTHER GUIDANCE FOR EMPLOYERS

Some frequently asked questions

Q Do the regulations only cover older employees?

A No. The regulations cover workers of all ages – young and old.

Q Can I ask for a candidate's date of birth on the application form?

A Yes. But asking for age-related information on an application form could allow discrimination to take place. Remove the date of birth/age from the main application form and include it in a diversity monitoring form to be retained by HR/personnel. In addition review your application form to ensure that you are not asking for unnecessary information about periods and dates.

Q Am I responsible for what an employment agency does?

A Yes. If you use a recruitment agency you need to be sure the agency acts appropriately and in accordance with your company's equality and diversity policies.

Q Do I have to do anything new or different when the legislation comes in?

A Yes. Include age in your equality policy. Consider adding all forms of discrimination and harassment (sex, race, disability, gender reassignment, sexual orientation and religion or belief) to your disciplinary rules. These rules should also include bullying.

Make sure all employees are aware (through training, noticeboards, circulars, contracts of employment, etc) that it is not only unacceptable to discriminate, harass or victimise someone on the grounds of age, it is also unlawful. Make it clear that you will not tolerate such behaviour.

Individuals should know what to do if they believe they have been discriminated against or harassed, or if they believe someone else is being discriminated against or harassed. This should be included in the grievance procedure.

Reminder: The Employment Act 2002 requires all employers, however large or small, to have both a disciplinary and a grievance procedure.

Check your policies for retirement and redundancy. Upper age limits on unfair dismissal claims and redundancy payments will be removed. There will be a default retirement age of 65, making compulsory retirement below 65 unlawful unless objectively justified.

Give serious consideration to the benefits of flexible working. All employees will also have the right to request to work beyond 65 or any other retirement age set by the organisation. You have a duty to consider such requests.

Q Must I have an equality policy?

A No. However, an equality policy is the best way of demonstrating that you take discrimination seriously and have steps in place to tackle it. The policy should set the minimum standard of behaviour expected of all employees through recruitment right through to retirement. It also spells out what employees can expect from the organisation. It gives employees confidence that they will be treated with dignity and respect, and may be used as an integral part of a grievance or disciplinary process if necessary. If you would like help putting an equality policy in place Acas can help – call our helpline on 08457 47 47 47.

Q Do these regulations cover all workers?

A Yes. The regulations apply to all workers, including office holders, police, barristers and partners in a business. They also cover related areas such as membership of trade organisations, the award of qualifications, the services of careers guidance organisations, employment agencies and vocational training providers, including further and higher education institutions.

The regulations also cover anyone who applies to an organisation for work, or who already works for an organisation – whether they are directly employed, work under some other kind of contract, or are an agency worker. You will also be responsible for the behaviour of your employees towards an individual working for someone else but on their premises, for example someone from another organisation repairing a piece of your equipment.

Employees are sometimes harassed by third parties, such as customers or clients. Where possible you should protect your employees from such harassment and take steps to deal with actual or potential situations of this kind. This will enhance your reputation as a good employer and make the organisation a welcoming and safe place to work.

Many organisations provide visitors and visiting workers with guidance on health and safety matters. It may be appropriate to include some comments on your organisation's attitude to harassment.

However the default retirement age and the duty to consider procedure apply only to a narrower group of employees – this does not include office holders, partners, barristers etc. Refer to the regulations for the precise definition.

Q I am a partner, am I covered by the regulations?

A Yes, you are covered by the regulations except for the provisions covering retirement and the right to request. Partnerships will need to objectively justify their decisions on age issues and for retirement. It would be sensible for partners to have clear records of these decisions at partnership meetings to show they meet business objectives, are properly considered and regularly reviewed. Such records may help support any case for objective justification.

Q No one in my organisation has ever complained of discrimination or harassment so I don't need to do anything new, do I?

A People do not always feel able or confident enough to complain, particularly if the harasser is a manager or senior executive. Sometimes they will simply resign. One way to find out is to undertake exit interviews when people leave and to ask them if they have ever felt harassed, bullied or discriminated against in the workplace. If it is possible, exit interviews should be undertaken by someone out of the individual's line of management, for instance a personnel officer.

Discrimination includes harassment which can take place without management being aware of it. Make sure all your employees understand that harassment means any unwanted behaviour that makes someone feel intimidated, degraded, humiliated or offended.

This includes teasing, tormenting, name calling and gossip and it applies to whoever the perpetrator may be. The victim's perception of the effect of the behaviour is also important.

Take all possible steps to make sure employees understand that they and their management teams will not tolerate such behaviour and that they will deal with whoever is causing the problem.

Q Should I take positive action to promote age diversity?

A Your business could benefit from employing people of different ages. The law allows you to introduce positive action measures where you can demonstrate that employees of a particular age are at a career disadvantage or are under represented in the organisation (see page [219]).

ANNEXES

Annex 1: An age healthcheck

Purpose

These questions are designed to kick start the planning and thinking process in your organisation. The answers to these questions should tell you if:

any key personnel decisions are influenced by age

your recruitment is attracting people from everyone in the local community.

The Checklist

1   Look at your records to establish your company age profile – insert 16–21, 22–30, 31–40, 41–50, 51–60, 60–65, 65+ (These age bands are for illustration only; you may wish to choose different ones to suit your company circumstances.) Compare this to census data available from websites, libraries, business and Chambers of Commerce. What do you find?

2   Look at your application forms for recent recruitments and compare with your age profile. Are you missing out on potential talent? Yes/No

3   Is your equality and diversity policy visibly supported by your board and chief executive? Yes/No

4   Do you train employees to recognise and tackle age discrimination? Yes/No

5   Is age ever used as a factor in staff recruitment/selection or training and development? Yes/No

   If yes, can it be justified? Yes/No

6   Do you offer variable and alternative working patterns to employees regardless of age? Yes/No

7   Are your managers aware of what behaviour could be perceived as harassment on the grounds of age? Yes/No/Not Sure

8   Do you have an action plan to ensure you are compliant with the age regulations in October 2006? Yes/No

Annex 2: Age action plan – some potential quick wins

Purpose

To make your action plan successful:

- Agree who is responsible for the plan
- Launch it with the support of the head of your organisation
- Agree who should be involved and consulted, for example line managers, personnel staff, trade unions, other stakeholders
- Make sure your partners and suppliers support your action plan
- Agree and publish timescales for when you will do things and prioritise key objectives before October 2006
- Get feedback from employees and address their concerns/questions.

Some quick win areas for the action plan

1 Recruitment, promotion and selection

- Remove ageist language (see page 12) from job and promotion adverts and focus on the needs of the job. In the short-term make someone responsible for 'vetting' the wording
- In performance assessments challenge phrases that make assumptions about an individual and focus on actual performance
- Look at where you advertise and how you advertise to ensure you reach the whole labour market
- Train selectors in anti age discrimination
- Monitor and publish your results to show you mean business.

2 Hearts and minds

- Deliver a programme of age awareness training to all employees to focus on:
  - tackling deep seated stereotypes; and
  - bullying and harassment.
- Review company literature for age bias, look to how your organisation might be perceived by younger or older employees. If someone feels fully engaged with an organisation they are likely to be more productive.

3 Retirement and knowledge management

- Recognise that senior employees have a wealth of experiences that are valuable and can help the organisation. Set up a system to capture this knowledge.

- Make your retirement policy well known and treat requests to stay after retirement as an opportunity to retain knowledge.

Annex 3: Practical impact assessing for age bias in policies

Purpose

Impact assessments are designed to measure the impact of policies and processes on different groups of people. They can help to inform planning and decision-making.

Ask yourself:

- What is the purpose of a policy or practice?
- What is it achieving?
- Do any age groups benefit and, if so, do any not? And how?
- What are the differences and adverse outcomes (if any) by age group.

To answer these questions you will need to look at:

- Your monitoring data (see section 'Know your staff' and Annex 4)
- Anecdotal views from managers and employee representatives about the way a policy is working locally
- Attitude surveys, focus groups, exit interviews and specific research and evaluation exercises you may wish to carry out
- What has worked elsewhere and why by comparing your data with that of other business groups/employer organisations.

This process will give you evidence of different outcomes by age groups. It is important to remember that not all differences are necessarily wrong and you need to ask the question "is it justifiable for this to continue?" Our guidance on objective justification can give some pointers here.

We would suggest that it would be good practice to undertake these assessments openly in the organisation as a sign of your commitment to tackle unwitting age discrimination.

Annex 4: Age monitoring – a framework

Monitoring the effect of the anti-age discrimination regulations can help you to:

- identify any problems
- gather evidence that might be needed by the courts for objective justification of any age discrimination (see page 30).

The following age bands might provide a useful starting point for gathering your information:

16–21, 22–30, 31–40, 41–50, 51–60, 60–65, 65+

Keep records on how all your employees fit into these age bands. Also keep data on employees who:

- Apply for jobs (and those who are successful)
- Apply for training (and those who receive training)
- Apply for promotion (and those who are successful)
- Are being assessed to measure their performance
- Are involved in disciplinary and grievance processes (and the outcomes of these processes)
- Leave the organisation.

Another source of monitoring information are staff attitude surveys that can be used in concluding a business benefit when considering the exemptions surrounding service-related benefits.

Staff consultation groups and trade unions can also be valuable sources of information that can add to raw data figures.

Annex 5: Fair retirement flow chart

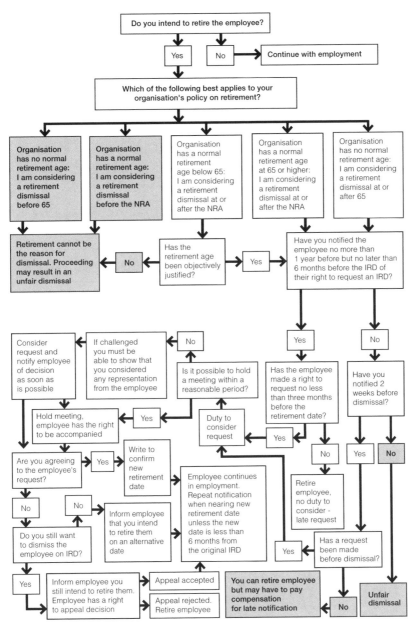

Notes: NRA means normal retirement age IRD means intended retirement date

Annex 6: Request to work beyond retirement flow chart

Annex 6: Request to work beyond retirement flow chart

Employer – Pre-Retirement

If you intend to retire the employee you must inform the employee of the retirement date, in writing, no more than one year but no later than six months before the intended retirement and that they have a right to request to work beyond the retirement age.

Employee – Responding to your employer's notification

When your employer has notified you of your intended retirement date and your right to request, if you want to request working beyond retirement age you must inform your employer no less than three months before the intended retirement date. Your request to your employer must be in writing and state whether you wish to continue work:

- indefinitely
- for a stated period
- or until a certain date.

You may only make one request in relation to each intended retirement date. If your employer has failed to notify you of your intended retirement date six months before that date, you may still make a request not to retire at any time before you retire.

Employer – Responding to your employee's request

When you receive your employee's request you must normally hold a meeting with your employee to discuss the request. If you accept there is no need to hold a meeting; simply amend the employee's contract of employment to reflect the new intended retirement date, and if required, the new employment pattern.

If after considering the request, you decide that you do wish to continue with the retirement you should hold a meeting with the employee. This will enable the employee to put their case to you. The employee has a right to be accompanied at the meeting.

The companion can be:

- chosen by the employee
- a worker or trade union representative employed by you or the organisation.

The companion can:

- address the meeting but not answer questions on behalf of the employee
- confer with the employee during the meeting.

The meeting must be held within a reasonable period after the request has been received from the employee. If the meeting cannot be held within a reasonable period, you may inform the employee of your decision in writing as long as you have considered any representation made by the employee.

Employee – The meeting to consider your request

If your employer does not accept your request, they must still offer you a meeting to discuss it. This is your opportunity to put your case before your employer. You have a right to be accompanied at the meeting.

The companion can be:

- chosen by you; but must be
- a worker or trade union representative employed by the same employer.

The companion can:

- address the meeting but not answer questions on your behalf
- confer with you during the meeting.

It is important to remember that your companion cannot answer questions on your behalf. You must take all reasonable steps to attend the meeting, although if it is not possible to hold the meeting within a reasonable period your employer may inform you of their decision in writing.

(continued)

Annex 6: Request to work beyond retirement flow chart (continued)

The meeting
The meeting is an opportunity for the employee to put their case before the employer. At the end of the meeting the employer may decide that whilst they cannot accept the employee's stated request, there may be a compromise solution. It is perfectly acceptable for the employer to propose alternative working patterns and retirement dates, other than those proposed by the employee, if the employer is persuaded by the employee's case not to be retired.

Employer – Post-meeting action
If, after the meeting, you decide to accept the employee's request you should inform them that you have accepted the request and state the new employment pattern and when the new intended retirement date will be.

Where the decision is to refuse the request you should confirm with them that you still wish to retire them – either on the original intended retirement date or an alternative later date.

Any decision should be given in writing and should be dated.
The employee has a right to appeal the employer's decision, or a decision on a new intended retirement date if it is shorter than the intended retirement proposed by the employee in the employee's initial request.

Employee – Post-meeting
The employer will inform you as soon as is reasonable after the meeting of their decision. If the employer rejects your request or proposes a new intended retirement date that is less than that in your original request, you may ask for an appeal meeting.

Appeal meeting
The appeal meeting is the final opportunity for the employee to put their case before the employer. At the end of the meeting the employer may decide that whilst they cannot accept the employee's stated request, there may be a compromise solution. It is perfectly acceptable for the employer to propose alternative working patterns and retirement dates, other than those proposed by the employee, if the employer is persuaded by the employee's case not to be retired.

Employer – Post-appeal meeting action
If, after the meeting you decide to accept the employee's request, you should inform them that you have accepted the appeal and state the new employment pattern and when the new intended retirement date will be.

Where the decision is to reject the appeal you should confirm with them that you still wish to retire them and the date that the dismissal is to take effect.

Any decision should be given in writing and should be dated.

Employee – Post-appeal meeting
The employer will inform you as soon as is reasonable after the appeal meeting of their decision. If your request is accepted, or a compromise solution is reached, the employer should inform you in writing of that decision.

If your appeal is rejected the employer is obliged to inform you of this in writing and of the date of your retirement. The employer does not need to give a reason why your application has been rejected.

Annex 7: Example of a letter informing employee of their retirement date

Letter to inform employee of their retirement date and of their right to make a request.

Note to employer: You must inform the employee no more than one year but no later than six months before their retirement date what the intended retirement date is and that they have a right to request not to be retired. Failure to inform the employee of the date and their right may mean that the dismissal is unfair. This letter should only be used if you are complying with the above time limits. If you do not, you are under an obligation to consider a request made by the employee at any time before retirement takes effect. You can get additional guidance on retirement from Acas.

Dear: Staff Number:

Date:

1   I am writing to inform you that your retirement date will be *[insert date]* and that you have a right to request not to be retired.

1a   I will give careful consideration to any request you may make to work beyond this date and will inform you if I cannot let you. I am not required by law to give a reason.

2   Your request not to be retired must be returned to *[insert name]* no later than three months before the date stated in paragraph 1. Failure to do so will mean that you lose your statutory right to have your request considered and you will be retired on the retirement date above.

Annex 8: Example of a letter informing employee of a meeting to discuss a request not to retire

Note to employer: The meeting to discuss the request should be held within a reasonable period after the request has been received. The employee has a right to be accompanied at the meeting.

The companion can be:

- chosen by the employee
- a worker employed by you or the organisation. The companion can:
- address the meeting but not answer questions on behalf of the employee
- confer with the employee during the meeting.

Dear: Staff Number:

Date:

I am writing to inform you that after receiving your request not to be retired that there will be a meeting to discuss your request.

The meeting will be held on *[insert date]* at *[insert time]* at *[insert location]*.

You have a right to be accompanied at the meeting by a fellow worker or a trade union representative. Your companion may be someone that you have chosen, but they must work for *[insert name of organisation]*. Your companion can address the meeting but not answer questions on your behalf although you may confer with your companion during the meeting.

After the meeting if it is decided to continue your employment beyond the intended retirement date of *[insert date]* you will receive written notification reflecting these agreed changes to your contract.

If no agreement is reached you will receive further notification confirming your intended retirement date and informing you of your right to appeal.

Annex 9: Example of a letter confirming retirement on the intended date

Note to employer: If after the meeting to discuss the employee's request not to be retired, you decided that you still wish to retire the employee, you must inform them as soon as is reasonably practicable. You must also inform them that they have a right to appeal

Dear: Staff Number:

Date:

I am writing to inform you that after our meeting held on *[insert date]* to discuss your request not to be retired, that *[insert organisation]* still intends to retire you on *[insert intended retirement date]*.

You have a right to appeal this decision. If you wish to appeal you must inform *[insert name]* as soon as is reasonable. Failure to do so may mean that you lose the right to an appeal meeting and *[insert organisation's name]* may consider your appeal without holding a meeting but they will consider any previous representations that you have made.

Annex 10: Example of a letter to employee notifying the result of their appeal

Note to employer: You must hold the appeal meeting to discuss the employee's appeal not to be retired as soon as is reasonably practicable. If it is not reasonably practicable to hold an appeal meeting within a period that is reasonable you may consider the appeal without holding a meeting as long as you consider any representations that the employee has made.

Dear: Staff Number:

Date:

I am writing to inform you that after our meeting held on *[insert date]* to discuss your appeal not to be retired, that *[insert organisation]* still intends to retire you on *[insert intended retirement date]*.

Annex 11: Example of a letter to employee confirming new retirement date

Note to employer: You should use this letter if you accept the employee's request or appeal.

Dear: Staff Number:

Date:

I am writing to inform you that following our meeting to consider your request not to be retired/appeal meeting *[delete as appropriate] [insert organisation]* has agreed that your new intended retirement date shall be *[insert date]*.

As agreed at the meeting to discuss your request not to be retired/ appeal meeting *[delete as appropriate]* your new working pattern will be as follows. *[Delete this paragraph if no new working pattern is agreed]*.

Annex 12: Retirement – transitional arrangements applicable up to 1 April 2007

Transitional arrangements apply to retirements from 1 October 2006 to 31 March 2007 because the DTI recognises that:

Where an employee is due to retire soon after 1 October 2006 the procedures for ensuring a retirement dismissal is fair are summarised below.

Notice given before 1 October 2006

If the employee is given notice before 1 October that they are to be retired after 1 October 2006 but before 1 April 2007:

- notice must be at least the period required by the contract of
- employment; or
- where the employee is already serving a long period of notice required by the contract that exceeds four weeks, the employer must give at least four weeks notice before the 1 October 2006 to ensure the employee is aware and given the statutory minimum period of notice for retirement.

On 1 October, or as soon practicable afterwards, the employer must write to the employee telling them of their right to request working longer.

The employee can make such a request after their contract has been terminated but not more than four weeks afterwards.

A meeting to discuss the request, and any subsequent appeal meeting, must be held within a reasonable period. The employee can ask to be accompanied by a companion.

Notice given after 1 October 2006

If the employee is given notice after 1 October that they are to be retired before 1 April 2007 the employer must:

- write to the employee notifying them of the intended retirement date
  - giving the longer of contractual or statutory notice; and
- tell them in writing that they have a right to request working longer.

An employee who wants to exercise this right should make a written request:

- where possible, four weeks before the intended retirement date; or
- as soon as reasonably practicable after being notified of the 'right to request'.

The request can be made after the employee's contract has been terminated but not more than four weeks after termination. A meeting to discuss the request, and any subsequent appeal meeting, must be held within a reasonable period. The employee can ask to be accompanied by a companion.

Anyone retiring on or after 1 April 2007 will be subject to the full retirement procedure set out in the Employment Equality (Age) Regulations 2006 and described in this guidance.

INDEX